—

What Every Middle School Teacher Should Know

—

What Every Middle School Teacher Should Know

Second Edition

DAVE F. BROWN AND TRUDY KNOWLES

NMSA

HEINEMANN
Portsmouth, NH

Heinemann

361 Hanover Street
Portsmouth, NH 03801–3912
www.heinemann.com

National Middle School Association
4151 Executive Parkway
Suite 300
Westerville, OH 43081
www.nmsa.org

Offices and agents throughout the world

The authors and publisher wish to thank those who have generously given permission to reprint borrowed material:

Excerpts from *Turning Points: Preparing American Youth for the 21ˢᵗ Century*, a report of the Carnegie Council on Adolescent Development. Copyright June 1989 by the Carnegie Council on Adolescent Development, a program of the Carnegie Corporation of New York.

Library of Congress Cataloging-in-Publication Data
Brown, Dave F.
  What every middle school teacher should know / Dave F. Brown and Trudy Knowles. — 2nd ed.
    p. cm.
  1st ed. gives Trudy Knowles as first author.
  Includes bibliographical references and index.
  ISBN-13: 978-0-325-00953-7
  ISBN-10: 0-325-00953-8
  1. Middle school education—United States. 2. Adolescence—United States.
I. Knowles, Trudy. II. Title.
  LB1623.5.K56 2007
  373.236—dc22   2007009285

Editor: Lisa Luedeke
Production editor: Sonja S. Chapman
Cover design: Jenny Jensen Greenleaf
Cover and interior photographs: Dave F. Brown
Compositor: SPi Publisher Services
Manufacturing: Louise Richardson

Printed in the United States of America on acid-free paper
13   EB   7 8

Dedication

To those middle level educators whose students know you care through your concern, support, and encouragement for their overall growth.

D. F. B.

To Rachel, who has the heart and soul of a middle school teacher. I love being your mom.

T. K.

Contents

Foreword by James A. Beane   xi
Preface   xv
Acknowledgments   xix

1. You Want to Be a What?   1
   Who Are Young Adolescents?   2
   Becoming a Middle Level Teacher   5

2. Understanding the Young Adolescent's Physical   10
   and Cognitive Growth
   Physical Development   12
   Cognitive Development   26

3. Who Am I? The Social, Emotional, and Identity   37
   Trials of Young Adolescence
   Social Development   38
   Moral Development   48
   Emotional Development   50
   The Search for Identity   52
   Concluding Reflections   65

4. Designing an Appropriate Middle School: Influences   67
   from the Past to the Present
   A Typical Day   68
   Emulating the Factory   70
   The First Junior High Schools   74
   The Promise of a New Design   76

Contents

Support for Genuine Middle Schools   79
The Carnegie Council on Adolescent Development   81
Content Standards Influence the Middle School   84
Concluding Reflections   89

5. Creating a Safe Haven for Learning   91
Middle Schools and Student Stress   92
Establishing a Caring Environment   94
The Dangers of Bullying   102
Encouraging Risk Taking   105
Recognizing and Responding to Diverse Learners   107
Sharing Decision Making   108
Creating Collaborative—Not Competitive—Learning Environments   110

6. Student-Designed Curriculum   113
What Is Curriculum?   115
Beliefs About Middle Level Curriculum   116
Basic Approaches to Curriculum Organization   121
What Students Want   129
*Curriculum Integration Model: A Different Way of Thinking
    About the Curriculum*   131
Curriculum Integration in the Middle School Classroom   135
Concluding Reflections   151

7. Facilitating Meaningful Learning   152
How Learning Occurs   153
Collaborative Learning   159
The Teacher's Role   161
Culturally Responsive Teaching   173
Living with Content Standards   177
Concluding Reflections   179

8. Assessment That Promotes Active Learning   180
What Is Assessment?   180
Connecting Assessment to Curriculum and Instruction   189
Alternative Assessment   190
Students' Roles in Assessment   190
Authentic Assessment Leads to Meaningful Learning   195
Performance Assessment   196
Student-Led Conferences   200

Contents

9. Real Teachers Using Genuine Curriculum Integration   203
   Revisiting Scott Clark   203
   The Alpha Team   204
   Soundings: An Eighth Grade Curriculum Integration Experience   216
   Starting with Our Little Corner   220
   Concluding Reflections   223

10. Altering School Structures   225
   Teaming—The Heart and Soul of the Middle School Concept   226
   Advisory Programs   235
   Alternative Scheduling   243
   Exploratory Curriculum   249
   Looping   251
   Concluding Reflections   251

11. Being an Advocate for Young Adolescents   253
   Misunderstanding the Middle School Concept   255
   Support for the Middle School Concept   257
   Supporting Young Adolescents   260
   The True Middle School   261

   References   265
   Index   287

Foreword: We Really Should Know This

James A. Beane

As anyone who's ever done it can tell you, teaching middle school is a very tricky business. Whether it's good or bad depends largely on how you see things. Young adolescents are in a real serious life transition and they bring the ups and downs of that to every teacher they meet. If teachers see those ups and downs as a problem or inconvenience, middle school teaching can be very frustrating.

Worse yet, as parents and guardians see the dependence of childhood slip away and the press for independence get underway, they often expect teachers to influence their children's lives in ways they cannot seem to themselves. So the so-called "problems" posed by young adolescence end up compounded by their family's expectations that teachers can do what they can't. Meanwhile education authorities and policy makers who may never have actually taught middle school make demands about what and how to teach. Too often those demands assume young adolescents have nothing but schoolwork on their minds and can't wait to move from one piece of content to the next. Now the whole business of teaching is buried under the weight of being expected to teach a group of "up and down" young people things they do not want to know as prescribed by authorities who never tried to do it themselves.

On the other hand, if you see what young adolescents bring to your classroom as a promise rather than a problem, middle school teaching can be one of the most exciting and satisfying things you will ever do. The fact is that young adolescents have tons of questions and concerns about themselves and their world, and their imagination and curiosity work around the clock. They love new ideas if those ideas shed some light on topics that are personally and socially significant. They love to explore and debate issues of fairness and justice. They love to learn new skills that will help them do something they want to do or think is worth doing. They love to dig deep into projects that are about big ideas or problems. And if you see young adolescents this way and learn how to teach like that, along the way they will learn more and learn better than if you see who they are as a problem you have to solve in order to teach them some abstract content that they, and maybe even you, don't really care about. When this happens you really see that young adolescents can do well and you put yourself in a position to help parents and guardians see the same.

There is a world of difference between seeing the promise in young adolescents and seeing them as problematic. Seeing the "promise" is at the center of *What Every Middle School Teacher Should Know*. From start to finish young adolescents are treated with dignity and respect, and their education is more an adventure worth having than a trial to be endured. In a way, saying what every middle school teacher should know may seem pretty pretentious, but what is offered here really does make sense. How can you be a good middle school teacher if you don't know something about young adolescence, or effective curriculum and teaching approaches, or what middle schools are for, or how middle schools ought to be organized? And how can you be really good if you don't see yourself as an advocate for the young adolescents you work with?

Teachers seem to work with one of two general theories. Some hold to the idea that, "if only the kids were different, we could do a great job." But because young adolescents are who they are and cannot be someone or something else, this theory can only lead to frustration for both teachers and students, and more than a little conflict between them. Others believe that, "if only we did things differently, the kids could do a great job." In the end, it is this second theory that leads toward worthwhile experiences for teachers and students because teachers can shape and reshape classroom life so that young adolescents can do great work. *What Every Middle School Teacher Should Know* is full of ideas and information to support that second theory. And that is why every middle school teacher really should know what's in this book.

Preface

Writing the first edition of *What Every Middle School Teacher Should Know* (2000) gave us an opportunity to listen to young adolescents and middle level teachers. We engaged in many hours of interviews with middle schoolers and were enlightened by *their* stories. In that first edition, we touched on young adolescents' physical, social, emotional, and cognitive development, trying to emphasize that young adolescents are different from elementary children and high school students. We also addressed what was known by researchers in the field about effective middle schools at that time.

In the seven years since that first edition, much more research has surfaced on young adolescents' growth processes. We now know that their brains are different from older adolescents and that this affects their behaviors and their learning. We know more about how their behaviors are affected by specific hormones. We've learned that specific instructional behaviors are better at meeting the learning needs of young adolescents than those we may have used in the past. Plus, we've witnessed middle school teachers using curriculum integration in democratic classrooms. It's been an exciting and educational seven years.

Now we want to share with you what we've been studying, including the impact of how this information can improve learning for your students. Teachers armed with this information can provide an environment of care and support—two affective aspects of learning that are significant to all students. In this second edition, we're still listening and adding more young adolescents' voices. As important, though, are the new findings by middle level researchers on the components of the middle school concept: teaming, advisory programs, flexible scheduling, exploratory curriculum, and looping. We also explain the power of democratically designed classrooms and student involvement in choosing curriculum. These middle level structures can and do make a difference in our effectiveness in meeting young adolescents' varied needs.

Chapter 2 has been expanded. In it we discuss the amazing new findings of the differences in physical development among all young adolescents and between females and males. We've added sections on the impact of being an early physical maturer, young adolescents' need for sleep, and appropriate diets. We've addressed the new cognitive development findings, in writing about the distinct differences between concrete and formal operational thought, brain wiring, why adolescents take the risks they do, and that pesky undeveloped prefrontal cortex and its impact on student behaviors that drive teachers crazy.

There is now a separate new chapter (3) on young adolescents' social and emotional needs. We have expanded those sections, added the research on moral development, and tackled the ever present issues on young adolescents' search for identities: sexual, gender, and ethnic, among others. We also describe the challenge of student self–esteem and how it is affected by the changes occurring during young adolescence.

No book on education written in the beginning of the millennium would be complete without noting the impact of standards and that federal legislation—dare we say it—No Child Left Behind. Chapter 4 examines these influences, where we've been in middle level education, where we are now, and how we arrived. We provide suggestions from the new *This We Believe: Successful Schools for Young Adolescents* (National Middle School Association 2003) and *Turning Points 2000* (Jackson and Davis 2000).

We explain in Chapter 5 how teachers can create a healthy classroom for young adolescents, with an expanded section on the impact and causes of bullying and teachers' roles in preventing it. We've added a historical perspective on the theory and practice of curriculum integration in Chapter 6, with additional research on its effectiveness and value for students.

Chapter 7 discusses effective instruction expanded to include how teachers can help their students move from Piaget's concrete to formal operational thinking, the power of knowing your students' learning needs through kid watching, ethnically and culturally responsive instruction, and an explanation of the value of differentiated teaching.

The original chapter on assessment has been changed to include a major emphasis on student responsibility for self-assessment, including an explanation of student-led conferences and strategies for including students in their assessment processes. As well, we explain the problems associated with standardized tests and the significance of assessment *for* learning instead of assessment *of* learning.

Chapter 9 is entirely new, with in-depth thoughts from a few middle level educators—Meghan O'Donnell, Cynthia Myers, Mark Springer, and Gert Nesin—who have implemented and sustained curriculum integration classrooms. We've added comments from students and parents who have been fortunate enough to experience such dynamic learning.

In Chapter 10 we provide recent research that supports the middle school concepts of advisory programs, teaming, and flexible scheduling. Exploratory experiences and looping are also presented as new material in this chapter.

We believe teaching is a journey, one in which the challenges are often unpredictable and seemingly mountainous. Simultaneously, being with young adolescents daily provides one with an exhilaration that is rarely matched. We hope that the journey is satisfying and to that end have written this second edition in an attempt to provide you with the tools and knowledge to design an exciting world within your classroom. Enjoy your professional travels with young adolescents—there is no journey like it!

DAVE F. BROWN AND TRUDY KNOWLES

Acknowledgments

In 1997, when Trudy talked me into writing the first edition of this book, I embraced the opportunity. We met in Indianapolis for my first National Middle School Association conference and spent hours exchanging ideas and writing rough drafts. It was the process of writing—that is, those conversations—that helped me develop my philosophy on teaching in general, but especially on teaching young adolescents.

The most significant part of writing that first edition is the new doors that have opened into the world of researching young adolescents. Those "doors" have meant being able to have genuine conversations with teachers and students about what their lives are like in and out of school. After thirteen years of public school teaching, I thought I knew plenty about my students, but it wasn't until I started really listening to the young adolescents we interviewed that I realized what I didn't know about their lives. I thank all of those young adolescents who have been gracious enough to speak to us over the past five years. I wish to thank the students and teachers at Upper Merion Area School District for their assistance in completing this book.

When I try to describe to my younger daughter what I do every day, I simplify it by saying, "I teach teachers." Actually, that's a lie. Every time I start a new class, whether it's with urban, rural, or suburban teachers, I end up being the learner! Teachers are actually teaching me through our conversations and, once again, through my listening to them. I want to thank all the teachers who are brave enough to spend an hour, a day, or a week in one of my classes. I am inspired by your energy, passion, and commitment to this business of teaching.

Acknowledgments

Many of the teachers whom I meet in my courses each year share with me a genuine commitment for adding to their knowledge of young adolescents and the middle school concept. I want to thank Maria Shollenberger and Janel Brogley, two of those teachers who shared their passion, understanding, and commitment for the middle school concept and in so doing taught me something new as well.

Some teachers have been especially helpful in the past six years in "schooling" me. I visit Mark Springer's room every semester, and he invites me in as if I am family. Mark has been an inspiration to me since I've learned of the Watershed program and studied Soundings. Mark's coteacher, Mary Canniff, is every bit as committed to curriculum integration and students' voices as Mark. Thank you both for sharing your classroom as a shining example of how to engage students in learning. To Gert Nesin, Meg O'Donnell, Cynthia Myers, and Mark Springer, thank you for contributing to this book and making the theory and principles of student-engaged learning real.

My new colleague Heather Leaman has direct experience with teaching middle school and is an avid researcher who understands the meaning of listening to students and telling their stories. Thank you, Heather, for encouraging me and listening to my concerns about how to meet our university students' needs and the needs of young adolescents.

Lisa Luedeke, our editor, has been extremely patient with us throughout this writing process. Thank you for taking us on, despite, I'm sure, your almost impossible professional schedule. We deeply appreciate and value your guidance.

The National Middle School Association Conference is an event I wouldn't dream of missing for many reasons. It's exciting to witness middle level teachers and researchers presenting what works, and I especially enjoy the conversations with colleagues. I thank Vince Anfara Jr., Dick Lipka, Jim Beane, Nancy Doda, Kathy Roney, Micki Caskey, Barb Brodhagen, Carol Smith, Gert Nesin, and of course, Trudy, for engaging conversations and happy times. Each year we meet, I walk away excited for the future of the middle school movement because of the energy and commitment that you all bring to it.

Trudy initiated this second edition—and as usual, she was right about the need to update and improve on our first efforts. I grow professionally with every conversation we have. Trudy knows what young adolescents are like and what the true middle school should look like because she listens and she's curious enough to ask the right questions. Thank you, Trudy, for your insights and your huge heart.

It's almost impossible to describe how families always provide the support you need, always knowing when you need it. I thank my dad and Betty for the example of responsible parenting that they always set and their constant support. For my siblings, Carol Ann, Bob, Brian, and Kenneth, thank you for reading all that crap I send you. Even if you don't agree, I know you're listening. You are all always in my heart despite the distance between us. I also want to acknowledge the encouragement I receive from my "East Coast family," Sandy and Bill Shusta, and thank them for always being supportive of the work that Dana and I do.

For my daughter, Lindsay, I've missed you so and look forward to future conversations. For Taylor, you bring me joy every day with your excitement for life and your great questions—keep asking them. I so much love seeing you write, and I hope you'll continue to add to my collection of your stories. Dana, my wife, I am happy to say, is my colleague, confidant, advisor, and the love of my life. Her teaching is an inspiration to me. I thank you, Dana, for always listening and standing up for what's right for your students, the world, and for me.

—Dave F. Brown

When Dave and I first thought about writing a book for middle school teachers, we knew that we wanted it to be grounded in the voices of young adolescents. They are the ones who can lead us into developing schools that respond to their needs. The middle school students whom we interviewed for the first edition of the book are out of school now. They are in the world, being citizens, creating their lives. And yet their words speak to us today as they did ten years ago. Because of their willingness to share their lives with us, we were able to create a resource that comes from them. I thank them again for that trust.

I never thought we would be writing a second edition of a book that was so long in coming the first time. I am grateful that middle school teachers and administrators have embraced this book and used it as a framework and resource for what they do every day in the classroom with students. I continue to be impressed with the thousands of middle school teachers who love their job and their students. I thank them for choosing to work "in the middle."

My belief in the importance of and necessity for democratic classrooms drives all that I do. I believe that we must listen to what our students say about their lives and their learning. I am fortunate to have connected with amazing educators who share that belief and who spend their professional careers advocating for kids. They are at the heart of true middle level reform.

I first want to thank Jim Beane for his friendship, his words, his life, and his legacy. No matter what he says, he will never retire. I won't let him.

There are a number of other inspirational middle level educators and colleagues who push me to the progressive edge but won't let me fall. I particularly want to thank the four teachers who shared their stories for this new edition. Meg O'Donnell and Cynthia Myers from the Alpha team in Vermont, Mark Springer from the Soundings program in Pennsylvania, and Gert Nesin from the University of Maine are incredible educators who believe strongly in the power of democratic classrooms and spend their days making it happen.

And there are more. Nancy Doda is my friend and inspiration, an amazing middle level advocate. Carol Smith and Barb Brodhagen are proof that democratic teaching can become a reality and can transform the lives of young people. Ann Yehle is a principal who believes so strongly in every child's right to quality learning. Her fight for justice inspires me. Dave Braun y Harycki and Bill McBeth are college professors who are opening up the eyes of future teachers to the power of democracy. Pat Clem is a principal who always pushes her teachers to do what's right by kids.

A special thanks to Holly Pasackow, a parent from the Alpha team, who was willing to share her experiences and to the other anonymous students and parents who so honestly and eloquently were able to put into words what was in their hearts and minds.

Acknowledgments

I have to thank Dave. It was as much fun writing this edition as it was writing the first. Dave did most of the work on this edition and is still letting me have my name on the cover.

And always, always, always, I thank my family: my sibs, my in-laws, my nieces and nephews, my kids—Mellissa, Rachel, Robert, Ariel, and Austin—and my husband, Dan. They support me, are proud of me, and love me unconditionally.

—Trudy Knowles

ONE

You Want to Be a What?

Middle school is very complicated.

Robert, age thirteen

Imagine that you are a new skier standing on the top of a mountain. You look down with fear. The only way to get to the bottom is to ski down, so you push your poles into the snow and begin. Suddenly you hit full speed. You are flying. You've never felt such exhilaration. Just as quickly, you lose control and fall down, not once, but again and again and again. You are ready to quit, but you are only halfway down the mountain, so you stand up one more time and promise yourself that if  you just make it down in one piece, you'll never attempt to ski again. You dig in your poles, take off, and soar to the bottom. Before you know it, you're on the ski lift again. You are halfway up the mountain before you realize you'll have to go down again. You know you'll fall, but you also know you'll fly. It's that one brief moment of flying that makes it all worthwhile.

You are about to take a ride as a middle school teacher. Going to school each day is exhilarating because you love your students. Sometimes you realize, however, that your emotional state matches that of your students, with all the ups and downs. You fall and get up again and again and again. You go home exhausted, wondering why you ever chose teaching as a career. The next day you're back in the classroom and you're soaring. You feel that you could teach forever. Teaching middle schoolers is not an easy trip, but the ride is exhilarating.

Who Are Young Adolescents?

What Are They Like?

What are they like, these young adolescents attending middle school? You've seen them. They're everywhere—walking in the mall, hanging out on street corners, living in your house. In fact, you were one, perhaps not so long ago. You know what they're like.

- They eat all the time.
- Their music is too loud.
- They take social issues very seriously.
- They frequently exclaim, "You don't understand."
- They cry a lot.
- They laugh a lot.
- They're sure that nobody has ever felt what they are feeling.
- They like hanging out at home and being with their parents.
- They hate hanging out at home or being seen with their parents.
- They have difficulty attending to something for more than a minute at a time.
- They will spend hours on a computer.
- They care passionately about the world.
- They are plagued with acne.
- They are seldom satisfied with the way they look.
- They're loyal to their friends.
- They talk behind their friends' backs.
- They outgrow their clothes every few months.
- Their voices crack when they sing in mixed chorus.
- They want to be independent.
- They don't want to let go of their childhood.

This time of vast emotional, social, physical, and cognitive change has been called *pubescence, transescence, emergent adolescence, early adolescence,* and *young adolescence.* Students at this stage are often called *difficult, obnoxious, hard to handle, impossible,* and *hormonally driven.* We would like to characterize this stage positively.

What should we call this time of change? *Transescence* is out. It is hard to say and sounds like a form of alien abduction. *Pubescence* suggests that the only significant aspect of this age is emerging sexuality. *Emergent adolescence* focuses too much on the future—on what will be instead of what is. What's left is *early* or *young adolescence.* Those are the terms we will use in this book.

How Do We Define Young Adolescence?

Should we define *young adolescence* according to age? Grade level? Physical attributes? Behaviors? Family or peer interactions? Emotions? Cognitive abilities? All of the above?

This period of time is characterized by vast developmental changes. Physical changes are more dramatic than at any other time in life except *in utero* and early infancy. Cognitive changes create vast leaps in thinking ability. Social and emotional changes result in a move from dependence to independence. The development of various identities, from personal to ethnic to sexual, occupy young adolescents' minds as they search for a persona that fits who they want to be. Some children begin these developmental changes at age ten, some not until fifteen. Most are somewhere in between. The definition of *young adolescence* is as complex as the people we are attempting to define.

Perhaps we don't need a definition. Perhaps, for purposes of this book, it is better to define *young adolescence* as the time a child spends in middle school. But that definition can also be complicated. Middle level grade configurations are not consistent. The most common grouping is sixth through eighth grade. You will also find middle schools that contain the fifth and/or ninth grades. And some only have seventh and eighth grades. Grade configurations in most circumstances generally don't affect students' social, emotional, or cognitive development. Definitions, however, are not what the young adolescent is all about. Perhaps descriptions are a more appropriate way of explaining this age.

What Changes Occur During This Time?

The changes that young adolescents undergo are distinctive. Adolescence is not like any other time of life, and no young adolescent is like any other.

Growth at this time is inconsistent from one individual to the next. Developmental stages are uneven and follow no set timeline. Middle school students can be physically mature young women or girls who have not yet experienced their first menses; they might be fully grown young men who shave often or boys barely five feet tall who seemingly will never need a razor. Their social and emotional actions can range from childlike behaviors to adult perceptions. Take a look in the middle school cafeteria and you'll see them all.

Other transformations are occurring. Young adolescents are making the transition from the dependence of childhood to the independence of adulthood. They are moving from the safety and security of their families to the insecurity of finding a place in the adult world.

During early adolescence, children develop a sense of who they are independent of anyone else; they learn to interact socially and act responsibly. They develop their values and character, expand their interests, and pursue their dreams. If we want students to be successful in middle school, we must be aware of and respond to the changes in their development, understand the challenges that lie ahead of them, and listen to what they say.

Time for Reflection
Why do you or did you want to be a middle school teacher? What characteristics do you think a middle school teacher needs to have?

Becoming a Middle Level Teacher

Middle Level Certification

Some middle school teachers come from the ranks of elementary-certified faculty. Teachers might explain, "I really wanted to teach second grade but this was the only job I could get." Others come from the ranks of certified high school educators: "I really wanted to teach eleventh grade American history and government, but this was the only job I could get." Approximately twenty-five states have specific middle level teacher certification based on required courses such as young adolescent development and the practices associated with genuine middle level schools. Middle level certificates prepare educators to teach students in grades four or five through eight or sometimes nine. In those states that don't require specific middle level certification, teaching certificates are now granted based on teachers' knowledge as determined by a score on a standardized content area test. These tests are required in many states as a result of the No Child Left Behind legislation (2001). In these states, no other requirements exist to become a middle level teacher if one is certified for any other grade level.

Understanding one's content is one criterion for successful teaching—but only one. Effective educators at all grade levels possess something more significant than content knowledge: a deep understanding of their students. Comer (2005) noted the following in studying over a thousand schools across the United States:

> [I]t became clearer that both academic and behavioral success were more likely in places where teachers and administrators bought into the value of basing their work on the principles of child and adolescent development. The focus on child development that is largely missing from the preparation of educators probably contributes more to creating dysfunctional and underperforming schools than anything else. (757–58)

The developmental characteristics of young adolescents are unique. Knowledge of these traits is imperative for you to experience

5

the success you expect to have as a middle school teacher. We fear, as Comer (2005) has discovered, that those teachers who become middle level educators without proper course work on effective middle school practice and young adolescent development will focus on content while ignoring the developmental and academic needs of their students. The result may be student and teacher dissatisfaction and may be detrimental to the success of many students at this crucial period.

So, what should you know before you become a teacher of young adolescents? For beginners, we suggest that you consider young adolescent behaviors that you'll frequently experience. Students will

- ask personal questions about your life and family
- question the way you dress
- surprise you with their sophisticated questions that demonstrate their deep concern about the world
- wonder about the type of car you drive
- ask about how much money you make
- swear at you occasionally
- ask you if you've considered plastic surgery or a makeover
- act completely socially inappropriate on occasion, yet surprise you with their social graces at other times
- experiment with their personality
- fall "in love" and "out of love" weekly
- pass notes
- text message one another during class
- act emotionally out of control one day and completely mature the next
- completely depend on you some days but act totally independent on others

We consider these behaviors demonstrations of growth. Teaching middle school is not a job for those whose primary aspiration as an educator is the transmission of content. Until you become somewhat knowledgeable of and responsive to the lives of young adolescents, you'll be a frustrated teacher. McEwin and Dickinson (2001) clearly described the value of knowing young adolescents:

> The most important quality that middle school teachers bring to their classrooms is their commitment to the young adolescents they teach. Without this commitment, there is little substantive progress for either party, and teaching and learning is reduced to some mechanical act, the consequences of which fall most heavily on the young adolescents, their families, and ultimately the nation. (11)

Characteristics of Effective Middle Level Teachers

If you are in a middle level certification program or hold a middle level teaching certificate, consider yourself fortunate. Being enrolled in a specific middle grades certification program and getting your teaching certificate, however, is not enough. Passing content area tests will also leave you searching for answers for how to succeed with young adolescents. You will need several personal and professional characteristics that you demonstrate daily as a classroom teacher. How does your list of characteristics match ours?

As a middle level teacher you will need:

- a sense of humor that you share with students regularly
- flexibility that you demonstrate in your instructional and curricular planning and delivery
- the ability to actively listen to your students
- the ability to show unconditional caring for your students
- a contagious passion for learning
- a willingness to move beyond the boundaries of your subject area
- a philosophy and action plan that places students at the center of the learning process
- a belief in the process of collaborating with students regarding instruction and curriculum
- the confidence to guide students on their path to learning
- an awareness of adolescent health issues and a willingness to address these issues with students

- a strong sense of your own identity
- a wealth of knowledge about young adolescent development
- a belief in all students' ability to succeed
- knowledge and skills to help all students achieve success

Naturally, the list could go on. The one trait, however, that your students will notice clearly each day they see you is a positive attitude. Nechochea et al. (2001) described its importance:

> A positive attitude for teaching adolescents is a necessary element for becoming an effective middle level teacher. Because of its elusive nature, teacher attitude is difficult to teach, but by all means needs to be incorporated into teacher education programs to instill a sense that middle school teachers can make a significant difference in the lives of young adolescents. (176–77)

Making a significant difference may take on several definitions and many distinctive behaviors. As you read through this book, ask yourself if you have the characteristics necessary to be an effective middle school teacher.

Time for Reflection
What questions or concerns do you have about young adolescents or the structure of the middle school?
What questions or concerns do you have about being a middle school teacher?
What do you think is the most important thing a middle school student can do or learn in school?

Your answers to the first two questions will become the basis for your inquiry into middle level education. Your answer to the third will develop into your philosophy of learning at the middle level. This book will enable you to explore your questions concerning middle level education. Chapters 2 and 3 focus on the development of the young adolescent and build a framework for a developmentally responsive middle school. Chapter 4 provides a historical overview of the middle school movement, while Chapter 5 explains how to develop communities of learning. This initial framework allows you to design a middle school environment that is developmentally responsive to young adolescents' needs and will help them move successfully toward becoming independent adults.

Chapters 6, 7, and 8 explore the important issues of curriculum, instruction, and assessment, focusing on how to create positive learning environments within democratic classrooms. Chapter 9 is primarily written by successful middle level educators who have taken the risks necessary to advance the learning of their students through curriculum integration and the effective assessment that follows this type of student-engaged learning. Chapter 10 examines structural and organizational issues relevant to appropriate middle level education and a true middle school. We end in Chapter 11 with a discussion on how to be an advocate for middle level education, young adolescents, and the middle school concept.

We hope that you will find the answers to many of your questions in this book. We suspect that in your reading of it, you will generate additional questions. In fact, we hope this is the case. Learning begins with asking questions, and the most effective teachers are inspired by their own quest for learning.

So hold onto your hat. We believe working with young adolescents will be the most exhilarating ride you will ever take.

TWO

Understanding the Young Adolescent's Physical and Cognitive Growth

Being a young adolescent is very cool because you're going through lots of changes—like, your body is changing and your voice is cracking and it's a new environment. And I'm meeting lots of people I never met before and switching class. I don't have recess anymore.

ERIC, AGE THIRTEEN

If you choose to teach middle school, you must understand that if you intend for students to genuinely learn something, you must first comprehend the details of your students' social, emotional, physical, and cognitive growth. Your success as a teacher will be determined by both your comprehensive knowledge of young adolescents and your ability to respond to their varied needs.

Young adolescence can be a tough time for children. Their bodies and minds are changing, creating a preoccupation with self-examination as they strive to discover and craft a personality. As the young adolescent begins to foster independence from the family, social interaction with peers becomes very important. It's not always easy to cope with such rapid and dramatic changes. One thirteen-year-old, Evan, described the difficulty he experienced: "It's a really tough time. You're not a teenager but you're not a baby. I think it would be easier if you were an adult or younger."

Young adolescents are not children and, alternately, not full-grown adolescents. They are literally in between the more comfortable stages of life in which we can often more clearly define who we are and what we want. Popular culture often uses the term *tweens* to describe young adolescents. And don't think the public doesn't notice them: three separate news magazines, *Time*, *U. S. News & World Report*, and *Newsweek*, devoted almost entire issues to young adolescence from 2003 to 2006.

Creating a school environment that is responsive to the changing needs of young adolescents requires an understanding of their developmental changes. More importantly, however, it requires an understanding of how young adolescents perceive those changes. Their perceptions become their reality.

Here is how Lindsay, an eighth grader, describes herself in both poetry and art.

What's on the Inside

I am an artist,
who draws what she feels, sees, and encounters,
I need love from my friends and family,
I need affection to help me be successful in life,
I want to be all I can be,
To do this I will work hard to achieve,
I am human,
I make mistakes and learn from them,
I will not give up and therefore,
I will be the best by being me.

LINDSAY HAMILTON

LOVE
FAITH
FRIENDS
FETISHES
DREAMS
CHERISH
HOPES
NEEDS
WANTS
FEELINGS
LIVES
ENCOUNTERS
WONDERS
FREEDOM
GROOVES
PEOPLE
NATURE
LIGHT
DARK
FLAVOR
INDEPENDENCE

Angel

Lindsay's self-description

Time for Reflection

Dig through some old pictures of yourself and find one from your middle school years. Write a few thoughts about how you felt about yourself during that time of your life.

Physical Development

The greatest problem for middle schoolers is growing up too fast.

BESSIE, AGE THIRTEEN

I've changed physically. I've gotten so out of shape. I come home so tired every day. All I want to do is eat. I gained twenty pounds this year.

DAN, AGE TWELVE

Photo day arrives at Smith Middle School. Students line up from shortest to tallest and march into the gym to have their pictures taken. There they stand: from four feet nine inches to six feet two inches. Six months ago, they were much more similar in size. What is happening to these kids?

It's *puberty*—a word that strikes fear in the hearts of parents and confusion in the hearts of young adolescents. When does it start? When does it end? Does puberty start when the physical changes begin? For some of your students, that may be as early as ten or as late as fifteen. Does it start when the child goes to middle school? That may be fifth, sixth, or seventh grade. If we can't even define when it starts, how will we know how to address it? How do these changes affect our students? How do these physical changes affect our attitudes and expectations toward our students?

The National Middle School Association (NMSA) clearly states, "Successful schools for young adolescents are characterized by a culture that includes educators who value working with this age group and are prepared to do so" (NMSA 2003). Being prepared for teaching young adolescents requires knowing what they are like.

Physical development is an overriding concern of young adolescents. Looking at themselves in every mirror they can find, they will often see an alien body staring back. Whether it's the reflection in the bathroom mirror at home or the one hung in their locker, in the window of a car, the doorknob to their classroom, or a cafeteria spoon, middle school students watch themselves, convinced that everyone else is watching them too. They want to know, "Am I normal?"

A story a former school administrator tells emphasizes the need young adolescents have for self-examination (Blackburn 1999). A middle school principal was receiving complaints from teachers in the building that students were constantly asking for the restroom pass during class time. Annoyed by the students' need to leave the room during lessons, the teachers were looking for solutions. The perceptive principal asked the central office administrator to purchase mirrors for every classroom. The mirrors were placed strategically inside the door of each classroom. The result was an amazing drop in the number of student requests for restroom breaks.

Young adolescents' concerns about their bodies are manifested in social and emotional reactions that may affect their ability to learn. Our understanding of physical development is therefore vital if we want to create an environment conducive to learning. The rate of physical development in young adolescents may vary from one student to the next, but there are common mileposts.

The Growth Spurt

Individuals experience a growth spurt of the skeletal and muscular systems that begins at about age ten for girls and twelve for boys and lasts for two to three years. The sequences of the changes tend to be somewhat consistent, although individual variations occur. What is less standardized is the age and speed at which the changes happen (Rice and Dolgin 2005).

Height gain may be as much as four or more inches a year in young adolescents, with usually two years of fast growth followed by three years of slow, steady growth. That could mean the addition of ten to twenty inches in just five years. Average height gain during adolescence for females is seven inches; for males, it is nine to ten inches.

Weight gains equal eight to ten pounds a year. Many young adolescents gain as much as forty to fifty pounds before it's all over. One middle schooler told us, "I gained ten pounds in six months. I'm not too proud of that." Another student added, "In the last year I've grown a lot—four or five inches."

Girls' growth spurts peak about two years earlier than boys'. Attend a middle school dance, and you will observe this phenomenon firsthand: five-foot-five-inch girls dancing with five-foot-one-inch boys. Suddenly girls are taller, stronger, and more mature than most of the boys their age.

Middle school teachers must be aware of and respond to these physical differences because they are constantly on students' minds.

They may not be saying it to teachers or parents, but young adolescents notice the physical differences, and these affect their attitudes toward each other and everyone else in their lives.

Skeletal and Muscular Changes

A defining characteristic of the physical development of young adolescents is rapid and uneven skeletal change. The bones in the legs may grow when nothing else seems to be growing, giving young adolescents the appearance of being all legs. The feet may grow while height remains constant. Many of us can recall when our feet seemed huge while the rest of our body appeared to be the same size as when we were nine years old. Arms may lengthen while the torso stays the same. The hands may seem disproportionately large. The result is "the awkward stage." In June of one year, the body is well proportioned; the student is an exceptional athlete. The following June, the child is lanky and graceless. What happened to the physical coordination of just a year before?

To complicate matters further, bone growth tends to surpass muscle growth (Tanner 1972). This variable development is significant particularly in physical education and sports programs: kids are often encouraged to lift heavier weights, jump higher, throw curve balls, and run faster when their muscles cannot sustain the effort. This information is something male and female athletes need to understand, but it's probably more critical that their coaches do.

Van Hoose and Strahan (1988) reported that another result of the changing skeletal structure of young adolescents is that the three tailbones fuse and harden into their final adult form. It is a process that can cause pain and discomfort. Eric told us, "Sometimes when the teachers are not looking, I need to stand." When Tom, age thirteen, was asked what he would change about school, he commented, "I would change the chairs. We have rock-hard chairs and it hurts after awhile."

Long bones, awkwardness, underdeveloped muscles, pain in the tailbone, huge feet, long hands—no wonder the young adolescent is concerned. Despite these uncomfortable growing pains, we put them in a setting where they have to sit for most of the day.

Hormones

> Scientists have identified almost fifty different types of human hormones. They are essential to everyday life, and they are at play every moment of our lives, every year of our life. So, if hormones regulate all sorts of bodily functions for all ages of people, why would we blame hormones for the teenage daughter's sudden [emotional] outburst?
>
> (WALSH 2004, 61)

Hormones have gotten a bad rap in discussions about young adolescents; they are often blamed for behaviors that many adults don't seem to understand. It is true that hormones play a powerful role in development. If we understand their role, we can better understand young adolescent behaviors.

The body begins preparing youth for full sexual maturity during early adolescence. Males and females experience increased amounts of the hormones testosterone and estradiol during puberty that affect sexual development. The most dramatic increase for males is in testosterone. Walsh (2004) reported that testosterone affects the male brain as well as sexual characteristics: "While testosterone does all sorts of good things, it is also likely to trigger surges of anger, aggression, sexual interest, dominance, and territoriality" (62).

The primary increase for females is in the hormone estradiol, or estrogen; levels are approximately eight times what they were before puberty (Nottelmann et al. 1987). Estrogen along with progesterone "[H]ave a powerful influence over neurotransmitters. The main neurotransmitters that are active in the adolescent brain are norepinephrine, dopamine, and serotonin. All three have a big influence on mood" (Walsh 2004, 63). We'll talk more about the social and emotional impact of hormones in Chapter 3.

The sex hormones are not the only hormones undergoing changes in a young adolescent's life. Hormonal secretions dictated by the pituitary gland also increase, often in an irregular way. For example, sudden secretions of adrenaline into the body from the adrenal gland could make the young adolescent want to run around the school building ten times just when asked to sit and do a worksheet. At other times, the gland is underactive, resulting in lethargy (Van Hoose and Strahan 1988). Peter, a sixth grader, describes the result of these physical changes: "One of the hardest things for me is just waking up in the morning and going through the day without pulses of tiredness. Sometimes I get real restless because I get really tired."

Sweat glands also become very active, explaining why classroom windows are frequently open even in the dead of winter. Active sweat glands also contribute to oily hair and the development of that scourge of adolescence—acne. One middle school language arts teacher describes how she insists on giving her eighth graders the "deodorant talk" each year in late October, explaining that although they may not notice their body odor, she and others do. She continues to explain how their bodies are changing and the need to address those changes with proper hygiene.

Hormonal changes in young adolescents naturally impact their physical growth, but certain hormones also influence social and emotional behavior and how the brain processes information.

Female Physical Changes

The initial physical change that occurs among female young adolescents as they reach puberty is a change in height during ages ten and eleven (Rice and Dolgin 2005). Girls generally grow taller before they experience maturational weight gains. The body also prepares for full reproductive capability. The major benchmark is menstruation—accompanied by the fear in girls that they'll be the last in their peer group to experience it.

Other changes include breast development—often accompanied by behavioral changes such as the wearing of baggy shirts, the adoption of an erect, proud walk, or a slumping of the shoulders in an effort to conceal development; the growth of pubic and underarm hair; and rounding of the hips.

The beginning of menstruation creates challenges for many females. Many girls have a negative view of it, particularly those girls who mature before the age of twelve (Rice and Dolgin 2005). Medical research reveals that puberty and physical sexual maturity are occurring earlier than they did a century ago (Rice and Dolgin 2005; Rimm 2005; Walsh 2004). For example, in the United States in 1900 the average age of a female's first menstruation was just over fourteen years. Herman-Giddens, who studied the onset of puberty for over a decade, noted that from 1963 to 1990, the average age of a girl's first menstruation dropped by approximately a month for every ten years (Bower and Caplan 2005). The average age today for first menstruation is slightly over twelve (Rice and Dolgin 2005). The theories that explain these earlier changes are an increase in the amount of fatty foods young adolescents eat, medical advances leading to better overall health, exposure to certain chemicals in the environment, use of infant formula containing soy, and a better diet for many (Rimm 2005).

Researchers have noted that African American females reach puberty several months earlier on average than Caucasian females (Daniels et al. 1998). Researchers also discovered that girls from families in conflict are more likely to reach menarche earlier (Ellis 1991; Kim and Smith 1998; Wierson, Long, and Forehand 1993).

Both male and female teachers may be called on to provide support during this transition. Keep in mind, though, that females often have a difficult time sharing this information with anyone else—especially their friends. The fifteen-year-old females that Koff and Rierdan (1995) interviewed also suggested that information about menarche be a continual process that starts long before their first time and continues long after.

While earlier physical development may sound like a good thing, the challenge is that young adolescents may lack the cognitive, social, emotional, and psychological maturity necessary to understand those changes. Several researchers report that early developing females may be at greater risk of developing mental health issues because they are not prepared for the physical, psychological, and social challenges brought on by puberty (Brooks-Gunn, Peterson, and Eichorn 1985; Hayward et al. 1997). For instance, girls who are early maturers "are more likely than other girls to exhibit depressive, eating, and delinquent symptoms as well as general behavior problems" (Graber et al. 2002, 40).

Early physically maturing females may experience low self-esteem because they are so different from their peers: they're heavier, taller, and more developed sexually. Another possible result of this early development is that females will spend time with older males, which may lead to early sexual behavior (Flannery, Rowe, and Gulley 1993).

In her study of 335 adolescents over a three-year period from sixth through eighth grade and during their last year of high school, Petersen (1987) found that late or early maturation affected individual satisfaction with appearance. The girls Petersen studied in the seventh and eighth grades seemed less satisfied if they were early maturers. Although these girls were seen as more popular, at a personal level they were often self-conscious and insecure.

An adolescent's physical maturity is no guarantee of simultaneous social or emotional maturity. Adults' unrealistic expectations of mature social and emotional behaviors can add to the undue pressure that physically early-maturing young adolescents may already experience. We hope that every school for young adolescents provides a health education curriculum that addresses these issues and encourages all teachers to be willing to address sensitive physical growth issues when they arise. We believe every middle school teacher is a *health* teacher because young adolescents have a constant stream of questions about their health, questions that may never be asked of parents.

Male Physical Changes

> I know everything I need to know about being an adolescent. You grow hair on your chin and want to have sex all the time.
>
> ROBERT, AGE TEN

Males generally begin the physical maturation process later than females. The growth spurt begins between the ages of eleven and a half and thirteen. Most males don't reach their full height until age seventeen. The greater physical changes for most males occur between the ages of thirteen and sixteen. The voice deepens now because of the rapid growth of the larynx (Adam's apple) and a lengthening of the vocal cords across it (Rice and Dolgin 2005). The cracking of the voice from low to high and vice versa may continue for some until age seventeen.

A primary physical maturational characteristic for males is testicular and penile growth. Adolescent males are often worried about the size of their penis. Frequent erections are common during adolescence and may cause a lot of embarrassment (Rice and Dolgin 2005). Most young adolescent males experience nocturnal emissions, also called "wet dreams." The first ejaculation, called "semenarche" or "spermarche," occurs for most males before their thirteenth birthday. This event, unlike females' first menses, is usually hidden from others, since many males have no knowledge that this will occur. Paddack (1987) reported that boys who are taught about these physical changes have more positive feelings about their occurrence. We hope, once again, that as a middle school teacher, you can understand the importance of disseminating information to young adolescents about these personal changes.

Other later physical signs of male physical maturity include a broadening of the shoulders, more regularly occurring facial hair growth, and muscular development. While some young adolescents experience these changes by eighth grade, others may be far from any need to shave.

Males who don't begin to mature physically by age fifteen are more likely to suffer negative effects than on-time or early-maturing males are. The first challenge is what Rice and Dolgin (2005) refer to as "locker-room syndrome": males begin to notice in the shower after physical education class that they have less hair in places, have an underdeveloped penis, are considerably shorter, and have less-developed muscles (91). Males who reach puberty much later than their counterparts may experience feelings of inferiority due to poorer athletic skills and a less mature appearance (Graber et al. 2002). These researchers also noted in their study that "late-maturing boys reported more self-consciousness, more conflict with parents, and more trouble in school" (47). These findings again point to the need for assurance from adults in their lives that the onset of physical maturity is highly varied for each person.

Early maturers enjoy many social advantages because their superior height and advanced muscle development often provide success in athletics, greater leadership roles, and more popularity among peers and adults (Ge, Conger, and Elder 2001). Petersen (1987) reported in studies she conducted in the 1960s that early-maturing males were more successful at peer relations during middle and high school. These individuals excelled in athletics, demonstrated confidence in social situations, and became the school leaders. The studies showed, however, that when the late-maturing boys reached their thirties, they seemed to have a stronger sense of identity.

Rice and Dolgin (2005), on the other hand, noted that early-maturing males generally have greater expectations for behavior and responsibility placed on them from adults in their lives. This may lead to less freedom to act "their age" and participate in activities that are more age appropriate. For instance, one of us taught an eighth grade male who was six feet four inches tall and an accomplished player on the school's basketball team. He enjoyed skateboarding with friends, but when he got hurt doing that, the coach was upset by his participating in a "childish" activity. Some physically mature males are expected to begin working full time after school or during the summers before they are fifteen or sixteen, even though they are not necessarily ready for nor do they desire this type of responsibility.

Some early-maturing males are given greater freedom by adults in their lives and, thus, are less supervised than others their age. The result could be more socializing with older males and the possibility of committing delinquent acts (Dubas, Garber, and Pedersen 1991). You may say as a teacher that these issues are not your problem; however, you see these young adolescents in your school each day, so your guidance may have a positive effect on the choices they make outside school.

The Appetite—Insatiable and Peculiar

Young adolescents require a lot of nutrients because of the rapid growth of the skeletal system and other physical changes. It is not uncommon for young adolescents to eat continuously from the time they get home from school until bedtime. Active young adolescents need anywhere from two to three thousand calories a day. Females generally need fewer calories due to a smaller stature and a lower metabolic rate (Rice and Dolgin 2005).

Physical type and size as well as activity levels should determine how many calories an adolescent needs. Unfortunately, given the cultural prevalence of fast food in this country, many of these kids are not eating foods that give them the maximum benefit.

Several factors exist that prevent adolescents from eating well. Young adolescents often choose snacks high in fat, inappropriate carbohydrates, and sugar while eating only small quantities of nutritious foods. For instance, Rice and Dolgin (2005) reported, "One quarter of all vegetables eaten by teens are french fries" (114). Adolescents may skip breakfast so they can sleep later and often don't eat regular healthy meals with their families. Social pressures often present a view of constant dieting among females.

The structure of the middle school day can also contribute to poor nutrition. Imagine your students catching the bus at 7:00 A.M. but not having a lunch period until 12:45. That span of time without food can have an impact on learning. In addition, students who eat lunch at 10:30 may not be getting the appropriate nutrition they need for effective learning later in the day, since school isn't over until 3:00. Most schools prohibit any eating in the halls or classrooms, meaning that many students are going through their busy days without eating for as long as five hours. Add an extracurricular activity to that after school and students extend their time without food even longer.

The choices students have at school are often poor and highly unhealthy: vending machines with soda, chips, cookies, ice cream, and candy; school lunches that are so flexible that students are able to choose a limited source of carbohydrates such as pizza. A haphazard school policy can often lead to life sentences of excess weight, obesity, and chronic unhealthy eating habits.

Childhood obesity rates have been increasing since the mid-1970s. Ozer et al. (2003) reported that African American girls and Mexican American boys have the highest rates (above 25 percent) and Caucasian youth have the lowest rates (around 12 percent) of obesity. There are many health risks associated with obesity, but among adolescents, issues of social rejection and low self-esteem also affect their lives (Rice and Dolgin 2005). Rimm (2005) noted that both males and females who were overweight had considerably less confidence and generally didn't believe they were above average intelligence. Rimm's story of an overweight female's description of how her eighth grade teacher encouraged her is something that every middle school teacher should hear:

Ever since I was a little kid, I was fat, and that made me feel different from other kids. Kids left me out of their groups. A wall kept going up separating me from everyone. This year my teacher liked me. She told me I was good at writing, math, and music and that I had a good personality. Her confidence made me feel different, but in a good way. I started making friends and felt smart and better about myself. (205)

The other side of unhealthy adolescent eating behaviors is that the ideal American body image leads some adolescents to deny even minimal nutritional needs. Female students are particularly susceptible to eating disorders such as anorexia nervosa or bulimia. Researchers note that about 1 percent of female adolescents have anorexia (Anorexia Nervosa and Related Eating Disorders [ANRED] 2006). Males also develop anorexia, but they only make up about 1 percent of those who struggle with eating enough. Some males succumb to a habit of taking steroids in order to develop what they believe is an appropriate body type.

Adolescents' Sleep Needs

Ask middle school teachers about their class schedules, and some will tell you that they despise teaching first period because their students are so tired they may be comatose or close to it. Some teachers want their worst-behaved students first period for the same reason—they're too tired to be a disruption. Parents suffer more than teachers in their efforts to wake their adolescent sons and daughters each morning for school.

Carskadon (1999), a sleep researcher, explained the process that affects adolescents' sleep needs. The hormone melatonin is secreted into the bloodstream and regulates the sleep time continuum. Melatonin is secreted later at night as teens progress through puberty (Wolfe 2005). That translates into teens being unable to go to sleep early at night and just as incapable of waking early in the morning. In addition, teens need nine hours and fifteen minutes of sleep to function effectively during the day (Carskadon). Telling them to go to sleep earlier isn't necessarily the solution since melatonin prevents them from falling asleep, keeping them awake approximately two hours later than a child or adult.

The importance of sleep is that it aids in the release of hormones needed by adolescents for growth and sexual maturation (Wolfe 2005). Adequate sleep is also necessary for the brain to regenerate and operate efficiently during the day. Sleep deprivation causes numerous problems for adolescents:

- contributes to poor reasoning
- causes difficulty focusing
- impairs functioning memory
- increases the stress hormone cortisol, which compromises the immune system
- affects alertness
- impairs ability to process glucose, which contributes to excess weight (Walsh 2004, 182)

Sleep deprivation may also lead to mood disorders in which feelings are more intense and may lead to difficulty controlling emotions. Armed with this information as a middle school teacher, your reaction to students' emotional outbursts becomes more tolerant.

Wolfson and Caskadon (1998) studied sleep patterns among adolescents and found that students earning C and D grades were getting about forty minutes less sleep per night and stayed up later on weekends than students receiving As and Bs. Teachers can't control when students go to bed at night or the habits that exist in their students' homes. They can, however, advise adolescents and their caregivers that middle school students need a great deal of sleep and that there are serious consequences to their ability to learn when they ignore those needs.

Impact of Physical Changes

Young adolescent development does not follow a strict timeline. Individual differences occur both between and within each gender. Everyone is developing at a different rate and yet everyone is on track. These variations make it difficult for young adolescents to find someone with whom to compare their bodies. How do they know if they are all right—if they are "normal"? Milgram (1992) explained:

> The pace of the physical changes taking place is different for each child and for each sex. In the egocentric, comparative world of the young adolescent, these differences are generally translated into feelings of inadequacy and deficiency. . . . It is important to remember that all adolescents at one time or another feel badly about some part of their bodies. (19)

This inadequacy undoubtedly has something to do with gender stereotypes, put forward by the media, dictating that females should be attractive while boys should be rugged. Media images remain a powerful force. Rarely do adult perspectives have the kind of influence that peer opinions and advertising campaigns have on young adolescent minds.

Not surprisingly, talking about the physical changes seems to be more difficult for the young adolescent than talking about newfound friends, mood swings, or what they'd like to see their teachers do in the classroom. The physical changes have such a dramatic impact on emotions, learning, and social interactions that discussing them can make perceived inadequacies seem even more real. Think back on your own early adolescence. How willing were you and your friends to discuss breast development, underarm hair, wet dreams, or vocal changes? Instead, less emotionally charged issues like shoe size tend to be discussed instead of the more serious topics that affect an individual's sense of self.

Ask seven-year-olds about the growth of their bodies and typically they'll express disinterest. Four years later the young adolescent is obsessed by these physical transformations. Few adults have positive memories about the way they looked during young adolescence. Wright, in a 1989 study of body image in adolescence, commented, "Preoccupation with one's body image is strong throughout adolescence, but it is especially acute during puberty, a time when adolescents are more dissatisfied with their bodies than in late adolescence."

Teachers must be aware of the facts of young adolescent physical development and be ready and willing to discuss developmental issues with their students and, perhaps, with students' parents. Students must be made aware that they are developing normally, whatever their rate or sequence of physical maturation. Young adolescents have many questions about their physical growth. They spend much time listening to inaccurate stories from friends and classmates about their bodies. Middle school faculty and administrators have a responsibility to respond to students' concerns in many ways—from designing curricula that address their needs to providing, in several formats, information that addresses their questions and provides accurate details about their growth processes.

Physical development is only one aspect to consider when looking at the young adolescent. Although physical changes are the most obvious and visible of the changes, it is the impact of physical maturation on cognitive, emotional, and social development that has the greatest influence on how young adolescents view themselves, school life, and those around them.

Cognitive Development

Effective educators are knowledgeable of their students' cognitive capabilities. The term *developmentally appropriate practice* has been used for well over twenty-five years in educational research and literature and is a defining description of teaching young children—especially at the prekindergarten and primary school years. That same term, however, is also used in the research on teaching young adolescents. Teaching to the cognitive needs of young adolescents in some way defines the difference between the original junior highs and genuine middle schools. The past few years have brought much scientific knowledge about the adolescent brain. Just how different are young adolescents from their earlier cognitive selves?

For years, scientists believed that adolescents' brains were fully developed by the time they reached puberty. The brain of an adolescent is fully grown if one is measuring its physical size, but it's what's going on inside that influences the behaviors, attitudes, and learning capabilities of young adolescents. Recently, by using new medical technology, medical scientists have been able to peer inside adolescents' brains (Walsh 2004).

Of particular importance to teachers are the continued "blossoming" and "pruning" of brain connections and the myelination of brain cells. Blossoming and pruning are especially prevalent during growth spurts. Blossoming occurs when dendrites in the brain are going through hypergrowth—that is, more brain connections are being made. This hypergrowth peaks for females around age eleven and for males around twelve and a half. All these new brain cells don't survive; those that are not regularly used shrink and eventually disappear. This is called *pruning*, but it is a positive rather than a negative process. Walsh (2004) stated, "The periods of blossoming and pruning are critical in brain development. Experiences during these periods, more than any other time, physically shape the brain's neural networks and have a huge influence on how the brain gets wired" (34). Walsh added that critical areas of the brain undergo blossoming and pruning *only* during adolescence (his emphasis).

Myelin is a white fatty substance, an insulator, that covers the main cable of the neuron—the axon—making nerve-signal transmissions faster and more efficient. Walsh (2004) reported that the myelination process in certain parts of the adolescent brain "actually increase[s] by 100 percent from the beginning to the end of adolescence" (37). The result of pruning and myelination is fewer but faster connections in the brain, making it more efficient (Park 2004). More myelination improves short-term memory, which may in turn lead to better reasoning and problem solving (Kail 1997).

More efficient processing takes time to develop in middle school students—they're not yet adults. Young adolescents need meaningful, challenging learning experiences in order to develop and sustain cognitive growth processes. Cognitive processing won't improve or develop as well if students are consistently taking notes or memorizing dates without opportunities to make genuine connections between content and their experiences.

The Prefrontal Cortex: Its Effects on Behavior

Some of the most significant changes occurring during young adolescence are changes to the prefrontal cortex (PFC) of the brain. The PFC is considered the CEO of the brain, influencing one's abilities and skills in making appropriate decisions, considering the impact of certain behaviors, planning for the future, and organizing materials. Walsh (2004) described it as a major "construction site," noting that it is far from being fully developed throughout all of adolescence (43). Since the PFC is far from mature during young adolescence, middle school students may lack many of the organizational and social skills that teachers expect.

From an academic standpoint, the PFC affects students' abilities to plan in relation to such decisions as writing assignments in notebooks, organizing their lockers, prioritizing completing homework over socializing, choosing the appropriate books and materials for class, organizing an essay, or choosing the right strategies for solving problems. When we asked experienced middle school teachers "What are the most important concepts and principles for students to learn during their middle school years?" one of their frequent responses was, "To learn how to be organized." Given young adolescents' developing PFC and teachers' learning priorities, it's easy to see how teachers might become frustrated with their efforts to help students gain these skills.

The corpus callosum that connects the right and left hemispheres also develops extensively during young adolescence. This process affects students' communication abilities—interpersonal skills—and they need guidance in order to develop these skills appropriately. The corpus callosum tends to be thicker in females than it is in males. The result is that females often do better in language arts classes, since they are better than males at using both sides of their brains simultaneously; males tend to use one hemisphere or the other for certain tasks (Walsh 2004).

Boys' literacy skills may improve if their teachers help them find appropriate stories that match their interests. Kinesthetic learning activities are also often effective in helping students learn principles more efficiently.

Middle level teachers can design learning experiences that best meet the needs of young adolescents' expanding intellectual capabilities when they understand their unique brain development processes. It is critical for educators to challenge students with meaningful learning opportunities that match their interests while helping them acquire the cognitive strategies needed to organize, prioritize, and take

28

responsibility for their learning. Teachers who adopt this guiding approach demonstrate to students the partnership required for optimum cognitive growth during the middle level years.

Piaget's Findings

Jean Piaget (1977a) provided the first distinct description of what may be happening intellectually to young adolescents. Piaget developed a theory about how people make sense of their world. In this process, he identified four stages of intellectual development. Each of the stages reflects characteristics related to a person's cognitive ability with respect to object perception. The stages are sensorimotor (birth to two years), preoperational (two to seven years), concrete operational (seven to eleven years), and formal operational (twelve years to adulthood). Individuals pass through each stage in sequence, but at varying rates.

Concrete Operational Thought

Middle level educators need to be aware of the differences in the last two stages: concrete and formal operations. In the concrete stage, students can do and understand the following:

- classify and order objects into hierarchical relationships
- understand reverse processes (comprehend that all actions, even mental actions, have an opposite)
- think logically about concrete objects
- arrange objects in order from large to small or small to large
- conceptually combine objects to form categories, for example, "boxes" and "jars" into container (Rice and Dolgin 2005, 124–25)

Elkind (1970) warned however, that the learner in the concrete stage of cognitive development can understand only two classes or relationships at the same time. Comprehending more than two categories at once is possible only when one has reached formal operations. Elkind also noted that those children in the concrete stage "can only reason about those things for which they have had direct, personal experience" (Rice and Dolgin 2005, 125).

It is clear then that students who process information at the concrete stage need direct experiences and do better with real as opposed to abstract objects or thought. Middle level students in this concrete stage are better able to cognitively grasp higher-level principles when ideas are taught with the use of hands-on activities and real materials rather than presented in a lecture or by reading a textbook. Students also often misunderstand lessons when teachers "cover" vocabulary words too quickly for them to understand the new concepts and principles associated with these words. Teachers must be aware that most middle school students remain in this concrete operational stage through eighth grade (Newman, Spalding, and Yezzi 2000; Muuss 1988; Piaget 1977a).

Middle level teachers should stock their classrooms with many genuine objects (manipulatives) so students can touch and see the concepts they are learning. Although manipulatives, role-playing, and hands-on activities are important during all stages, they are particularly important during the concrete stage—in other words, all of middle school.

Formal Operational Thought
In the formal operational stage, students have developed the capability to solve abstract and hypothetical problems. According to Piaget (1977a), "This period is characterized in general by the conquest of a new mode of reasoning, one that is no longer limited exclusively to dealing with objects or directly representable realities, but also employs hypotheses" (33). Formal thought includes several elements. One part is an increased ability to think in hypothetical ways about abstract ideas as well as to generate and test hypotheses systematically. When asked how his thinking had changed, Rob (age fourteen) responded, "I think I examine problems more and try to put the problem with something else I already know." Formal operational thought implies that students can also understand the multidimensional nature of problems.

Another formal operations skill is the ability to think about the future and therefore to plan and explore, often with an extremely idealistic perspective—hence middle school students' sudden preoccupation with life plans and their concern for the world around them.

One of the most powerful growth processes during this stage is the development of metacognition, or the ability to reflect on one's thoughts. Caine and Caine (1994) describe *metacognition* as "thinking about the way we think, feel and act" (160). When a seventh grader doesn't understand something, he or she can suddenly think about not understanding. Such thinking may not lead to understanding and may in fact lead to frustration. Indeed, many of the frustrations middle school students experience may result from this new reflective thought—this thinking about thinking. They may even worry about why they are thinking about their thinking.

For the early adolescent, the growth of metacognitive abilities generates greater understanding of abstract principles and results in more meaningful learning. Metacognitive growth includes the ability to monitor and reflect on on-task academic behavior. This occurs when a student realizes, "I can't recall what I just read. I'd better reread that paragraph." A critical component of metacognitive growth is an awareness and control of attitudes toward learning. For students, the internal conversation may go something like this: "I usually hate social studies, but these map activities are kind of fun. I can do this." Another essential aspect of metacognition that students own is taking responsibility for their academic effort. In other words, students may proclaim, "I'm going to work harder on this assignment than I have others." Students tap into their metacognitive skills when they choose among a set of strategies to use to solve problems or complete assignments. They might realize, "If I can't solve this problem this way, I'm going to try that new method we learned in science today." A final aspect of metacognition is an awareness of their personal learning profile: "I know I will understand this better if I draw a picture."

Teachers can help students develop these strategies by explicitly modeling them—literally saying out loud, "When I can't solve the problem this way, I think, 'Maybe I'll try reversing those numbers to see what effect that has on solving this problem.'" Some middle schools help students identify their preferred learning style. Teachers must also explain to students that they are in control of their attitudes and effort toward learning. Conversations with entire classes about attitudes and effort may help to improve student motivation as students learn how their attitudes affect learning.

Final traits of formal thought are one's idealistic beliefs and an ability to expand one's thinking. The middle school student's mind is suddenly open to a myriad of ideas, solutions, and imaginings. The ability to think hypothetically produces unconstrained thoughts and a sense of unlimited possibilities. "Reality" is no longer the benchmark of thought, having been overtaken instead by "what is possible."

Piaget delineated two substages of formal operational thought and believed that young adolescents are actually in the one titled "emergent formal operational thought," in which they are able to demonstrate formal operations in some academic situations but not others (Rice and Dolgin 2005, 126). Researchers have made it clear, though, that some adolescents and adults never reach the final stage of formal operational thought, because their intelligence and life experiences are limited (Muuss 1988).

Moving from Concrete to Formal Thought
We can assume that most students will be in the concrete operational stage as they enter middle school and experience periods of formal operational thought by the time they leave. Middle school then becomes a period of cognitive transition. Although this idea sounds good in theory, many students remain primarily in the concrete operational stage of development throughout their middle school careers, with only about one third of eighth graders consistently demonstrating an ability to use formal operations (Newman, Spaulding, and Yezzi 2000; Piaget 1977b).

Lounsbury and Clark (1990) indicated that academically talented eighth graders often experience confusion because they are adjusting to and accommodating more powerful cognitive strategies. An eighth grade teacher describes her frustration: "I think my biggest challenge is getting all the kids in the class to reach the same conclusions and the same level of thinking—which I can't do. So, when I ask *why* something happens, I have some kids who are wondering *what's* happened."

Variations among students are common. So are variations in individuals with respect to different subject areas. The young adolescent may be capable of abstract thinking in mathematics yet not be able to set up a scientific experiment. Students move back and forth between concrete and formal operational thought. These variations have great implications for instruction, as Van Hoose and Strahan (1988) noted: "Planning instruction is like shooting at a moving target due to rapid, individual changes" (16).

When young adolescents use their formal operational thinking abilities, they begin demonstrating traits of intellectual growth in the following ways:

- persevering when the solution to a problem is not immediately apparent
- decreasing impulsivity and deferring judgment until adequate information is available
- using flexibility in thinking and sustaining problem-solving skills until an answer is found
- checking the accuracy of their work
- initiating questions themselves instead of relying on teachers to ask questions
- transferring knowledge beyond the classroom to real life
- using more precise language in speech and writing
- enjoying problem solving on their own (adapted from Forte and Schurr 1993, 201)

Teachers must cognitively challenge young adolescents to help them take advantage of their intense brain growth. We don't want teachers to believe that because most middle level students haven't reached formal operations the curricula must be "dumbed down." Young adolescents are ready for many intellectual challenges that lead them to capitalize on their cognitive potential. It is the manner in which lessons are presented and the opportunities students have to interact intellectually with new concepts, principles, ideas, and theories that determine if your lessons will contribute to their movement from concrete to formal operational thought. As Rice and Dolgin (2005) noted: "The highest levels of reasoning are attained when individuals are given the chance to discuss, argue, and debate with people whose views are different from their own" (137). Using interactive learning and engaging students in the process of curriculum decision making are significant strategies for effecting cognitive change.

These components of effective middle level practice are discussed in detail in Chapters 6 and 7. In Chapter 7, we describe how teachers can assist students in moving into formal operations.

The Curiosity Factor

Middle school students are learners in the purest sense of the word. With their developing capacity for abstract thinking, middle school students are curious about life and highly inquisitive about everything life has to offer. They challenge principles that don't fit their view of the way things work. This curiosity leads to the desire to participate in practical problem solving and activities that reflect real issues.

The curiosity factor is clearly evident in the following poem written by a college student reflecting on his middle school years.

I Wanna Know

I wanna know
How trees are made
And why money's paid
I wanna know
How stars are so bright
And why lights light
I wanna know
How animals mate
And why people hate.
I wanna know
How pollution starts
And why mountains fall apart.
I wanna know
How people breathe
And why birds fly with ease.
I wanna know!

RICHARD BORDEAUX

The bodies of young adolescents are physically maturing; their minds are thinking in new and deeper ways. Both of those developmental changes affect social interactions and impact the young adolescent's emotional life.

Adolescent Risk Taking

> Even the meekest, smartest, most obedient, and sensible teenager will, at some point or another, find himself or herself facing the angry, disbelieving face of an adult who shouts, "What were you thinking?"
>
> WALSH (2004, 55)

All these cognitive changes among young adolescents create another challenge for the adults in their lives: a need for risky behaviors, that is, a time of physical, social, and emotional excitement and impulsivity beyond the daily routine. (You didn't want to be bored as a teacher, did you?)

A result of expanding thought processes is the sense of personal uniqueness and infallibility. Middle school students are certain that no one has ever thought the thoughts they are thinking or felt the feelings they are feeling. As they get caught up in their personal worlds, young adolescents can become removed from reality and begin to feel indestructible. The belief that "it won't happen to me" contributes to risk-taking behaviors.

Teachers are the second most likely to experience adolescent risk taking (parents are the first, of course). As parents and former teachers, we've seen adolescents do and say some pretty absurd things. Part of the problem is the incomplete wiring of the PFC. The effects cause what may appear to be many apparent unconscious behaviors, including poor decision making, quick mood changes, and confusing feelings (Walsh 2004). Specifically, middle school students might suddenly

- say something completely inappropriate to fellow students, teachers, or visiting adults in the school
- begin crying over something that appears minor to adults
- physically and verbally bully other students
- try physical stunts that are incredibly dangerous

Middle school teachers have a responsibility to remain calm in the face of possible insults, swearing, and other demeaning behaviors. Teachers who overreact in these situations demonstrate to their students that they are also not in control of their impulses. Guidance is the key role that adults can play here. We suggest teachers

- act calmly and professionally when unruly behaviors occur
- create a space for students to cool off
- provide opportunities for conflict resolution among students
- guide students to appropriate decision making when major and minor incidents occur
- brainstorm possible consequences for future behaviors
- encourage students to self-evaluate inappropriate behaviors

Teachers have a responsibility to guide students through adolescent years. If it sounds as if we expect teachers to be more like counselors instead of merely teachers, then you are beginning to comprehend the role of effective middle level practitioners.

Although we separated them into sections for organization's sake, all of the developmental processes of being a young adolescent are intertwined. Changing bodies and advancing intellectual capacity create more than just larger, smarter children—these changes also impact social and emotional processes, which are always connected to cognitive processes.

THREE

Who Am I? The Social, Emotional, and Identity Trials of Young Adolescence

The fact is that teens sometimes have a tough time getting along with themselves, let alone with their parents and family.

WALSH (2004, 17)

Although the growth of abstract thinking allows early adolescents to revisit their self-systems, early adolescents' self-theories are not very coherent.

AZMITIA (2002, 170)

As if the physical changes aren't enough for young adolescents, the changes in their cognitive awareness create another challenge—specifically, a search for a true identity when months earlier they were quite possibly content with their persona. Every young adolescent at some time from sixth through eighth grade experiences questions about his or her place in the social milieu. Some of the questions that arise might include: Are my current friendships appropriate? Should I find new friends? What about having a girl- or boyfriend? Should I join

that particular peer group? Who do I sit with at lunch? Should I call or email that person?

Beyond the social questions are essential concerns about who they are and who they should be. Young adolescence sets into motion a search for identities: social, sexual, gender, ethnic, cultural, familial, socioeconomic, and spiritual, all related to who they think they are now and who they want to become as adults. Their future lives seem more immediate to them, although they are years from taking on the responsibilities of mature adults.

Beliefs related to their own maturity lead to many assumptions and much confusion about how much independence they have, are entitled to, and want. Adult expectations often wreak havoc on their need for dependence. Their constant search for a persona often leaves the adults in their lives confused as well. Teachers need to address young adolescents' social and emotional concerns and identity issues through curriculum, school programs, and the development of a personal healthy relationship with each student.

Social Development

> Although family, church, and community are important sources for developing friendships, for most students school is a primary place to acquire a sense of social group belonging and to practice skills necessary for making and keeping friends.
>
> SHEETS (2005, 71)

At a time when dramatic physical and intellectual changes are occurring, children are taken from the safety and security of the self-contained elementary school and put in an alien environment. They often go to larger schools with students they've never met before. They change classes and are responsible for being at certain places at certain times. As frightening as this new setting appears, it also provides the exciting and challenging prospect of meeting new people and gaining increased control of their lives. Bordeaux (1993–1994) reflected on this prospect in the following poem.

Finding a Place In the Group

Alone
In the back of the room
with this growing sense of doom
Laughter to the left of me
Smiling to the right.
Alone in the middle
No land in sight
Drowning in fright
Hey, somebody
Anybody
throw me a line
and I'll be fine
I'll pull myself in
Show you what's within
Give you the straight poop
And maybe
Just maybe
Find my place in the group.

Sheila, a seventh grader, was asked what she liked best about middle school. She responded, "Coming and seeing my friends and stuff." Asked what the most important thing to learn in school was, Peter responded, "How to make friends and how to act. Some people are just naturally more popular than others and they make friends more easily for some reason. But I think if you're not one of those people you have to learn the harder way—worrying about if people like you, or hate you, or whatever." Eric, also a seventh grader, agreed: "Social abilities are the most important thing to do and learn—getting in touch with the world and knowing what's going on and being able to talk in front of people."

In interviews with many middle school students, one eighth grader provided Doda and Knowles (2007) these revealing comments about friendships and peers in middle school:

I think every middle school teacher should know, or try to understand, the social whirlwind of statuses that forms and so quickly

39

hardens with every student in their place. What may seem, to a teacher, a classroom full of students peacefully working, may be exactly the opposite to a student. It becomes a room full of pitfalls, danger signs, and safe havens situated carefully in familiar territory. Every student, throughout the day, moves cautiously on "safe" paths from room to room. They will not read in another level's territory. They will not mix; everyone knows their place. Only a teacher or a student from a higher level will cause them to mix.

The separation between boys and girls is even more pronounced. Boys have territory separate from girls, and their own divisions in that. Boys and girls will absolutely not mix, except in the rare groups of girls and boys that are friends; these groups are either absolute highest status or the very bottom. Every student, boy or girl, has their place, their territory, their paths, the people they can stay with on their level. I think middle school teachers should know of, and try to understand, this code of the students. This network of statuses and levels is ever present in middle schools. While some students may not be directly aware of it, they always have a subconscious understanding of where they fit.

Teachers agree that developing friendships during the middle school years is important. Asked about the most important thing a middle school student should do or learn in school, they have surprisingly similar responses: "how to get along"; "social interactions along with social responsibility"; "socialization"; "social interaction with fellow peers and adults." Although academics remain important in preparing these students for life, teachers acknowledge the vital role that socialization plays during the middle school years.

Sheets (2005) reported that young adolescents begin to understand "the need to be satisfied by friendships and to value the importance of sustained relationships. Mutual aid, intimate self-disclosure, trust, commitment, and loyalty become important functions of friendship in adolescence" (71). Friendships have the power to affect so much of an adolescent's life: from healthy cognitive and emotional development to opportunities to negotiate social problems, become leaders, and improve cooperation (Sheets 2005).

Females have different friendship needs than males do during this stage of development, seeking intimacy and emotional support from their female friends. Males seek friends who can provide material support and who will stand by them in times of trouble.

Socialization skills, however, do not always come easily to young adolescents. Friendships during middle school years can be highly unstable. An underdeveloped prefrontal cortex (PFC) of the brain is one reason that causes young adolescents to completely ignore or misread facial expressions of others (Brownlee 2005). Adolescents may interpret messages of surprise or concern as anger, threats, or insults. Misreading these messages may lead them to exaggerate their intensity and intention: for example, saying, "Ms. Green yelled at me today when I wasn't doing anything wrong!" when the teacher calmly and politely asked the student to stop talking.

Young adolescents frequently need guidance in their social interactions with both friends and teachers. Some teachers seem to enjoy complaining that their students don't have any social skills or manners, but where else than in school would students have as many opportunities for socializing? It's their training ground, and they're going to make mistakes.

Wise teachers purposely plan lessons that offer social opportunities: collaborative research projects, debates, readers theatre, writing workshop, simulation games, and role-playing activities. Placing students in mixed social groups in academic situations during adolescence may help them better develop their social skills (Sprenger 2005). Manning (1993) summarized the following benefits of providing social experiences for young adolescents:

1. Relationships and conversation between friends can boost young people's self-esteem and reduce anxiety as trust and respect develop.
2. Friends help young adolescents develop their sense of identity.
3. Friendships contribute to the development of interpersonal skills important for future intimate relationships. (17)

The Role of Peers

Making friends in middle school is probably one of the first true choices a child has the opportunity to make. The child doesn't get to choose his or her parents or where to go to school. During elementary school, your friends were usually the children who lived in your neighborhood or attended your school. Prior to middle school the only models of behavior were family members, teachers, adults in the community, and maybe sports or entertainment stars.

A new world opens up during middle school. This expanding social landscape creates questions in young adolescents' minds about how to get peers to like them. They begin to see that some kids are popular while others aren't. They wonder how that happens and how they can become part of the popular group. They question where they stand and wonder what their peers think of them (Rice and Dolgin 2005).

The idea of "being popular" affects peer group orientation and choice. Middle school students' perceptions of popularity are often based on who they think is the most well known (Eder 2002). In some schools "being known" is associated with athletic success. In other schools, popularity may be associated with other activities such as being in the band or in the drama club. In addition, males found "physical and verbal fighting skills, use of humor, and willingness to be daring" instrumental in determining social status (Eder 154). For females, appearance, particularly the clothes they wear, was critical to being accepted. Sixth graders in a school that did not have an athletics program felt a greater sense of equality in terms of social acceptance (Eder). The idea that popularity even matters is a testament to the changing social landscape for young adolescents.

The young adolescents' world has changed: new lifestyles and new ways of thinking, values, and ideas are continually presented. The peer group is the primary source of new standards and models of behavior. Being part of the group helps young adolescents develop different points of view and try out new ideas. Experimenting with different ways of thinking and behaving is a vital component of the search for personal identity. Peers aid in this development by offering feedback on clothes, appearance, behavior, and anything else that interests them. The feedback allows young adolescents to gauge their new patterns of behavior in search for what fits.

The desire for peer approval is an extension of the desire to have their personal choices validated. Being part of a group also allows young adolescents to cover up what they believe are inadequacies. Since young adolescents no longer know what is normal, they lean heavily on peers to provide a structure for new behaviors and count on their peers to lead them in the right direction. This conformity to behavioral norms can have both positive and negative ramifications.

Although interest in the opposite sex emerges, often in the form of "puppy love," same-sex affiliation remains dominant and is preferred by the middle school student (Milgram 1992). Sex roles begin to change, but it is often parents, teachers, other adults, or the media that encourage that change and stress opposite-sex relationships. Informal and sometimes formal dances encourage young adolescents to form relationships at a time when they may prefer friendly interactions, long phone calls, mixed-group activities, and casual flirting.

Peer pressure is real to the young adolescent. As young adolescents try to fit in, they become sensitive to what other people have to say about them, particularly if it is negative. One student, when asked about peer pressure, said, "You gotta fit in so you get good friends."

When asked what the greatest problem for middle school students is, Celeste, an eighth grader, responded, "Smoking, peer pressure, and trying to fit in." Her friend Melissa continued, "A few [students] got caught with marijuana; someone got suspended for carrying a pack of cigarettes; I also think graffiti—people draw on the walls. People were dyeing their hair with markers."

Why do they engage in such behaviors? To be accepted by a group. Parents may not approve, but middle schoolers are more encouraged by the approval of their peers than discouraged by the disapproval of their parents. When asked what the biggest problem middle school students have to face, Eric, age thirteen, said, "Not getting along with kids. Having them tease you."

Although parents and teachers worry about the peer pressures that lead to destructive behaviors, peer pressure can be positive when the peer approval focuses on academic success or encourages participation in plays, sports, clubs, or other activities. Being a member of a social group is, in fact, a vital link in learning successful adult social interactions.

The influence of peers follows students as they leave for home each afternoon. The ubiquity of cell phones and email leads to continued "conversations" for hours after leaving school. Many young adolescents say they prefer instant messaging (IM) for chatting with friends, and one in three students noted that they used IM every day (Hoffman 2003).

Social events in and out of school influence young adolescents' behavior toward one another, behavior that often extends to the classroom. Middle school advisory programs provide a forum to address the challenges of socialization during these years through explicitly designed lessons. The socialization of young adolescents is a developmental process that requires the support of teachers for students to successfully navigate the challenges they experience.

The Role of the Family

As young adolescents attempt to move from dependence to independence, their social affiliations broaden, with allegiance split between the family and the peer group. Although authority remains primarily with the family, young adolescents want to begin making their own choices about what to do and who to do it with.

Parents begin to lose their omnipotence and are no longer viewed as infallible. Suddenly the parents don't know all the answers to the homework questions, and their behaviors can be seen by the young adolescent as inappropriate. Parents may eventually become an embarrassment to young adolescents.

Early adolescents struggle with the conflict inherent in the need to depend on parents for support as they move toward independence. The seventh grader who occasionally asks her parents for assistance in doing homework may request that her father drop her off a block from school to ensure that he not embarrass her in front of her friends. At the end of the day, when the father returns to the same intersection to pick his daughter up, she might chastise him for not driving right up to the school building.

In order to conform to the desires of a new social group, early adolescents may appear to renounce any loyalty they previously had to parents. As peers gain importance, the young adolescent may reject directions or suggestions from the family and challenge previously held beliefs that the parents have so carefully inculcated. Although other adults may continue to have a strong influence, the young adolescent desires and searches for increased decision-making opportunities. Parents become confused about whether to offer assistance or let the child alone.

Despite this apparent rejection of parental authority, parents continue to play a primary role in the young adolescent's life. When asked who the most important person was in their life, young adolescents we interviewed almost universally picked one or both of their parents:

"I'd say my dad. He always helps me. He'll help me understand things better like in school."

"My parents. They pretty much make you the person you are. If you're little, they guide you. They teach you your manners, they teach you what to do."

"My parents. They teach me the important lessons."

"My parents because I love them so much. They take good care of me and they're nice to me."

"I think my parents. I have a really close relationship with them. I definitely think they help me a lot. I really look up to them."

"My mother because two years ago my dad died, and my mother had to take over two parts of the family."

"My parents because they kind of explain things to me."

Young adolescents need stability and security in a world that sometimes seems upside down and is certainly confusing. Although parents may be equally confused, they can provide the stability and security that the child needs. We encourage teachers to mention to parents and caretakers during beginning-of-the-year open houses and in parent-teacher conferences that they should continue to provide support and guidance even when their children appear to want to distance themselves.

The Role of the Community

In addition to the need for successful peer interaction comes an increased awareness of the broader social world with an accompanying concern for social justice. Young adolescents' sense of right and wrong is intense. If you want to find a solution to a social problem, give it to a group of middle school students. Their new awareness of the world around them, a need to be involved with their peers, and a mind that is open to all possibilities allow them to seek and act on solutions that are seemingly out of the realm of adult thought. Their new cognitive thinking skills come unimpaired by experiences of failure that often impede adults in devising solutions.

Although parents may be relegated to a lesser role in the influence they hold over their young adolescent children, these same children will listen to and emulate other adults. Whether it be teachers, parents of their friends, or community members, adults have the opportunity to influence and lead the young adolescent in positive directions. Their letter-writing campaigns, canned-food drives, volunteering, and political activism provide a wide range of experiences and a sense of empowerment and meaning within the group—all essential elements in young adolescent growth.

The Role of the Media

Believe it or not, what celebrities do affects the way some kids think. If you think a movie star is so great and you want to be like her when you grow up, you're going to do everything you can to be just like her.

FROM AN EIGHTH GRADE FEMALE (CITED IN RIMM 2005, 107)

On TV, people are always having sex with a one-night stand. There's more sex, more cussing, drug dealing, and violence now.

FROM AN EIGHTH GRADE MALE (CITED IN RIMM 2005, 108)

The adolescent's world cannot be understood without considering the enormous power of the mass media, especially television, but also movies and popular music. Together with the increasing penetration of cable television, videocassette recorders and computers in

American homes and schools, these electronic conduits for programming and advertising have become strong competitors to the
traditional societal institutions in shaping young people's attitudes
and values.

CARNEGIE COUNCIL (1996, 41)

Technology increases every new generation of adolescents' exposure to the world in positive and negative ways. Young adolescents
have immediate and constant access to the world through the Internet,
iPods, and the latest generation of cell phones. Understanding the constant bombardment of visual and auditory images is challenging for
young adolescents. Yet what they experience shapes their views of
the world and their perceived place in it. Young adolescents need
reasoned conversations about the images they see and their perceptions
of them.

Parents have the primary responsibility for engaging young adolescents in conversations about what they see and hear. However, middle
school teachers know that they will frequently become a part of conversations among their students about these issues. Many times, con-
troversial topics arise from the links that students make between the
curriculum they are studying and the images they see. Students, as
well, often ask questions provoked by specific conversations among
friends or by something they have experienced via the media.
Ignoring their questions is unwise. Students will gain information
through any means necessary. Teachers must respond to students' concerns when questions arise. Effective educators take advantage of
these situations when they occur to help young adolescents understand how various situations affect them.

Because they are susceptible to media advertising, young adolescents must become aware of the impact that it has in their lives. Often
it is the media that define for these children whether they are worthy
or not—whether they are normal. The media tell them that they are
too thin, too fat, too tall, not athletic enough, not hip enough to the
latest fashion trends. Magazines such as *Seventeen, Cosmo Girl, J-14,*
and *Teen People,* the four best-selling magazines for adolescent
females, frequently send developmentally inappropriate messages

about behavior and dress (Rimm 2005). The media also influence males, with their ad campaigns on television sports programming and the often inappropriate images of male and female roles presented on Music Television Videos (MTV).

The impact of the media on our youth cannot and should not be underrated. Helping young adolescents understand the media's power as well as pitfalls, ability to engage as well as addict, and wide source of accurate as well as erroneous information becomes a daunting but vital task for parents and educators. The middle school curriculum should address the impact of media on young adolescents' lives.

Moral Development

Moral development is an ongoing process throughout everyone's life. It is generally believed that as one matures cognitively, moral development advances as well (Kohlberg and Gilligan 1971). As young adolescents experience social interactions, process more cognitively, and develop relationships, they simultaneously experience moral dilemmas that they never before considered. They begin to see the world through more caring and sympathetic eyes, noticing the differences between their lives and that of less fortunate others. They are capable of more complex moral reasoning; that is, they are aware that two or three opposing viewpoints exist when previously one view was all that they could perceive (National Middle School Association [NMSA] 2003).

Adolescents' skills in moral reasoning improve when they are able to reflect successfully on their behaviors and ascertain the effects on others and themselves (Swanson and Hill 1993). The traditional elementary school mantra that each situation is as simple as making a "good choice" or "bad choice" may not fit the more advanced moral reasoning of young adolescents. They begin to see other possibilities they previously weren't able to imagine. They may initiate arguments about rules or policies, attempting to get to the root of the reasoning behind them and their application to them personally.

As young adolescents respond to peer influence and pressure, they generally move from the initial stages of moral development into "conventional moral reasoning" (Rice and Dolgin 2005, 335). In these stages, young adolescents may act at times "so as to gain others' approval and do what others think is right" (Rice and Dolgin, 335). Deciding what is "right" is often a cloudy process for young adolescents, depending on the situations that arise in their lives and from whom they seek approval. If peer influence dominates their perspectives, then their moral actions may not be those that the adults in their lives see as appropriate.

Disagreements about morals between adults and adolescents occur when adolescents believe that adults have interfered with some of their personal choices, often with regard to appropriate dress, hairstyle or color, body piercings, tattoos, or cell phone and computer use.

Young adolescents explore and examine their own moral behavior and ultimately develop their own personal values. Despite the disagreements they have with parents, the values they choose most often parallel their parents' values (NMSA 2003). Middle school teachers need to know that young adolescents may disagree with adults about moral issues yet clearly need (and may seek) the assistance of parents and other adults in deciding how to act in certain moral situations.

The developing moral maturity among young adolescents is a positive thing. Young adolescents have a strong desire for justice and are interested in idealistic plans for making the world a better place (NMSA 2003). They are frequently concerned about how to ensure worldwide peace, contribute to environmental issues, and create safe environments for animals. Young adolescents "believe that if they can conceive and express high moral principles, then they have attained them, and nothing concrete need be done" (Rice and Dolgin 2005, 130). By developing curriculum based on students' questions and concerns, teachers can provide an environment in which students can explore these issues and act on their beliefs.

Any typical middle school day presents many opportunities for conversations centered around "teachable moments" that involve moral decision making. Events reported by the media give teachers a chance to initiate meaningful conversations about how to act in specific situations that occur locally or nationally. Young adolescents' own peer group interactions can center on appropriate behaviors. Students can be

49

asked to help reason out what constitutes proper classroom behavior. Teachers should embrace the ever present moral development of young adolescents as an opportunity to guide them to further maturity.

One of the best ways is to model effective behaviors and verbal responses. Students spend much of their time watching their teachers and noticing their actions when fellow students misbehave. How teachers respond in these situations reveals their true beliefs about how people should treat one another.

Emotional Development

The middle school student confronts a number of diverse changes all at one time:

- accepting physical changes
- experiencing new modes of intellectual functioning
- striving for independence from the family
- establishing a unique identity
- adjusting to a new school setting
- relating to new friends

This period of transition between dependence and independence results in a multitude of needs and a dramatic change in self-concept. Physical changes and the hormones that cause them often trigger emotions that are variable and little understood.

Mood Swings

Eric, a thirteen-year-old seventh grader, was having a particularly rough evening. He had gone to school that morning his typical bouncy self. That evening, he lay around on the couch with his dog at his side, staring into space. Questions by his mom brought monosyllabic responses, "Yes," "No," "Nothing." When she didn't let up, he finally said (thanks to his school's comprehensive health curriculum and class unit on self-esteem), "Don't worry, Mom. I'm an adolescent now. I'm supposed to have mood swings."

Mood swings are a quintessential characteristic of young adolescence. Emotions change rapidly. Students are happy one moment and angry or sad the next; quiet one day and loud and boisterous the next; terrified with respect to one issue and overconfident about another; anxious on Monday and self-assured on Tuesday.

Too often mood swings are blamed on hormones and discounted as temporary aberrations. Although we can attribute some mood swings to chemical imbalances or rapid hormonal fluctuations, that's only part of it. If we consider the wide social and intellectual changes young adolescents are experiencing, as well as their continued brain development, their emotional variability seems understandable.

Effective middle level educators understand what's happening with their students and are respectful of all the developmental changes they are going through. They explain to young adolescents that there may be times when they will have difficulty controlling their emotions. Teachers need to help students develop strategies for taking responsibility for their actions and finding creative and appropriate ways to handle their excessive emotions.

Egocentrism

One aspect of young adolescents' thinking is a new form of egocentrism. Unlike the egocentrism of younger children, who assume that others think the same way they do about everything, young adolescents begin to understand that people have different beliefs and attitudes. They become immersed in their own thinking. They reflect on and analyze their thoughts and assume that everyone is as interested in their ideas as they are. A typical thought process is, "Because I am thinking about me, then everyone must be thinking about me. Because I notice my hair, everyone else must be looking at it. Since I pay attention to myself, everyone else must be paying attention to me."

Much of young adolescents' emotional energy is expended in responding to this imaginary audience (Buis and Thompson 1989). Since adolescents believe they are constantly being watched, they often react by being loud or acting provocatively, wanting to appear cool. Or, to avoid standing out from others they may try to fit in, to

51

conform. Because of their imaginary audience, young adolescents also have an increased need for privacy: when they are alone, they can relax. Self-consciousness is at its highest levels from the ages of fourteen to nineteen (Tice, Buder, and Baumeister 1985).

Young adolescents believe that their feelings and emotions are indeed unique—that no one has ever experienced what they have experienced. Elkind (1967) referred to this as "personal fable." In addition, they are convinced that they will live forever and that the horrible things that happen to others will not affect them. They'll never have an unwanted pregnancy, be in a car accident, or get a sexually transmitted disease.

The Search for Identity

> Identity is a patchwork of flesh, feelings and ideas held together by the string of the moment.
>
> BORDEAUX (1993–1994)

Developing an identity involves many aspects of one's personality. Young adolescents begin to form identities as they choose values and beliefs and set goals for themselves (Rice and Dolgin 2005). The middle school years are marked by an almost constant search for an identity in many areas: gender, ethnicity, culture, sexuality, spirituality, and concerns about one's future life (which job will I have, how much money will I make, will I marry and have children?).

More immediate concerns include taking music lessons, horseback riding, becoming a cheerleader, trying out for the school track team, joining the student council, taking a leadership role in scouts, trying out for the school play, or volunteering at a local veterinary office. Young adolescents can learn much about their interests and themselves by participating in extracurricular activities, whether school, community, family, or church sponsored. The search for identity is almost continuous as young adolescents try on different personas through the planned and unplanned events and activities that occur during these times of their lives.

Erikson's Theories

The search for identity is the defining characteristic of the young adolescent. The first comprehensive look at identity during early adolescence was done by Erik Erikson during the 1950s and 1960s (Erikson 1950, 1968). According to Erikson, during adolescence individuals struggle to find out who they are and where they are going in life. Young adolescents are just beginning this struggle, trying to integrate their childhood experiences with their developing bodies and biological drives, their new thinking capacities, and their ever expanding social roles. This search for identity doesn't begin and end during early adolescence. It involves a slow search for a lifestyle that is compatible with physical changes, intellectual understandings, and social interactions.

Asked about the greatest problem middle school students experience, Jesse, an eighth grader, responded, "I think it's definitely that people want to fit in—they don't want to stand alone. But I think it's also important to be an individual, too. There are a lot of cliques in middle school. People get into little groups, and I think that's bad because you need to stand as an individual."

Despite interest in conforming and belonging to a social group, young adolescents still want individuality. The need for confirmation by a social group is really a need for personal validation. Learning to be part of a social group is an important part of the successful transition to independence. More vital, perhaps, are attempts to understand the "self."

When Rob, a fourteen-year-old eighth grader, was asked what the most important thing to learn at school was, he commented, "Not caring what other people think. Most people, if they get made fun of, they'd take it personally. I've learned, and a lot of people make fun of me, that if you don't care, you have a lot more fun because you're not trying to impress people. It's getting your own style." When Rob was asked, however, to comment on the biggest problem facing middle school students, he replied, "Making your presence known." Like other young adolescents, Rob is developing his self-concept and self-esteem. Although we sense that Rob is socially well adjusted, he feels the need to develop a strong sense of identity and begs for personal acceptance as well as the acknowledgment of himself apart from the group—as an individual.

The search for identity often revolves around trying out new ideas and behaviors that would have seemed incomprehensible only a year before. It involves looking at situations through different points of view and making decisions about how to act in a given situation in an attempt to develop a public self that is congruent with the inner self and is validated by peers and society. Those decisions, never etched in stone, become the foundation of an identity that is ever changing throughout life. Those not measuring up to cultural and societal expectations may develop negative identities in order to be acknowledged by a peer group and recognized by society.

Marcia's Theory

James Marcia (1980) expanded on Erikson's idea of identity, using the notions of crisis and commitment. Crisis is defined as "a period of exploring alternatives" and commitment as "making choices." Marcia identifies four resolutions to the search for identity.

1. *Identity diffusion*—no exploration and no commitment. Students neither explore nor choose from the options available to them. They do not question alternatives or act. Someone is making decisions for them. Parents could choose their after-school activities, their friends, and their clothes. Most fifth and sixth graders are normally diffused. They haven't considered becoming someone different from who they are now. Older adolescents who remain in this stage may be quite insecure. They often lack self-confidence, have low self-esteem, lack meaningful friendships, and drift from one relationship to another (Rice and Dolgin 2005).

2. *Identity foreclosure*—commitment without exploration. Here, a choice is made about a lifestyle in the absence of opportunities to explore alternatives. Early maturers who become great athletes in the middle grades may experience

identity foreclosure. These students have been defined by their physical precociousness and either have not been given the opportunity to explore other options or have chosen not to. They often state that they want to become what others want them to become: for example, a doctor because that's what parents expect. They may marry early because everyone in their family does this and expects this behavior. Foreclosed adolescents seek security from significant others and generally seek to reduce anxiety in life (Kroger 2003).

Perhaps many of the risk-taking and sometimes dangerous behaviors of young adolescents stem from their need to explore life and all its options when they feel that their options are being denied. Teachers must be careful about labeling students prematurely—as great athletes, musicians, scholars, or leaders, for example—thus denying the opportunity for these students to experience other options and perhaps denying other students the opportunity to become an athlete, musician, scholar, or leader.

3. *Moratorium*—exploration but no commitment. Students search and explore without making a commitment to a lifestyle. Ideally, older middle school students should be at this stage. The existence of options and opportunities allows students to explore areas they might not have considered before. For example, providing musical or athletic opportunities for the late maturer may open a career that expands as maturation unfolds. All students who want to be in plays, sing in the chorus, play in the jazz band, cheer at ball games, or join the science club should be allowed to participate in these activities. Schools can encourage their students to explore by offering them opportunities to develop skills and interests in varied careers.

Middle schoolers in the moratorium stage may express themselves through exotic dress and diverse hairstyles and colors and demonstrate a wide variety of personality styles. Teachers and parents alike should embrace these behaviors as a sign that adolescents are exploring possibilities and further developing a sense of self, as long as their behaviors don't become dangerous to themselves or others.

4. *Achievement*—exploration of roles followed by commitment to a specific identity. Psychologists and adolescent researchers emphasize that youth between the ages of twelve and twenty cycle from moratorium to achievement several times in different areas (Meeus et al. 1999; Waterman 1993; Stephen, Fraser, and Marcia 1992). Adolescents' forays into each new area of identity become stronger during their later adolescent years and lead to more commitments.

Marcia's theory, although not universally accepted, does provide us with a view of how the process of identity development may occur and how we can better help young adolescents explore the many options the world has to offer. Too often we push students into making choices. We limit opportunities rather than opening them up. We let only the "best" be part of the jazz band or choral group. Only those who demonstrate acting ability can be in the play. When we limit opportunities, we pass on the message that a certain student is not capable enough, good enough, strong enough, or smart enough to make a contribution. Our job is to provide opportunities, not deny them. Middle school students should never be told they are inadequate. They just might believe it!

Few, if any, students reach their final identity states during the middle school years, nor should they. Young adolescence should be preserved as a time of identity exploration. Throughout high school, college, and into early adulthood, opportunities should exist for people to explore options and make decisions and choices about their futures.

Ethnic Identity

Generations of children are disenfranchised because the relationship between their ethnic background, cultural histories, and knowledge of their human developmental process has not been adequately addressed.

SHEETS (2005, 52)

Many African, Native, Hispanic, and Asian American students experience an additional challenge during adolescence in developing a personal identity that recognizes that they are not White European Americans (Howard 1999; Gay 1994; Ogbu 1991). Not only do these students have to go through a process of self-identification, they also have to develop a cultural identity (Gay 1994).

Cross (1991) established a five-stage theory of Black racial identity development.

1. *Preencounter*—This stage is "an attempt by African Americans to distance themselves from their own racial identity" (Howard 1999, 86). This stage mirrors the foreclosure stage mentioned by Marcia (1991).
2. *Encounter*—Once an African American experiences racist comments or notices being treated differently because of her or his color, she or he may be moving into the encounter stage—a phase in which students of color begin to notice that skin tone alone can lead to negative treatment. African, Hispanic, Native, and Asian Americans begin to identify their place in society based on their ethnicity and cultural differences to Whites. Because of their heightened self-consciousness, young adolescents are particularly aware of being treated differently. A barrage of media images also influences how ethnically different students perceive their place in society.
3. *Immersion/emersion*—When adolescents of color enter the immersion stage, they may begin to feel anger toward Whites and avoidance of the majority culture's ideals and ways of life (Parham 1989). In this stage "an individual . . . is deeply committed to Blackness and invests much energy in exploring the roots of his or her Black culture" (Howard 1999, 87).
4. *Internalization* and 5. *Internalization/commitment*—During these final two stages, students of color are more willing to cooperate with members of other cultures and ethnicities. Young adolescents do not generally reach the last three

stages of identity development. They usually remain in the preencounter stage.

Identity development theories also exist for Hispanics and Asian Americans (Broderick and Blewitt 2003). Teachers must recognize, though, that these categories of "Hispanic," "Latino," or "Chicano"; "Native American" or "First Nation Peoples"; and "Asian American" are far too broad to define the ethnic characteristics of many of their students from Hispanic or Asian countries or varied Native American tribes (Brown 2002b). Does *Hispanic* mean, for instance, that a student is from Mexico, Puerto Rico, Spain, the Dominican Republic, Bolivia, or possibly Guatemala among many other countries? As for *Asian Americans*, students could be from China, Vietnam, India, Pakistan, or South Korea among many other Asian countries. Pacific Islanders are also grouped into the category of *Asian American* despite the many differences in each of their cultures. Imagine how different each Native American tribe is. Umana-Taylor and Fine (2001) discovered great variety in the ethnic identification among Colombian, Guatemalan, Honduran, Mexican, Nicaraguan, Puerto Rican, and Salvadoran youth; all of them would be classified as Hispanic in the United States.

Each ethnicity denotes a diversity of traits that impacts students' and their families' perceptions, attitudes, interests, and efforts toward education. More important, though, with each student comes a different personality shaped by ethnic factors as well as the other influences on behavior and learning. The categories and labels are often useless in helping teachers understand and assist their students. Understanding the limitations of these simple labels and studying the developmental nature of identity are useful tools in guiding young adolescents to healthy behaviors.

Oppositional Identity
The behaviors of African, Hispanic, Native, and Asian American students may lead to what is described as oppositional identity (Ogbu 1991). Students who experience oppositional identity purposely ignore traditional and popular European American attitudes and

behaviors. Finn (1999) noted, "Members of the oppressed group come to regard certain beliefs, skills, tastes, values, attitudes, and behaviors as not appropriate for them since they are associated with the dominant culture."

Ethnically diverse students from many backgrounds may develop an oppositional identity attitude if they believe that their opportunities for educational advancement, better jobs, and a better quality of life are not possible because of their oppression by the majority culture. Demonstrations of oppositional identity include a Chicano student who refuses to speak English in school when addressing teachers or an African American student who refuses to do any academic work at school or at home since he doesn't want to fit into a "White" world. Young adolescents are acutely aware of how fairness, racism, prejudice, and discrimination affect them personally and affect their families, ethnicity, and culture (Sheets 2005).

Combating oppositional identity requires a commitment from teachers to develop personal relationships built on trust with those students who are convinced that the entire system is working against them. Changing students' attitudes as they enter middle school is a lengthy process of reversing beliefs that for some have been ingrained for many years.

Developing an ethnic identity is especially challenging when one's parents are ethnically different: for instance, an African American father and a Vietnamese mother; a European American mother and a Puerto Rican father; a Peruvian father and a Cuban mother. Often these students experience confusion when asked to identify themselves on a limited list of racial choices provided on a standardized test. Although their parents may have provided them with pride about their ethnicity, schools and teachers can quickly create embarrassment through traditional sorting systems and labels. This issue emphasizes the uselessness and negativity of the word *race*. Teachers can positively recognize students' family heritages through informal conversations, planned curriculum, and school advisory programs. Young adolescents need teachers to recognize and honor their ethnicity.

Gay (1994) indicated, "A clarified ethnic identity is central to the psycho-social well-being and educational success of youth of color"

(151). She goes on to say, "If ethnic identity development is understood as part of the natural 'coming of age' process during early adolescence, and if middle level education is to be genuinely client-centered for students of color, then ethnic sensitivity must be incorporated into school policies, programs, and practices" (153).

Brinthaupt and Lipka (2002) emphasized the role of middle schools in the identity development process: "The major argument is that efforts and activities of schools must be centered around the identity needs of the early adolescent in order for successful development to be fostered" (10). Teachers must deliberately create learning environments that attend to cultural, ethnic, and racial issues. As we talk about appropriate middle school practices in this book, we will present a framework for curriculum and instruction that responds to these issues.

Sexual and Gender Identity

Middle schools are powerful training grounds for the development of sexual and gender identity. Attitudes about the appropriate roles for males and females exist in the minds of young adolescents based on the modeling they see at home, in the media—particularly television—and in the messages received from peers. Teachers also influence how males and females view their roles in the classroom and later as adults.

Some researchers report that females often experience an overwhelming decline in confidence and self-esteem during the middle school years (Ornstein 1994; Brown and Gilligan 1992). Many girls perform well academically during their elementary school years, but during middle school low confidence results in poor academic performance, less assertiveness, and lower expectations for future educational plans and career paths. Broderick and Blewitt (2003) described this transformation:

> This phenomenon has been called the "loss of voice" by Gilligan and her colleagues (Brown and Gilligan 1992), who purport that a girl experiences a gradual silencing of an authentic, imperious, and often willful self in order to identify with certain culturally prescribed roles of women as self-sacrificial and pleasing to others. (238)

Middle level teachers who inadvertently reinforce traditional male and female career goals may discourage students from believing that they can succeed academically in a subject area or enter a career path that may match their academic interests, strengths, and potential.

Males also face stereotypes about the roles that they should play in life. Sadker (1999) revealed that three out of four males report that they were targets of sexual harassment (usually through challenges to their masculinity). Sadker went on to report, "Males who express an interest in careers typically thought of as 'feminine' also encounter social pressures" (24).

The middle school curriculum should directly address students' questions about the roles that males and females can play in life— roles that may be entirely different from the cultural and ethnic expectations of family and peers.

Developing a Sexual Identity

Sexual orientation describes a preference for sexual partners and is a central aspect of adolescent development. A large majority of adolescents identify themselves as heterosexual. Sexual orientation, whether heterosexual or homosexual, originates in the brain, and most geneticists believe that it is determined by a combination of genes affecting the concentrations of sex hormones in the brain when it is forming prior to birth (Walsh 2004).

Most middle school students are aware of the labels, views, and attitudes associated with homosexuality, though they may not fully understand the characteristics or reasons that one identifies as homosexual. Middle schools are breeding grounds for attacks on those students who appear to be different from mainstream social attitudes or behaviors. Many adolescents who may be aware of homosexual interests are reluctant to admit or ask questions about their sexual preferences due to their fears of retribution. Walsh (2004) described their concern:

> It can be difficult for an adolescent to deal with his or her homosexuality at the very time in life when it is so important to fit in and be accepted. The emotional and psychological torture that many gay and lesbian adolescents experience can be overwhelming. Studies

61

suggest that one third of all teens who commit suicide are gay or les-
bian. For them death can seem preferable to the pain of accepting a
sexual identity that their friends or family or culture find perverted,
sinful, or shameful. (109)

Transgender adolescents may feel they are trapped in the wrong body.
Young adolescent males who prefer to look and behave feminine are
frequently teased and bullied. Although cross-gender behavior is
somewhat more acceptable for females, they too experience instances
of verbal abuse. Transgender students generally have a life history of
being bullied which seriously affects the development of healthy self-
esteem (deVries, Cohen-Kettenis, Delemarre-Vander Waal 2006).
These students need accurate information about their sexuality;
unfortunately these are often forbidden topics in school. Parents are
just as likely to ignore or refuse to address transgender issues.

The social attitudes expressed by many create a sense of fear for
those adolescents who have many questions about how they fit into a
primarily heterosexual world. Teachers and all those who represent the
school community are responsible for protecting youth—under all circumstances. Young adolescents should clearly understand that it is normal to have questions about their sexual orientation. If adolescents
don't receive accurate information about their concerns about sex from
adults, such as parents, counselors, and teachers, they'll instead ask
peers and risk receiving flawed information and perhaps little support
(Pollock 2006).

Teachers may not have a great deal of control over which health-
related topics, in what depth, are taught in school. However, they can
provide a caring and supportive environment for all their students,
protecting them from sexual harassment during school hours and providing them with the resources and appropriate contacts to discuss
their specific sexual concerns.

Behavioral Issues

The search for meaning and identity can be a difficult—even
traumatic—experience. Young adolescents face a constant concern
about whether they are normal; a dissatisfaction with who they are,

how they look, what they believe; a belief that something is wrong with their physical development. It's no wonder that young adolescents exhibit behaviors that seem at times contradictory, bizarre, dangerous, or just plain rude.

Young adolescents can be kind and compassionate and mercilessly cruel. Sensitive to criticism and easily offended, they may become unhappy and take their frustrations out on others: family members, teachers, and especially their classmates. Insults, name calling, and pejorative labeling occur often among students.

Young adolescents' feelings of inadequacy and attempts to gain control over their constantly changing environments prompt much of their inappropriate behavior. Students find ways of protecting themselves. Lashing out against others is often the chosen path of self-protection. Asked about problems for their age group, Sarah, a seventh grader, reported, "People take [their frustrations] out on school, their friends, their school life. . . . They make their lives miserable for themselves instead of making them better."

On the other hand, middle schoolers can be intensely loyal to their peers, team, parents, and family. Behavior is subject to wild fluctuation. One never quite knows what to expect—except for the fact that if we wait a while, it will change.

Self-Esteem

Self-esteem often suffers as a result of the changes young adolescents experience during the middle school years. Self-esteem is an affective component of a person's reflection of self; that is, does one like him or herself? Rice and Dolgin (2005) described six perceptions one ponders about self that influence self-esteem:

- Who I really am
- Who I think I am
- Who others think I am
- Who I think others think I am
- Who I think I will become
- Who I think others want me to become (166)

63

Having an answer for each of these questions is quite elusive for young adolescents; yet the questioning is continuous in their search for a comfortable identity—at least for the day. The amount of self-esteem students have depends on their perceptions of four central issues affecting self-esteem:

1. The amount of perceived control over their circumstances
2. Whether they are accepted by those from whom they desire acceptance (peers)
3. A need to be competent in what they attempt and wish to accomplish
4. A sense of being virtuous to others

Maintaining an enhanced self-esteem is a lifelong challenge, but the onset of puberty triggers constant self-assessment. Many young adolescents experience a considerable drop in self-esteem brought on by frustration with longer limbs, big feet, curly hair, being too tall, being too short, or having acne. A parent's love and acceptance can provide solace during the elementary years. During the middle school years, however, one also needs to be accepted by peers to feel a strong sense of self-esteem. Greater academic expectations, more homework, and the higher-level thinking required often challenge young adolescents' beliefs about their competence as students. Self-esteem may be based more on a middle schooler's ability to join a peer group than on an ability to perform well academically. Despite their belief that they are virtuous, young adolescents may evaluate their value to others based on their ability to impress peers with inappropriate behavior rather than acting responsibly.

The self-consciousness that accompanies this stage of growth originates in the young person's perceived loss of control over his or her environment. If young adolescents are unable to establish positive feelings about themselves and develop healthy relationships with their peers, they are likely to feel alienated and may eventually choose to drop out of school (Mills, Dunham, and Alpert 1988). Rob, age fourteen, jokingly tells his friends, teachers, and family, "Seventy percent of middle school kids suffer from low self-esteem and you're contributing to the problem." Rob acknowledges that his statistics may be in error but senses the need among his peers for affirmation and success.

Young adolescence brings with it life's first identity crisis, in which students attempt to project an image consistent with the inner self, which they hope will be accepted by others who make up their world. Young adolescents' concerns are real, their problems are unique to them, and their bravado often masks fear and anxiety. Middle schools must provide opportunities for students to understand the growth they are experiencing and exercise their independence in supportive ways. Bessie, a seventh grader, stated the needs of young adolescents quite clearly: "My least favorite thing about school is being told what to do. I think that if you're going to find out what it means to grow up, you need to make your own decisions."

Concluding Reflections

Young adolescents face a multitude of changes throughout their middle school years, and these changes have a significant impact. Keith recalled his middle school experience in a statement he wrote as a college junior. "Overall, as I look back, [young adolescence] wasn't so bad. Back then, though, I probably would not have agreed with that statement. Every aspect—my friends, family, school, emotional and physical changes—all greatly affected me while I was growing up."

As we work with young adolescents, we must be aware of these changes. It is a time of transition between dependence and independence, a time to explore new alternatives and try out new identities, a time to experiment with new points of view, and a time to learn how to interact with others.

Think about these possibilities:

- What if we truly supported and encouraged young adolescents in their quest to develop a self?
- What if we based schooling on a knowledge of and respect for early adolescent development?

- What if we designed a school that acknowledges the physical changes that these students are going through?
- What if we developed a curriculum that responded to their changing intellectual and social worlds?
- What if we provided an environment that supported their need for social interactions and emotional stability?
- What if we listened to what they said?
- What if their questions became our questions?
- What if . . . ?

FOUR

Designing an Appropriate Middle School: Influences from the Past to the Present

Middle school is like a prison.

RYAN, SIXTH GRADER

You wake up early, you work all day at school, and then, they expect you to do homework.

ELIZABETH, SEVENTH GRADER

Middle school students are often given numerous and lengthy homework assignments that they may not be able to comprehend. They are expected to take notes during a lecture that has no meaning for them. In some schools, students have few if any opportunities for social interaction during the school day. Recess typically has been eliminated despite the overwhelming need for physical activity among young adolescents. Student involvement in curricular or instruc-  tional decisions is rare despite young adolescents' hypersensitivity to life's global issues and an understanding of their own learning characteristics and needs. Maybe school *is* like a prison! As some middle school educators begin to change school structures to meet the needs of their students, other teachers and principals persist in maintaining traditional structures that are inappropriate for young adolescents. In a country that values democracy, there seems to be very little of it in many of our schools.

Time for Reflection

- As you reflect on the developmental characteristics of young adolescents discussed in Chapters 2 and 3, brainstorm with your classmates or fellow teachers how a middle school could respond to the developmental needs of young adolescents.
- Work collaboratively with others in your group to write a description of what an ideal middle school would be like based on your understanding of how young adolescents develop, how people learn, and the needs of society.

A Typical Day

I feel like a cow. They herd us in the building in the morning trying to fit a thousand kids in two doors. Then they make us get into our stalls. Then they make us get into line and serve us all the same food. Then they give us fifteen minutes of pasture time after lunch, then herd us back into the classroom.

ROB, EIGHTH GRADER

The school bus arrives at the street corner at 7:25 A.M. Students arrive at school at 8:10 following a forty-five-minute bus ride. They sit quietly in the school gymnasium for ten minutes until the homeroom bell rings, giving them permission to go into the hallway to their lockers.

Students enter a long hallway filled with lockers that stand inches apart from one another. Three hundred students, at the same time, attempt to get into their lockers and avoid bumping into one another. Students with adjacent lockers are not able to get to them at the same time; there's not enough room. Lockers are only twenty centimeters wide, making it difficult to cram in coats, band instruments, and all those books and notebooks required by each teacher. Adding to the confusion is the fact that students have only three, maybe four, minutes to open their lockers and take out the appropriate materials for their first few classes.

Classes begin and students sit passively for forty-two minutes as they listen to a lecture, complete worksheets, answer questions in the back of the textbook chapter, or take written tests. When the bell rings at the end of each period, students file into the crowded hallway and play the locker game again, jostling for position. Finally, after three hours of classes, they have a lunch period.

The lunch line is long (it's not cool to bring your lunch from home). Lunch periods are a short twenty to twenty-five minutes (a time frame that prevents students from becoming too loud). If students are in the back of the line, by the time they sit down they will have about seven minutes to eat. The lunch menu is determined by administrators and does not allow for student choice. Lunchtime is the only opportunity for socializing that students will have until after school on the bus ride home. Those students who don't have enough time to eat their whole lunch won't get a chance to eat again until after school.

Students head back to class after lunch without any opportunity for physical exercise except an occasional run down the long hallway if there are no teachers in sight. Some students feel exhausted after eating lunch; nevertheless, they return to the classrooms for three more forty-two-minute classes.

Each teacher the students see assigns evening homework. Students need thirty minutes to an hour or more to complete the homework for each class.

Finally, students board the bus for a forty-five-minute trip home. If they begin their homework soon after they arrive home, they may complete it by 10:00 P.M., provided they don't spend any time talking to friends, exercising, or just hanging out for an hour or so.

Does the description conjure up fond memories of your own past experiences? Is this an appropriate way to educate young adolescents? Who designed such a stifling environment for students and why?

Emulating the Factory

Several societal forces have affected teachers' perceptions of their roles and have been instrumental in the way teachers provide instruction and make curricular decisions. The development of the factory assembly line in the early 1900s had an enormous impact on the structure of education. Factories were designed so that each person had a specific job to do and performed the same task all day long. Work started and ended with the blast of a horn or a bell. Breaks were granted to workers on a set timetable. Work was evaluated by the amount of time on task and the number of items produced each day. The boss' job was to keep the employees on task. Reflective thinking was not necessarily required and certainly not valued. Bosses wanted compliant employees who were highly productive during long hours on the job. They did not expect employees to question the work they were responsible for completing or how it was done.

During the early 1900s, schools were "concerned with producing a work force to staff and operate the factories" (Caine and Caine 1994, 13). Hence, school structure was based on the factory model. Schools contrived a seven- or eight-period day, with classes lasting approximately forty to forty-five minutes, ending with a bell as students filed out of their classes, into the halls for four minutes, and then into another classroom. Subjects were taught separately, and all of the learning outcomes were predetermined by textbook design or prestructured curricula chosen by central office administrators. Every student was expected to learn the same curriculum, at the same pace, and all students were taught in the same way. Compliant behavior was rewarded; creative and critical thinking were discouraged.

Influence on Teaching Beliefs

When education is designed according to the factory model, students are treated as raw materials to be molded and polished into something new without regard to the needs or variations of the original material. Several assumptions are implicit in this design:

1. All students have similar learning characteristics.
2. Teaching is a simple process whereby one style fits the needs of all students.
3. The amount of information students need to learn has an established limit.
4. The information that students are expected to know is unilaterally predetermined and involves a fixed set of concepts and principles.
5. All students are expected to perform similar responsibilities once they graduate.
6. Learning means memorization of facts.
7. Creative and critical thinking are not valued.
8. Connections do not exist between subjects.
9. Teachers are the unilateral decision makers with respect to events that occur in the classroom.

These assumptions ignore what researchers are discovering about cognition and the learning process, and they ignore what is known about young adolescent development.

You may be saying, "That was then. Look at us now." Look around you! Do schools continue to deliver information in forty-two-minute segments? Is the school day divided into six or seven periods? Are subjects taught separately? If so, you are experiencing the factory model of schooling.

Teachers may have a difficult time envisioning a schooling structure that looks different from the factory model. They often hold tightly to traditional views of learning because for many it's all they've ever experienced. Many parents expect their children's schools to continue using the same teaching and learning processes that they experienced (Brown and Rose 1995). These predominant belief systems are a challenging barrier for administrators, teachers, and university professors who are interested in implementing needed change.

Influence on Teacher Behaviors

The factory approach not only affects educators' choice of instructional strategies but also student socialization, student-teacher relationships, and the general quality of the school day. The factory model makes it more difficult for teachers to develop the kind of caring relationships with students that are required as a basis for learning. In a study in which researchers asked young adolescents what they wanted their middle school teachers to know about them, it became clear that students wanted strong personal relationships with their teacher (Doda and Knowles 2007). One student responded,

> The key to being a good teacher is to know the kids. You have to know every single one and have a relationship with every single one. I think that one thing that really allows me to work hard is knowing that my teacher knows where I am in life at that moment.

When the focus is primarily on the structure of the school and on the content of the classes, these warm relationships are more difficult to establish.

Researchers who understand the relationship between emotion and cognitive processing (Caine and Caine 1994; Goleman 1995; MacLaury 2002) have warned us of the negative effects of a sterile learning environment. Positive feelings associated with learning experiences foster meaningful learning. Forty-two minutes is not sufficient time for teachers to develop the kind of healthy, caring relationships with students that are necessary to promote meaningful learning. Adam, an eighth grader, describes one aspect of his "perfect" middle school: "Teachers would be friendly with the kids. Some are okay, but the teachers aren't close enough to kids." When students and teachers have opportunities and time to communicate with one other, they begin to care about each other in ways that make meaningful learning possible. Edith, a sixth grade teacher, explained, "I definitely think the middle school should be more nurturing. I find my role as a teacher is just one part of it. I feel like I am a counselor, a grandmother; it's much more than just teaching."

Similarly, forty-two-minute periods prevent teachers from identifying the cognitive needs of all their students, thus denying educators an opportunity to design curricula and instructional strategies in a way that ensures optimal learning. Forty-two-minute periods limit opportunities to complete curricula in a meaningful manner; instead, teachers are encouraged to cover topics briefly, move on to another topic, and complete the book. Sheila, a seventh grader, had this to say about the traditional lecture-style classroom: "Civics is so boring. We read our book and we do these answer-and-question pages. We never do anything as a whole class—we just read and take notes the whole time."

Students need longer blocks of time for meaningful learning to occur. They need opportunities to construct their own knowledge through discovery, to formulate and ask questions, to engage in in-depth problem solving, and to use critical and creative thinking processes. An eighth grader, Meg, put it this way: "We need fun ways to learn and more challenges. We need to expand our minds."

The factory model of schooling limits quality socialization among students. Short periods, four minutes between classes, large numbers of students in each class, predetermined curricular guidelines—these are but a few of the structures that discourage teachers from using collaborative learning experiences in their lesson design. Recognizing the social needs of young adolescents, teachers should design opportunities for students to learn collaboratively. Cooperative learning strategies take more time to implement initially, and short class periods may discourage teachers from using them. Edith, a sixth grade teacher, was in a middle school that moved to longer blocks of time for each period. She commented, "This year I started a double whole language period and then a math—it was fabulous. From 8:15 until 9:45 I have the same children. This is really advantageous to the students."

When students are forced to learn as much material as is expected in a six-period school day, it is unlikely that teachers will provide time for young adolescents' much needed physical activities. Teachers who work in schools that follow the factory model design lessons filled with content. Although many administrators and parents may applaud this type of time-on-task rigor, young adolescents are unlikely to be paying attention to the lessons because of their pent-up energy and physical discomfort.

Based on what is now known about how learning occurs and the developmental abilities and needs of young adolescents, middle schools must abandon the factory approach to schooling and evolve into more effective centers of learning. Some schools have recognized the needs of young adolescents and replaced the factory model with more developmentally appropriate structures. These structural and philosophical changes began to be incorporated thirty years ago.

The First Junior High Schools

The most common organizational pattern of education in the late 1800s was eight years at an elementary school and, if students were continuing their education past that (few were), high school. In 1893 concern about the inconsistencies in college preparation resulted in the formation of an organization of educators known as The Committee of Ten on Secondary School Studies (Gruhn and Douglass 1971). The committee recommended that secondary school begin in the seventh grade. The division into six years of elementary school and six years of high school lasted until 1909, when concern about the immaturity of sixth grade students and overcrowding of high schools led to the development of the first seventh through ninth grade school, in Columbus, Ohio. This school was recognized as a junior high school. In 1919 the North Central Association of Colleges and Secondary Schools provided a definition: "A junior high school is a school in which the seventh, eighth, and ninth grades are segregated in a building (or portion of a building) by themselves; possess an organization and administration of their own that is distinct from the grades above and below; and are taught by a separate corps of teachers" (North Central Association 1919, 4).

The junior high was originally designed to provide a program that would respond to the uniqueness of this developmental stage and offer a practical and active curriculum that would engage the young adolescent mind (Tye 1985). The junior high school curricula, however, were heavily influenced by the development and use of Carnegie Units in high schools around 1910 (Toepfer 1992). Carnegie Units are credits awarded for completing high school courses and were developed as a means of measuring the number of courses that students would be required to complete in high school in order to graduate. Junior high school educators were concerned that students needed to be prepared for ninth grade. Therefore, they chose the Carnegie Unit structure in an effort to bolster junior high school students' academic preparedness for high school.

False Hope

Approximately sixty-five hundred junior high schools existed across the country by the 1950s. Despite its popularity and the rhetoric of developmental appropriateness that accompanied its initiation, the junior high school never quite lived up to its promise of providing a distinct experience for young adolescents. Anfara and Waks (2002) reported, "Aubrey Douglass, an early advocate of the junior high, wrote in 1945 that the junior high had persistent problems, including a curriculum that was too subject-centered, teachers who were inadequately prepared to teach that level of schooling, a curriculum that was characterized as teacher or textbook controlled, and students who were tracked" (43). Many junior highs were and currently are staffed by teachers with little or no knowledge of young adolescent development who lack the strategies needed for meeting students' cognitive, social, and emotional needs (McEwin, Dickinson, and Jenkins 1996). Instead of developing practical and active curricula, junior high schools maintained traditional content-specific curricula and a factory design of six forty-two-minute periods throughout the day.

Throughout the 1940s and 1950s, the need for a distinct educational experience for young adolescents remained in the forefront of the minds of many educators and developmentalists. These educators suggested that junior high schools provide curricula designed for student exploration and integration of knowledge and also provide many opportunities for socialization. It was the Association for Supervision and Curriculum Development (ASCD) that responded to these calls for change in 1961 with the publication of *The Junior High School We Need* (Grantes, et al. 1961). The authors envisioned a school in which educators were specifically trained to use appropriate instructional strategies to teach young adolescents. They recommended smaller schools with flexible schedules. The authors' suggestions, unfortunately, were not implemented widely until the 1990s.

The Promise of a New Design

"What if?" some educators were asking. "What if we attempted to respond to the needs of young adolescents? What if we developed a school with the characteristics proposed by the ASCD?" Fueled by such powerful convictions, the middle school movement was born. In his edited collection of writing and reflections by early middle school visionaries, Robert David (1998) wrote,

> The middle school concept did not spring from sterile, educational thought. It was the result of the work of dedicated and inspired leaders who recognized that traditional secondary practices did not meet the needs of emerging adolescents. William Alexander, Donald Eichhorn, John Lounsbury, Conrad Toepfer, and Gordon Vars, identified as founding fathers of middle level education, . . . had the vision and determination to create a new and powerful educational reform effort for the 11- to 14-year old child. . . . Each focused on a vision regarding the programming and educational needs of the young adolescent. And they articulated a philosophy born out of the awareness that the middle level learner is a unique individual with special needs that call for a distinctive educational program. (ix)

William Alexander, often referred to as the "father of the middle school," first coined the phrase *middle school* in a speech, "The Junior High School: A Changing View," given at Cornell University in 1963 (David 1998). Alexander argued that junior high school should not simply be an extension of elementary school or a preparation for high school but that schools in the middle needed validity in and of themselves as places that met the needs of a unique age group. He called for one institution with three distinct parts designed to meet the developmental needs of students at those levels: the "lower, middle and upper level or a primary, middle and high school" (5).

Alexander outlined specific school programs necessary for educating the young adolescent. He called for a strong general education for all students with project-based instruction that allowed students to answer real questions through hands-on investigations. Alexander stressed the need for a flexible curriculum that differentiated instruction based on individual student needs. In addition, he cited the importance of a comprehensive health, physical education, and guidance program to help students cope with their rapid physical changes as well as an exploratory curriculum that would expose students to new topics and ideas. Alexander underscored the importance of understanding the social, emotional, and moral growth of students and that teachers should place an emphasis on student self-evaluation and learning to respect others while making judgments about what is right or wrong.

In his speech, Alexander also called for changes in the organization of the school. The best structure would be teams of from three to five teachers who would be responsible for a group of students. Each student would be in a small homeroom class with a teacher who knew him or her well. Groupings would be heterogeneous.

One of Alexander's most important recommendations was the call for teacher education programs to prepare teachers to work with the unique needs of the young adolescent. Alexander's ideas had an enormous influence on middle school reform throughout the next four decades and would become the core of the middle school concept. The vision of a unique school for young adolescents began to take form. In the mid-1960s Upper St. Clair, Pennsylvania; Centerville, Ohio; and Barrington, Illinois, were three of the first communities to implement this new middle school concept (George, et al. 1992).

In Upper St. Clair, assistant superintendent Donald Eichhorn not only talked about the need for reform, he was instrumental in creating a new middle school structure. As such, "he shook not only Upper St. Clair; he shook the nations' middle level schools and put into motion a process in Pennsylvania which led to the recognition of the middle grades as a distinctive level in K–12 education" (Brough 1994, 19). Eichhorn redefined instructional practice, established advisory programs to meet students' emotional needs, and developed multiage grouping. Perhaps his greatest accomplishment was his courageous willingness to question the validity of the existing traditional curricular structure. Although more middle schools were created throughout the United States shortly after the Upper St. Clair innovation, most of these were middle schools in name only and did not implement the innovations suggested by Alexander, Eichhorn, and the other educators who were working on true middle level reform.

Demographic Influences on Middle School Development

Many junior highs that changed their names to "middle school" did so because of demographic factors: the baby boomers completed high school, and a small "baby boomlet" flooded the elementary grades with overwhelming numbers of new students (George et al. 1992). Suddenly classrooms were available in high school buildings and a shortage of classrooms existed in kindergarten through sixth grade buildings. The school board's solution was to move the ninth graders into the high school, move the sixth and sometimes fifth graders into the junior high, and rename the junior high the "middle school." In response to the mandates of Brown v. Board of Education, other school districts moved to the middle school design in order to desegregate schools (George et al.).

Unfortunately, the unrealistic academic expectations required of these new students—specifically sixth graders—was as intense as that previously expected of seventh and eighth graders. Again, these were middle schools in name only—not in their design or in the ways in which students' developmental needs were addressed. Middle schools of the 1960s and 1970s frequently utilized features common to high schools, such as departmentalized instruction, forty-two-minute periods, and students tracked according to ability—in essence, the factory approach to educating students.

Support for Genuine Middle Schools

As more and more districts began to develop sixth through eighth grade schools, educators realized the need for a national organization to advocate for young adolescents. As a result, in 1973, the National Middle School Association (NMSA) was founded. In 1982, NMSA published the first comprehensive position paper outlining the role of the middle school in meeting the unique developmental needs of the young adolescent. The authors of this report asserted that simply designating an institution a "middle school" did not mean that it met the needs of young adolescents; schools must also be responsive to developmental issues. Entitled *This We Believe*, the work outlined the essential elements present in a true middle school and set the standard for middle school reform. Revised in 1995, *This We Believe* became an important statement about the vision of a middle school that fulfills its promises to young adolescents.

Seven years later, advanced research into young adolescent behavior, new understandings about teaching and learning, an analysis of successful practices in existing middle schools, and the focus on high-stakes testing to define school success led a group of middle school educators to review and revise the document again. Published in 2003, this third edition of the NMSA position statement, titled *This We Believe: Successful Schools for Young Adolescents*, was developed from a strong research base and is supported by a companion document, *Research and Resources in Support of This We Believe* (White et al. 2003). For the first time NMSA published a review of research studies that supports their position statement.

In the introduction to *This We Believe: Successful Schools for Young Adolescents* (2003) the authors stated,

> National Middle School Association seeks to conceptualize and promote successful middle level schools that enhance the healthy growth of young adolescents as lifelong learners, ethical and

democratic citizens, and increasingly competent, self-sufficient young people who are optimistic about the future. (1)

This newest revision centered around the idea that in order for middle schools to produce successful young adolescents, all aspects of the school must be geared to their needs. This new vision of a successful middle school is based on fourteen characteristics. Eight focus on the culture of the middle school and how teachers, administrators, communities, families, and students develop an environment to ensure success. The other six characteristics focus on the programs in the school that can exist in such a culture. These characteristics, listed below, include a look at curriculum, instruction, assessment, and other structures that support student learning. National Middle School Association (2003) believes:

Successful schools for young adolescents are characterized by a culture that includes

- Educators who value working with this age group and are prepared to do so
- Courageous, collaborative leadership
- A shared vision that guides decisions
- An inviting, supportive, and safe environment
- High expectations for every member of the learning community
- Students and teachers engaged in active learning
- An adult advocate for every student
- School-initiated family and community partnerships.

Therefore, successful schools for young adolescents provide

- Curriculum that is relevant, challenging, integrative, and exploratory
- Multiple learning and teaching approaches that respond to their diversity
- Assessment and evaluation programs that promote quality learning
- Organizational structures that support meaningful relationships and learning
- School-wide efforts and policies that foster health, wellness, and safety
- Multifaceted guidance and support services. (7)

The Carnegie Council on Adolescent Development

In the 1980s the Carnegie Corporation of New York was also working on behalf of middle level education. It established the Carnegie Council on Adolescent Development in 1986 out of concern for the high risks for drug and alcohol abuse, early pregnancy, school failure, and violence that adolescents faced. This group's task was to develop strategies to meet the needs of adolescents in a rapidly changing environment. Although many middle level educators continued to develop appropriate programs for their students, on a national level the education reform movement of the 1980s failed to provide specific suggestions for improving schools for young adolescents. Education became a central focus of the Carnegie Council: it established the Task Force on the Education of Young Adolescents. One role of the task force members was to determine why middle schools and junior high schools were not meeting the needs of young adolescents. The group reported the following:

- Middle and junior high schools contained large enrollments.
- The students had developed few meaningful relationships with the adults in the schools (teachers, administrators, counselors); that is, the adults did not become well acquainted with the students.
- The chosen curricula were irrelevant to students.
- The majority of instructional strategies used were better suited for specialized classes in high school or college.

The task force developed a proposal for educators and parents to suggest the design of a school that would better meet middle school students' needs. The group's report, published in 1989, was titled *Turning Points: Preparing Youth for the 21st Century* (Carnegie Council on Adolescent Development 1989). David Hamburg, chair of the council, provided this descriptive comment about young adolescents and the responsibility that schools had to these students:

The emerging adolescent is caught in turbulence, a fascinated but perplexed observer of the biological, psychological, and social

81

changes swirling all around. In groping for a solid path toward a worthwhile adult life, adolescents can grasp the middle grade school as the crucial and reliable handle. Now, the middle grade school must change, and change substantially, to cope with the requirements of a new era—to give students a decent chance in life and to help them fulfill their youthful promise. (14)

Task force members identified the kind of person they wanted middle schools to develop:

- an intellectually reflective person
- a person enroute to a lifetime of meaningful work
- a good citizen
- a caring and ethical individual
- a healthy person (Carnegie Council on Adolescent Development 1989, 15)

The Carnegie task force members provided eight recommendations that became basic guidelines for developing an appropriate educational setting for young adolescents. They clearly reflected the earlier work of Alexander, Eichhorn, and other educators who had called for middle level reform for more than two decades. Following is the executive summary of the task force's recommendations (1989):

1. *Create small communities for learning* where stable, close, mutually respectful relationships with adults and peers are considered fundamental for intellectual development and personal growth. The key elements of these communities are schools-within-schools or houses, students and teachers grouped together as teams, and small group advisories that ensure that every student is well known by at least one adult.
2. *Teach a core academic program* that results in students who are literate, including in the sciences, and who know how to think critically, lead a healthy life, behave ethically, and assume the responsibilities of citizenship in a pluralistic

society. Youth service to promote values for citizenship is an essential part of the core academic program.

3. *Ensure success for all students* through the elimination of tracking by achievement level and promotion of cooperative learning, flexibility in arranging instructional time, and adequate resources (time, space, equipment, and materials) for teachers.

4. *Empower teachers and administrators to make decisions about the experiences of middle grade students* through creative control by teachers over the instructional program linked to greater responsibilities for students' performance, governance committees that assist the principal in designing and coordinating school-wide programs, and autonomy and leadership within subschools or houses to create environments tailored to enhance the intellectual and emotional development of all youth.

5. *Staff middle grade schools with teachers who are expert at teaching young adolescents* and who have been specifically prepared for assignment to the middle grades.

6. *Improve academic performance through fostering the health and fitness* of young adolescents, by providing a health coordinator in every middle grade school, access to health care and counseling services, and a health-promoting school environment.

7. *Reengage families in the education of young adolescents* by giving families meaningful roles in school governance, communicating with families about the school program and students' progress, and offering families opportunities to support the learning process at home and at the school.

8. *Connect schools with communities*, which together share responsibilities for each middle grade student's success, through identifying service opportunities in the community, establishing partnerships and collaborations to ensure students' access to health and social services, and using community resources to enrich the instructional program and opportunities for constructive after-school activities. (9–10)

After the report was published, some middle schools began to implement the core recommendations. They developed team structures, thus creating the smaller communities for learning. Advisory programs were developed in some schools. Tracking was eliminated, on occasion, and instruction was designed to better meet the unique needs of the young adolescent.

Content Standards Influence the Middle School

The standards era was introduced and thrust upon schools during the 1990s, partly because the business community and legislative bodies were determined to influence education. Broad standards related to what students should know or be able to do when they graduated from high school were developed by most state departments of education, as well as many school districts. The emphasis to adopt content standards led most states to develop a set of curriculum frameworks to guide school content. The standards that were developed related to problem solving, communication skills, and being a participating member of society and gave schools broad latitude in designing curriculum when they were originally designed.

The federal government's reauthorization of the long-established policies for funding schools through the Elementary and Secondary Education Act under the new name of No Child Left Behind (NCLB) in 2001 changed the way standards were designed. Broad goals were quickly replaced by specific content standards that state what students should know as a result of studying specifically designated topics.

Perhaps no single event had a greater impact on the structure, organization, curriculum, instruction, and assessment practices of the middle school than the focus on content-standards-based teaching, coupled with high-stakes tests associated with the No Child Left Behind Act of 2001. NCLB policy required that each state develop benchmarks (minimum test scores) for student performance. Each school is required to meet an established level of "adequate yearly progress" (AYP). In most states, AYP is determined by the percentage of students reaching proficiency on a standardized test. If schools fail to meet the minimum required level of AYP for two years, they are labeled "in need of improvement." If schools fail to make AYP for five years, the district is required to restructure the school, replace the staff, and perhaps turn the school into a charter or private school (NCLB 2001).

Parallel to the standards-based movement was the call for teacher accountability. With the influence of NCLB policies, teacher accountability in the eyes of many administrators and legislators quickly became synonymous with acceptable test scores. Success in school was measured by a student's ability to reach a specific level (designated as *proficient* by NCLB policy) on a state-mandated test. If students achieve proficiency, according to popular belief, teachers have done their job.

Even teacher certification programs began to focus more on content knowledge at the expense of pedagogical expertise. NCLB policy defines "highly qualified teachers" at the middle school level as those who know their content area. The impact of highly qualified teacher policies was a change in certification requirements for middle school teachers in many states. Content area standardized teacher tests were developed by outside agencies, specifically Educational Testing Service, to assess potential and even experienced middle school teachers' knowledge of content with no regard for their knowledge of young adolescent development and middle school philosophy, practice, and curriculum. Experienced middle school teachers from some states were required by their state education department to take a content area test to ensure that they were "highly qualified" despite years of successful teaching in their content area.

As a result of the standards-based movement and the NCLB policies, many middle schools may be returning to the factory model. Teachers have abandoned innovative teaching and have become transmitters of information as they prepare students to reach proficiency on high-stakes tests. Many of these teachers are familiar with and have always used developmentally appropriate practices; yet they feel compelled to fill students with facts and knowledge because their administration fears being declared a school "in need of improvement." We would do well to remember these words from William Alexander's speech in 1963:

> There seems little disagreement that the youngster of twelve and above needs many and varied opportunities to identify and/or deepen worthwhile interests, and all of us would applaud what junior high schools have done to this end. However, the recent pressures on schools to give greater emphasis to the academic subject may be curtailing the exploratory feature. Earlier languages, more mathematics and science, more homework, may mean for many pupils less time and energy for the fine arts, for homemaking and industrial arts, and for such special interests as dramatics, journalism, musical performance, scouting, camping, outside jobs, and general reading. (David 1998, 5)

Alexander wrote these words six years after the Russian satellite, Sputnik, was launched in 1957. The launching of Sputnik sent shock waves through America as fear developed that the Soviets would surpass America in the space race and possibly develop the capability to attack the United States from space. Political pressure influenced American educators to increase mathematics and science instruction in the schools. The result, as evidenced in Alexander's quote, was another time in our educational history when rigorous academics became the focus of education at the expense of the individual needs of students.

Turning Points 2000

Following its initial report, in 1989, the Carnegie Corporation continued to be an advocate for middle school reform. The Middle Grade School State Policy Initiative was formed by the Carnegie Corporation to push for the adoption of the recommendations and to assess the success of implementation. After nearly a decade of observing and assessing schools that were implementing their recommendations, the Carnegie Corporation produced a new document, *Turning Points 2000: Educating Adolescents in the 21st Century* (Jackson and Davis 2000).

One of the findings reported in *Turning Points 2000* was that although many schools had undergone structural changes, such as connecting students via teams and involving parents and communities in the school, little change had been made in curriculum, instruction, or assessment. While the original eight recommendations continued to form the framework of middle level reform, *Turning Points 2000* centered its new recommendations on one broad goal: "ensuring success for every student" (23).

The new recommendations developed from a decade's worth of research on best practices that supported the success of all students. In response to the standards-based movement, the new document focused on the need for rigorous content standards for middle school students. The new recommendations are:

- Teach a curriculum grounded in rigorous, public academic standards for what students should know and be able to do, relevant to the concerns of adolescents and based on how students learn best.
- Use instructional methods designed to prepare all students to achieve higher standards and become lifelong learners.
- Staff middle grades schools with teachers who are expert at teaching young adolescents, and engage teachers in ongoing, targeted professional development opportunities.
- Organize relationships for learning to create a climate of intellectual development and a caring community of shared educational purpose.
- Govern democratically, through direct or representative participation by all school staff members, the adults who know the students best.
- Provide a safe and healthy school environment as part of improving academic performance and developing caring and ethical citizens.
- Involve parents and communities in supporting student learning and healthy development. (23–24)

Responding to Standards

In an attempt to raise student test scores and meet their AYP, school districts throughout the country began evaluating and reassessing many practices and policies. Middle schools seemed to be particularly under scrutiny. Some districts reverted to the junior high model with the belief that they must prepare students for high-stakes tests through traditional curricula that simulate high schools. Other districts, particularly in large urban areas, replaced middle schools with K–8 schools. The rationale for creating such schools included the desire to have smaller schools, to relieve overcrowding in some middle schools, or to improve discipline problems that may occur in large sixth to eighth grade schools. The bottom line, however, is that administrators wanted to raise test scores and believed that K–8 buildings would accomplish this (George 2005).

The danger in changing to K–8 schools is that schools will likely be based more on an elementary rather than a middle school model. In an analysis of K–8 schools throughout the country, researchers discovered that only a third of the schools reported using interdisciplinary teacher teams compared with 77 percent of the middle schools. K–8 schools offered fewer exploratory and extracurricular programs to young adolescents. Teachers in K–8 schools also had less common planning time, an important element for middle school success. In addition, it is essential that teachers who work with young adolescents be prepared to deal with the unique needs of this age group. When young adolescents are placed in K–8 schools with teachers whose primary knowledge of teaching is based on their content expertise, it is likely that effective preparation of middle school teachers will be less valued (McEwin, Dickinson, and Jacobson 2005). In their attempt to raise test scores, school districts must be careful about creating schools that ignore the unique needs of the young adolescent.

It is important, when looking at the success or failure of middle schools, to analyze how many of the recommendations from the original *Turning Points* and *This We Believe* were actually implemented. Are many middle schools simply junior high schools in disguise? A seven-year longitudinal study of middle schools implementing the recommendations of *Turning Points* to a high degree indicated significant academic and social growth, with students scoring higher than state norms on mathematics, language arts, and reading assessments.

Improvements were also found in student behavior (Felner et al. 1997). This study is discussed at length in Chapter 11. Continued research will help determine the effectiveness of the middle school concept, not by merely examining student achievement but by also examining how schools contribute to the healthy development of the young adolescent in all areas.

Middle schools continue to proliferate despite the return by some districts to K–8 buildings or junior highs. Lounsbury and Vars (2005) reported, "As of January 2004, according to Market Data Retrieval, there are 14,548 public middle schools and only 554 junior high schools of grades 7–9. The face of American Education has indeed been remade twice through the reorganization movement that began about 1910 and continues today" (11).

Whether a district keeps their middle schools, returns to a junior high format, or moves young adolescents into a K–8 setting, what is important is that an intentional effort is made to develop curriculum, instruction, assessment, and a school environment appropriate for young adolescents. As Tom Erb (2005b), editor of the *Middle School Journal*, noted, "The middle school concept is about organizing and delivering developmentally appropriate programs for young adolescents—not about what grades may or may not be housed in the school building" (3). School districts can change the name of the school, restructure the configuration of the classes, or move students into another building. Ultimately, however, it is the implementation of effective middle school practices that provide young adolescents with a meaningful learning environment.

Concluding Reflections

While many of the original recommendations of *This We Believe* and *Turning Points* drove the middle school movement through the 1990s, increasing accountability and high-stakes testing influenced educators' decisions about middle school practice into and after 2000. The idea of a middle school responding to the needs of young adolescents must be honored despite the focus on rigid content standards and teacher accountability. In attempting to respond to accountability concerns, we must not forget the inherent curiosity; the desire for curricular relevance; and the social, emotional, and physical needs of the young adolescent in designing their school day. Genuine accountability for middle school teachers occurs when they respond to the specific needs of each young adolescent they teach. Fear of accountability should not result in knee-jerk reactions to bureaucratic mandates.

We sincerely hope that preservice and inservice teachers will continue to work to develop middle schools that are sensitive to the developmental stages and needs of young adolescents and also implement democratic principles in classroom practice. The courage and actions of teachers change schooling more than the efforts of administrators or professors who write books! It is imperative that teachers comprehend their role and assume responsibility for improving middle level education.

Time for Reflection
- Return to the middle school design you devised at the start of this chapter. Compare your group's design with the thoughts put forth by NMSA and the Carnegie Report.
- Decide as a group how you would alter your design or change the design suggested by the NMSA and the Carnegie Report.
- Discuss how your school can meet content and performance standards while still meeting the learning needs of young adolescents.

FIVE

Creating a Safe Haven for Learning

Teachers wear a lot of different hats: teacher, doctor, social worker. With middle school age [students], you're wearing all of the hats—almost equally. I find myself playing an advising role all day long.

RODNEY, EIGHTH GRADE TEACHER

My own middle school years remain vivid in my memory. I was excluded, and I manipulated the exclusion of others. I could be mean, yet, in turn, I was deeply hurt by others. If my friends and I did speak to an adult about these problems we heard such clichés as: "There are plenty of other girls who would love to be your friends" or "Can't you just try to be nice to each other" or my all time favorite, "Sticks and stones may break my bones, but words will never hurt me." Words break your heart and scar you for life.

LANE (2005, 41)

Any student will tell you that teachers cannot feign caring and believing in students. Your students know what you feel about them. Naima, a seventh grader in an urban middle school, reveals this awareness: "Some teachers don't have respect for us. They only

91

come here to get paid. If they don't want to teach they shouldn't be here." Every student you teach will realize your commitment to teaching and be aware of the extent of your interest. Students have an entire class period to "size up" teachers to decide whether to cooperate with them or engage in learning with them.

You may be saying at this point, "I don't need to read this chapter. Of course I care about students, or I wouldn't consider being a professional educator!" You might be surprised by the kind of teacher behaviors and school policies that deflate students' attitudes and confidence. Middle level classrooms aren't always the caring learning havens that you would expect.

Time for Reflection

- Develop a list of characteristics that describe the best teachers you have known.
- Compare your list with others in your group.
- Write a description of the classroom where you learned the most as a student. Consider how students treated each other, how the teacher treated students, and what a typical day was like in that classroom.

Middle Schools and Student Stress

Many situations initiated by teachers can cause fear and stress in young adolescents. Here are a few:

1. frequently yelling at one student or an entire class
2. applying punishment inappropriately
3. threatening students
4. making fun of students
5. establishing unrealistic academic demands or expectations
6. requiring students to open their lockers, get the appropriate books and notebooks, and get to their next class on time— all in less than four minutes

7. pushing students to learn abstract principles that are beyond their cognitive capabilities
8. assigning extensive homework that requires at least an hour or more of work each evening for each subject
9. embarrassing students in front of their most significant audience—their peers

We know you're thinking, "I'd never do any of these things." But through more subtle actions, teachers may also unwittingly disrupt the emotional stability students require in order for learning to occur:

1. refusing to lend a pencil, protractor, or paper to students
2. caring more about completing the textbook than meeting each student's needs
3. treating each student the same regardless of differences in learning abilities or learning styles
4. preventing students from interacting socially during class time
5. assessing student learning in only one way
6. designing lessons that are primarily teacher-directed without hands-on opportunities for student learning
7. refusing to be flexible in curriculum design, instructional processes, or scheduling
8. using quizzes to "catch" students who may not understand material
9. ignoring young adolescents' stages of cognitive, social, and emotional growth

These negative actions affect more than students' self-esteem.

How Stress Affects Student Learning

Anxiety and stress affect the quality of students' cognitive processing, disrupting their ability to process information efficiently. Caine and Caine (1994) described what many students experience when perceiving a threat as a "narrowing of the perceptual field" (69). Students are likely to feel a sense of helplessness whenever a situation becomes threatening. Helplessness is followed by a loss of effective cognitive processing, described as "downshifting" (69). When stress associated with fear creates anxiety, people drift into a downshifted state and have difficulty using higher-order cognitive abilities efficiently and are unable "to see the interconnectedness . . . among topics" (70). Caine and Caine added that stress-related issues prevent our brains from forming permanent new memories. A number of studies have identified the relationship between socioemotional states of mind and cognition (Elias et al. 1997; Perry 1996; Brendtro, Brokenleg, and Van Bockern 1990). These studies indicate that "under conditions of real or imagined threat or anxiety, there is a loss of focus on the learning process and a reduction in task focus and flexible problem solving" (Elias et al. 1997, 3).

Many students consider schools to be the central, if not the only, place where a safe and trusting environment exists. Karen, an eighth grader in an urban middle school, commented: "Students in our school have pressure in the homes and stuff. They can't concentrate in school because at home they've got to be the adult. When they come [to school], they've got to be the child." Even in high socioeconomic communities, schools can be a safe haven for students who are not getting sufficient emotional support at home. A sixth grade teacher, Edith, who teaches in a wealthy neighborhood, spoke of the "emotional needs" of her students despite their high socioeconomic standing: "Because parents are so busy with their jobs, the children are neglected. Someone's not there to listen to them. There's an emotional component within these children that we have to be aware of."

Establishing a Caring Environment

Young adolescents, in moving away from the need for parental approval, need to know that someone other than their peers will provide a support system. This comment from John, an eighth grader in an urban school, emphasizes the importance of the teacher/student relationship:

> It's not supposed to just be, "I'm your teacher; I see you in school and that's all." It should be like a friend bond also; so you can talk to that teacher—be open to her. That way, they get to know more about you.

According to Elias et al. (1997), "Caring happens when children sense that the adults in their lives think they are important and when they understand that they will be accepted and respected, regardless of any particular talents they have" (6).

Researchers in one study discovered that showing care and respect for students "promoted learning and overpowered the comparative effects of instructional methodologies" (Goodman, Sutton, and Harkevy 1995, 696). Lipsitz (1995) added: "Caring did not substitute for learning; caring established an effective culture for learning" (666). When caring attitudes are demonstrated by teachers, "trust is established and caring interpersonal relationships are built in classrooms" (Chaskin and Mendley Rauner 1995, 673). Creating a caring environment should be a primary initiative for all teachers.

In an interview study with young adolescents, Bosworth (1995) asked students to describe caring teachers. Students reported that caring teachers:

- walk[ed] around the room talking to everybody to see how they were doing [and] to answer questions
- help[ed] students with school work
- noticed and inquired about changes in behavior
- recognized different learning styles and speeds
- sought to know students as unique human beings
- showed respect for students through actions such as "talking in a quiet voice or talking to you in private or alone"
- [did] a good job of explaining the content area, making sure that all students understand
- encourage[d] students to improve (691–92)

This sounds like a great deal of work to accomplish on a daily basis—and it is. Behind all of these suggestions, however, is probably one of the primary reasons we become teachers: because we really care about students—especially young adolescents!

When teachers show their acceptance of students, and students begin to see and understand that teachers care, school can be mutually satisfying to both students and teachers. You can show students you care by:

- sharing your life experiences with students and conveying your excitement for learning
- modeling one-on-one active listening
- helping students develop personal academic and social outcomes
- participating in daily activities such as lunch, recess, and after-school intramurals
- taking the time to discover what is important to your students outside school—hobbies, interests, family stories, pets
- attending your students' musical, athletic, and theatrical performances

Naturally, you'll think of many other actions once you get to know your students. Some teachers make it a point to spend the first and last few minutes of each class session just talking to students about their personal lives.

Genuinely Knowing Students

Barth (1991) proclaimed, "What needs to be improved about schools is their culture, the quality of interpersonal relationships, and the nature and quality of learning experiences" (45). Teachers are responsible for creating the kinds of interpersonal relationships with students that can improve the quality of learning.

You can test your personal knowledge of your students after the first month of the school year by writing down their names, then listing observations about each of them. Once a personal link with each student is established, you will notice that students begin to focus more effectively on academic issues and learn in more meaningful ways.

Remember that a caring relationship begins with the development of trust and mutual respect between students and teachers. Your job is to create that trust and to maintain a level of respect for each student throughout the year. Respect for students is demonstrated through your modeling of politeness, courtesy, and honesty. Respect is shared between students and teachers when teachers make it a point to recognize students for their efforts and talents—and not merely their academic abilities.

It is imperative to understand that teachers and students *together* have the responsibility for assuring that a classroom is a place in which all students have an opportunity to learn. In developing this collaborative environment, teachers must invite student cooperation. A more traditional view of a teacher's role is as someone who controls students' behaviors. Teachers do not control students! Students merely choose to cooperate with us. We suggest that you develop the kind of meaningful connection with each student that encourages students to want to cooperate with you and others. The beauty of establishing a mutually respectful classroom is that it enables students and teachers to reach a common outcome—a comfortable and meaningful learning community.

Developing a respectful community in a school and classroom also includes establishing ground rules for how students treat each other. Most middle school teachers realize, if you don't recall from your own middle school years, that students can be unkind to one another. Teachers have a responsibility to assist students in the challenges they face in responding to daily social pressures.

Communicating Effectively with Students

Many teachers consider themselves to be effective communicators with students and colleagues. You might use the words *good listener* to describe how friends and family members think of you. Would your students, however, similarly describe you? By the time students arrive in middle school, they have been listening to teachers in formal learning environments all day long for at least six years. As McCarthy (1999) pointed out, "During adolescence they want and need the chance to share their feelings and ideas. . . ." (4–5). Developmentally, young adolescents experience a social awakening. Their social needs eclipse other interests and are often a priority in their lives. They are certainly concerned with interacting with peers, but they also enjoy conversations with adults.

Teachers must provide opportunities for students to be heard, both formally through collaborative lesson design and informally through private conversations. Students notice teachers who genuinely listen to them in conversations about something other than school. When Ladson-Billings (1994) asked a group of eighth graders what they liked about their teacher this is how they responded:

> She listens to us!
> She respects us!
> She lets us express our opinions!
> She looks us in the eye when she talks to us!
> She smiles at us!
> She speaks to us when she sees us in the hall or in the cafeteria! (68)

You may not realize that students notice these behaviors in teachers, but obviously they do—and it matters to them.

Teachers' nonverbal actions are even more noticeable to students than what teachers say. Responding verbally to students without a corresponding and congruent nonverbal action sends a message—but perhaps not the one intended. We explained in Chapter 3 how young adolescents' brain development affects their ability to adequately process verbal and nonverbal messages sent by others. Teachers can send a message of listening through the following actions (as suggested by Brown 2005):

- make frequent eye contact
- face the student
- listen actively
- rephrase a student's comments when he or she is finished speaking
- listen completely until the student is finished speaking (13)

Active listening is a critical component of mutual respect between teachers and students. Effective educators find and make time for listening every day and all day.

Roadblocks to Effective Communication

We can all recall our parents' responses to difficult situations that arose during our childhood or adolescent years. They usually tried to resolve the problem for us or gave us sound advice for how to resolve the problem ourselves. When our students say something to us, we often lapse into familiar patterns of communicating with them through the voices of our parents. These traditional responses to student behaviors and concerns are often roadblocks to listening and communicating effectively with students.

Englander (1986) described some of these roadblocks:

- ordering: "Go over and apologize to her for what you said."
- moralizing: "Life isn't supposed to be fair."
- interpreting: "It's not that big of a deal."
- reassuring: "You shouldn't be nervous about that; you always get good grades."
- questioning: "Why did you act that way?" (64)

These sound like innocent and supportive comments. We've heard them for years from the adults in our lives. The difficulty is, when adolescents hear these comments, the problem is not solved and their feelings and frustrations may linger for hours. Brown (2005) noted: "These roadblocks, unfortunately, send a clear message to young adolescents: 'This person isn't interested in hearing what I think, believe, or feel'" (14). These traditional responses usually indicate that the adults using them are dominating the conversation and imposing their own values and solutions to others' problems (Englander 1986).

The alternative to using roadblocks is "empathetic listening," or "getting inside the heads" of students:

You make yourself aware not just of their words, but of their deeper hopes, fears, realities, and difficulties. The way to do this is to listen within the student's frame of reference as child or adolescent rather than from your frame of reference as adult teacher. This is the student's perception of reality. (Charles 2000, 52)

Empathetic listening requires listening without judging or moralizing. Empathetic listeners encourage students to be responsible for their own behavior by having them reflect on and begin to resolve their own problems. Young adolescents are more likely to develop an internal locus of control of their behavior, taking more responsibility for their actions and words, when teachers use empathetic listening. With a conscious effort, teachers can become better listeners and thus create a classroom of mutual respect.

Young adolescents are often consumed by emotional energy. Their verbal outbursts that follow emotional situations are often quite inappropriate. The reaction from teachers during these emotional situations is key to maintaining a cooperative spirit with students. It is easy to feel hurt and angry when a fourteen-year-old swears at you, but a teacher's reaction in that situation can cause even more problems if not designed to defuse emotions and demonstrate mutual respect. A teacher's response to an emotional outburst is also observed by the entire class as evidence of a teacher's professionalism and care for students. Teachers who react calmly despite their own frustration model ways of responding to aggression and can also defuse a problem more quickly. Brown (2005) provided a few defusing responses:

- "Swearing is a common response to being embarrassed; however, it offends me and possibly others as well. Plus, it's not acceptable behavior in a public forum such as school. Can you think of something else to say when you're angry that's not so disrespectful?"
- "I noticed you're late again. Is there anything I can do to help you get here on time? It means a lot to me to have you here when class begins."
- "I see you don't have a pencil again. What can *you* do to resolve this problem? Do you need my help in getting supplies?"
- "How do you think your behavior might affect others?"
- "I see you're quite upset. Do you want to talk about it?" (14)

Each response encourages student self-reflection and ultimately also notifies students of teachers' feelings and intent to help. The most inappropriate response is to use sarcasm or to belittle students in any way when they act emotionally. Teachers cannot afford to take young adolescents' unpredictable behavior personally.

Encouraging Positive Student Relationships

Young adolescents must don a strong suit of armor when they interact with peers. You can probably recall your own middle school days and the way you were treated by classmates who were your friends one day and your enemies the next. Middle school's social battlefields may best be described as a place of survival of the fittest, and many students don't have the strong social strategies they need to defend themselves. Adults who don't regularly see young adolescents together may not understand the many ways that middle school students can hurt each other through their words and actions. Every middle school teacher has seen the havoc that young adolescents can create socially and emotionally for other students. Although many teachers may believe that it is not their place to settle student-to-student conflicts, wise educators take a more proactive role in ensuring that middle level students are polite to one another. Teachers, at least within their classrooms, have a responsibility to provide a safe and secure environment for social interaction.

For most students, middle school presents an entirely new social setting in which they see few of their elementary school friends. Young adolescents who enter middle school as fifth or sixth graders usually begin to establish relationships with many new students from varying demographic backgrounds. Creating safe havens for learning begins with designing classroom activities at the beginning of the year that allow students to interact with one another for the purpose of feeling comfortable together. Until students begin to share aspects of their lives with others, they will not experience the sense of trust needed to cooperate with one another or with the teacher.

Safe and secure classrooms are social environments in which teachers provide opportunities for students to become acquainted with one another and with you as the teacher. Teachers should begin the school year with activities that encourage student-to-student interaction, such as:

- inviting students to share their life histories
- having students meet in pairs to write newspaper reports describing their partner to the rest of the class
- creating cooperative base groups in each class, in which four students work together and accept responsibility for one another's understanding of material and completion of assignments
- pairing students for safe travel between classes
- helping students learn and practice conflict resolution strategies

Another primary responsibility for teachers is establishing and enforcing appropriate behavioral expectations. Middle level teachers can frequently take a hand in preventing students from embarrassing each other or inflicting emotional pain. Teachers and students together can develop a set of appropriate social expectations in each classroom and enforce those expectations when violations occur, thus ensuring that the classroom is a place of mutual respect and a safe haven for learning. Charney (1991) values the actions of teachers in creating a community classroom environment because of her belief that "part of our mission is to create communities with fewer nightmares, where self-control and care for others minimizes the possibilities of violence" (17). A peaceful classroom environment is a place where students care about and support each other through their daily interactions.

The Dangers of Bullying

Nearly every young adolescent gets victimized by a peer or group of peers at some time or other during the middle school years. That is a fact of life for our children. The push and pull of social gathering during early adolescence creates outcasts and crises by the dozen.

GIANNETTI AND SAGARESE (2001, 90)

102

Bullying is characterized as an imbalance of power and control in relationships among students. In normal conflicts, each person usually shares equal power. Bullies change that balance and create fear or distress in their victims, who are generally younger or weaker (Rigby 2001).

Pardini (1999) defined bullying as "ongoing, relentless infliction of physical, verbal, or emotional abuse by one or more students. It can take many forms, including teasing, threats, extortion, assault, theft, sexual harassment, and social isolation" (26). *Direct* bullying involves face-to-face confrontation and may include verbal as well as physical acts of aggression. With *indirect* bullying, there is no direct contact. It usually involves verbal or written comments about others, often circulated via the Internet or cell phones. Another form of indirect bullying is *relational* bullying, which involves rejecting or excluding others (Banks 2000). Males and females can and often do engage in all three types, although males are more likely to use physical, direct bullying and females, verbal and relational.

The relational bullying that is common among females who know one another can involve

> ignoring someone to punish them or get one's way, excluding someone socially for revenge, using negative body language or facial expressions, sabotaging someone's relationships, or threatening to end a relationship unless the friend agrees to a request. In these acts, the bully uses her relationship with the victim as a weapon.
>
> SIMMONS (2002, 21; CITED IN LANE 2005, 43)

This type of bullying is used to destroy relationships or prevent others from becoming members of cliques. It can lead to serious disagreements or fights. Lane noted, "Because girls crave close relationships and inclusion, relational aggression causes great emotional suffering for many girls" (43).

Relational bullying may begin at school but can erupt into intense viciousness against another student through cyberbullying—on-line conversations and accusations usually posted in writing, sometimes anonymously (Chu 2005). Long (2006) wrote, "Instead of passing notes in class or whispering secrets in the schoolyard, students use cell phones, text messages, emails, instant messaging, and digital cameras as tools to tease and taunt their victims from anywhere, at any time" (33). Chu (2005) emphasized the difficulty in controlling bullying via the computer and instant messaging: "If parents and teachers think it's hard to control mean girls and bullying boys in school, they haven't reckoned with cyberspace" (52). In recent surveys among middle school students, as many as 18 to 21 percent reported being cyberbullied (Chu). Females report cyberbullying almost three times as much as males. The rumors and innuendo that result from the comments about others on the Internet can be devastating to many young adolescents and negatively influence behaviors in school.

Teachers' Responsibilities with Bullying

Teachers are responsible for preventing as much bullying as possible. Bullying patterns are normally established within the first six weeks of school, and students usually don't bully someone whom they know well (Kerr 2006). Teachers thus have a specific responsibility to develop a community in the classroom so that students do know and care for one another.

Teachers in the past tended to let students handle these problems themselves. Teachers' roles in responding to bullying are much clearer now. The average length of a bullying incident is approximately thirty-seven seconds, and if onlookers step in within the first ten seconds, it is likely that nothing more will happen (Kerr 2006). Early intervention is thus clearly schools' and teachers' responsibility. All educators can discourage bullying when it occurs.

A key finding among bullies who were interviewed is that they knew they could get away with their bullying. This confession reveals that supervision and surveillance are essential. Teachers need to take notice of school spaces where students are isolated and hidden from others as well as specific times during the day when bullying is likely to occur. Effective programs against bullying may begin with anonymous questionnaires to determine the nature and extent of bullying problems. Bullying can be reported via short written forms placed in a school mailbox or a special telephone number (Kerr 2006). Specific advisory sessions devoted to bullying are also helpful.

Lane (2005) suggested that encouraging girls to describe their feelings in journals (through words or pictures) can help them handle their hurt and anger. Lane also advised that teachers get to know those students who are often alone and provide them with social strategies to become more involved with others.

Preventing bullying is a responsibility of every faculty and staff member in schools. There are many books and on-line resources available for dealing with bullying. This issue should become a priority in schools through faculty meetings and in-service sessions.

Encouraging Risk Taking

As an educator you are responsible for ensuring the success of all of your students—for encouraging them to develop higher levels of motivation and commitment toward their own growth. A part of this challenge is to invite the types of risk-taking behaviors required for genuine cognitive growth to occur. Without taking cognitive risks, students limit their learning potential.

We teach reading and writing at all grade levels from kindergarten through high school. We challenge students to use their minds to solve problems, create stories, and respond to issues and ideas that they've never before encountered. We encourage our students to think critically and generate hypotheses. Behind all successful students is a belief that they can and will succeed at the academic challenges that teachers present. But what about those students who don't do particularly well at reading the first two years of formal schooling? What about the students who never develop effective writing strategies? What about students who have been persuaded by their teachers that mathematics is not their strong suit? Many of these students never develop or use the necessary risk-taking behaviors required for substantial cognitive growth.

One characteristic of "good" thinkers is risk taking (Glatthorn and Baron 1991). Risk taking is also a characteristic of effective readers and writers at the elementary school level (May 1998). Taking risks is a joy to many of us, but for students who are seldom recognized for academic success, taking a risk, such as reading out loud to the other students in class, is viewed as a losing prospect. Students who meet with minimal success in school because of academic difficulty, learning disabilities, or behavioral problems ask the same question daily: "Why play a game that I will never win?" To protect themselves, these students refuse to participate out of fear that they will never receive recognition for their efforts, only for their products. Their schoolwork may never meet the unrealistic standards often developed by state legislators, local school boards, or their own teachers. These frustrations create a constant feeling of inadequacy.

No adult would be foolish enough to participate in a losing effort for 180 days a year for thirteen consecutive years; yet we expect struggling students to return to school year after year despite their inability to succeed. Let's face it, if you don't believe that you can succeed at something, why would you continue to try—only to fail over and over again? For example, perhaps you don't play tennis well. Every time you play, you become frustrated by your inability to hit the ball, place it in the "right" place on the other side of the net, win a game. Imagine your horror if every day a yellow bus came into your neighborhood and took you to the tennis courts for another day of failure! Yet every day, thousands of students get on the bus and head for school knowing that they will not succeed at many of the tasks they are asked to undertake.

Without the confidence, encouragement, or support to attempt new reading strategies, writing experiences, or to learn new mathematical principles, many students wander aimlessly through school, afraid of looking like a fool. Many children begin to believe that they will never succeed as students even before they reach young adolescence. These students are quite capable of learning, but their learning doesn't involve academics and seldom occurs at school!

Teachers need to reach out to these students. Professional educators are hired to meet the needs of all students—not merely the gifted and talented ones. Meeting cognitive needs is secondary to meeting students' emotional needs for a safe learning environment that encourages them to take risks.

For students, academic safety means that

- no one laughs at them when they attempt to ask or answer a question
- teachers establish realistic academic expectations and outcomes for each student
- students' efforts are recognized as well as the products of those efforts
- teachers eliminate competitive situations that create inequity among students
- teachers develop cooperative grouping strategies that encourage students to collaborate in their learning and share their knowledge and expertise with one another
- teachers play the role of learning facilitator to encourage student independence
- teachers choose alternative instructional strategies to meet each student's learning style
- teachers recognize and appreciate talents other than academic skills

We understand that providing this type of attention to each student may seem impossible. If you're not sure you are up to meeting the challenge, ask yourself this: "If schooling were not mandatory, how would my behavior as an educator encourage each student to return to my class every day?" You affect many young lives as a teacher. Interacting positively with your students is imperative.

Recognizing and Responding to Diverse Learners

If you care about young adolescents and their need to learn, you will spend much of the first few weeks of the school year studying how each student operates in the classroom. After discovering what works well for each student, you will provide the conditions needed for his or her learning and the tools each student will need to succeed at new cognitive challenges. A most important characteristic of becoming an effective, caring educator is the ability and commitment to recognize individual learning differences among students.

Ineffective teachers use the same materials, lesson plans, and testing practices with every student year after year, disregarding individual learning needs. Effective educators ask, "What can I do to help each student to learn successfully this year?" Effective teachers design classroom learning experiences that match the needs of all students: those with different ethnic backgrounds, those with special learning disabilities, those from low socioeconomic neighborhoods, and students who excel in all academic areas.

Although much has been written about strategies for teaching diverse and at-risk student populations, our view is that a responsive middle level teacher takes all students' characteristics into consideration when planning and delivering instruction and assessing students. Effective teachers who recognize and react to diverse learners are extremely flexible in how they present information to students, allow students to complete assignments, and assess their students' learning. In the typical classroom with a range of diverse learners, student learning may be facilitated in many different ways. Each student develops a separate set of expectations and outcomes based on his or her needs. We believe that committed, caring teachers make an effort to discover the strengths and weaknesses of their students and adjust their teaching to meet individual needs.

Sharing Decision Making

Many preservice and in-service teachers believe that their role is to "take control," "discipline students," and make sure that students don't "get out of line." They view themselves as an authority figure, unilaterally responsible for making the rules, enforcing them, and revising them. We live in a country founded on democratic principles. Teachers can be instrumental in helping young adolescents develop democratic ideals when students are permitted to influence the policies and procedures that govern their behavior.

The fear associated with the idea of a democratic classroom stems from adult skepticism that young people are capable of making appropriate decisions about their education. Educators who share this mistrust of students fail to recognize that classrooms designed to provide opportunities for student choice are much more meaningful learning environments than those in which all decisions are made by the teacher.

You might be asking yourself, "Where is the middle ground? How do I create a classroom in which students participate in the learning process without infringing on my authority?" Your next question might be, "How do I perform in the role of teacher if I relinquish control over how the classroom is organized or what the rules are?" Remember that young adolescents are curious about authority and are beginning to question the rules and policies they have subordinated themselves to unthinkingly for so long. It is an exciting and, to some, a threatening thought that students are beginning to dismantle the entire moral, behavioral framework that others have built up around them. They are chipping away at previously accepted rules, finding serious flaws in their structure. What an excellent time for teachers to engage students in dialogue on topics such as civic order, the reason for authority, self-regulated behavior, accepting responsibility, and appropriate and reasonable decision making.

Teachers don't need to do the work of establishing class expectations and policies by themselves—why waste the growing cognitive powers of young adolescents? Now is the time to have students participate in designing the classroom atmosphere. Initiate discussions on the role of students and teachers in creating an effective and dynamic learning environment. Use class meetings to decide how to appropriately handle violations of trust and foster respect among students and between students and teachers.

Shared decision making lays the foundation for a classroom that operates as a community. When students view their classmates as partners in a joint venture, involved in a process of learning from one another, the classroom becomes a democracy, where each individual's contributions are valued.

Student Involvement in Curricular Decision Making

Inviting students to collaborate with teachers on curriculum development marks a radical departure from traditional schooling practices.

After all, many educators question whether *teachers* should participate in curricular decision making, let alone students! But schools must become places in which the information that students learn has meaning for them. Curricular outcomes designed without the voices of middle school students are likely to have little impact on influencing the lives of young adolescents. As stated in the National Middle School Association's *This We Believe: Successful Schools for Young Adolescents* (2003), "Consonant with their varying capacities to handle responsibility, students must be nurtured in making choices and decisions about curricular goals, content, activities, and means of assessment" (22).

How relevant to their lives will their class work be if textbook writers, curriculum supervisors, or teachers make unilateral decisions about content intended for the young adolescent? The curriculum is meaningful only if it responds to the personal questions and concerns that students have. Strategies for involving students in curricular planning are discussed in Chapter 6.

Creating Collaborative—Not Competitive—Learning Environments

One of the most disturbing aspects of the traditional school experience is pitting children against one another. Young adolescents clearly understand how diverse their academic abilities are. Teachers who create competitive learning situations accentuate the weaknesses and strengths of students. The public comparison is embarrassing for less able students. As a result, they refuse to take the risks necessary for learning to occur. If being "the best" is what success means—and that is the idea in many schools—most students will fail. Kohn (1986) stated that a competitive learning environment "distracts you from a task at a given moment, makes you less interested in that task over the long run, and this results in poorer performance" (60–61). Contrary to what you may have been led to believe, competitive environments do not result in increased learning.

Students in collaborative classrooms work together to solve problems, plan presentations, design projects, develop questions, and resolve personal differences. Kohn (1986) explained that "a cooperative classroom is not simply one where students sit together or talk with each other or even share materials. It means that successful completion of a task depends on each student and therefore each has an incentive to want the other(s) to succeed" (6).

Collaboration among students doesn't automatically occur just because teachers ask students to work together. The teacher's role is to plan instructional activities that encourage student cooperation and to help students develop the social strategies needed to work together successfully. After group work sessions, middle level students should be asked to evaluate their collaborative efforts to determine how to improve their skills in this area. Students may rate their skills as team members in categories such as

- effectiveness in listening to one another
- ability to accept various individual responsibilities
- willingness to alter original beliefs to reach consensus
- ability to establish and meet deadlines

Such reflection will help students improve their collaborative skills.

Educators must question traditional practices that foster hostile learning environments. Most of us experienced these ourselves when we were students. You can change such negative conditions to create a more positive learning environment. Students, like plants, grow well when they are cultivated with care. The more comfortable and secure your students feel when they are with you each day, the more growth they will experience.

Time for Reflection

- Based on your reading to this point, add to the list of effective teacher characteristics that you developed at the beginning of this chapter.
- Review your list with a classmate or fellow teacher who has also written one, and compare the similarities and differences.
- How do you think the role of teachers has changed since you were a middle school student? How have teacher roles remained the same?
- Discuss with your classmates or fellow teachers your views on the importance of using class time to develop a learning community.

SIX

Student-Designed Curriculum

I think the curriculum should change. There are teachers that I have who photocopy the same sheet for ten years, the same worksheet, every year the same thing. Like Germany, the teacher said, "Write East and West Germany." I would make teachers have to change their curriculum. Every year they would have to modify it.

EIGHTH GRADER

Some curriculum is pretty dull in regular classes. Learning what you want to learn is motivating. Every day I wanted to come to class!

EIGHTH-GRADE CURRICULUM INTEGRATION STUDENT
(CITED IN BROWN AND MORGAN 2003, 19)

Middle level schools have not lived up to their billing as developmentally respon-sive schools for young adolescents; they have failed to address the fundamental element of the school—its curriculum.

BRAZEE (1995, 16)

113

While many positive changes have been made in the education of young adolescents, most schools have not tackled the hard and often political question of the middle school curriculum. Teachers have changed *how* they teach but in many cases they have not changed *what* they teach. Educational content is often the same from middle school to middle school; it looks surprisingly like that of the junior high school, which looks surprisingly like that of the high school, which looks surprisingly like that of schools fifty to seventy-five years ago—despite dramatic changes in the way *life* looks today. As Sue Swaim, executive director of the National Middle School Association (NMSA), said in 1993, "While a continually increasing number of schools have moved to implement interdisciplinary teams, teacher advisor programs, broad exploratory experiences, skill development programs, and other recommended characteristics, the basic questions of what we teach and how we teach remain for the most part, unanswered and little challenged" (xii). Her statement is as valid now as it was then.

A developmentally appropriate middle school curriculum should be the central focus of any middle school. If a school has implemented changes in school structure, the school day, and modes of instruction but has not changed the curriculum to respond to developmental issues, it cannot meet the needs of young adolescents.

Time for Reflection

- What qualities make a job satisfying to you?
- Why are chores (laundry, house cleaning) sometimes so frustrating?
- Why do so many students look forward to ending their formal education even though that might mean facing the world of work (perhaps menial work) and having a standard of living lower than when their parents supported them?

CLARK (1997)

Look at how you answered the above questions. Now think of schooling at the middle level. According to the criteria you devised in answering the first question, would middle school be satisfying? Does it have any of the characteristics of a task that is frustrating? What is it about school that makes so many students want to escape or drop out? If middle level students had a choice, would they sign up for the teachers that they are assigned to? Would they voluntarily sign up to be in your class? Would they return to school each day if schooling were not compulsory? Why is achievement so important in our lives, and how can that translate to middle level education?

What Is Curriculum?

Before we look at what the curriculum of the middle school should be, let's clarify terms. Curriculum *is not*:

- a collection of textbooks or guides
- a fixed course of study
- that which the teacher prefers to teach
- a program of study that must be completed before the end of the school year
- a set of content standards that teachers must cover

Curriculum *is*:

- the total experience of students at school
- a plan that involves students in learning
- a construct that enables students to access, process, interpret, and make connections to information
- the organizing focus of a school

Curriculum permeates the school life of adolescents; they are immersed in it. It is their life from the moment they walk into the building until they leave at the end of the day. It includes everything: social times, club times, athletics, lunch, after-school programs, drama, music—every planned and unplanned event.

115

Beliefs About Middle Level Curriculum

Early Thinking

Educators always discuss what should be taught in the schools. The general public has its opinions as well. These discussions center around what people think the purpose of schooling is. We continue to have, in Kliebard's (1986) words, "the struggle for the American curriculum." Should the curriculum be designed to help meet the needs of business? Should it be designed so that students can compete with other students around the world? Should it be designed to meet the individual needs of students? Should it be designed around the disciplines of knowledge? Should it be designed around a set of mandated content standards? Or should it be designed around problems and concerns that arise out of students' questions? Should the curriculum emulate the kind of democracy we all value?

Progressive educators in the early part of the twentieth century advocated for a child-centered curriculum that not only met the needs of students but also focused its content on issues in society. These early visionaries wanted a problem-based/project-based curriculum relevant to the lives of the students. The call for such a curriculum resulted in a landmark study during the 1930s, the *Eight Year Study* (1942), based on the idea that

> the conventional high school curriculum was far removed from the real concerns of youth. . . . Young people wanted to get ready to earn a living, to understand themselves, to learn how to get on with others, to become responsible members of the adult community, to find meaning in living. The curriculum seldom touched upon such genuine problems of living. (Chapter 1)

In this study, participating high schools throughout the country offered an experimental curriculum collaboratively designed by teachers and students. The curriculum was experience based without regard to specific discipline subjects and centered around problems of concern to the students. These students, in other words, did not take the traditional high school subjects—four years of English, two years of

116

social studies, two years of science, or other traditional course work. These high schools were supported by a number of colleges and universities who were willing to forgo the traditional requirements for college admission.

Through this curriculum, students were provided with the opportunity to live and experience democracy and to learn social responsibility at a time when, according to the report, five out of six high school students were not attending higher education institutions. The educators wanted the experience of high school to be as powerful as possible for all students, not just for the one of six who planned to attend college.

An analysis of the results of this study indicated that those students who were part of this project did as well or better on standardized tests than students who had attended traditional high schools. Those who went to college earned a slightly higher grade point average and received more academic honors. More importantly, those students involved in the program tended to be more curious and resourceful and have more drive and a clearer vision of where their education would take them, and they continued to be more concerned about world affairs than those students from traditional high schools.

Finally, here was a curriculum that engaged students in thinking about their world, a curriculum based on significant social issues and concerns. These students did not have to take traditional high school subjects; yet, in college they performed as well or better than those who were exposed to traditional curricula (except in the foreign languages). Achievement aside, the students involved in the study had many affective and social gains not seen in students from traditional schools.

So what happened? If this approach was so powerful, why wasn't it introduced in high schools throughout the country? In short, World War II interrupted the process. As the country became immersed in the war effort, the results of this significant study became less and less noticed.

The style of curriculum developed in these schools became known as the "core" curriculum. Lounsbury and Vars (1978), early middle school visionaries, defined core as "a form of curriculum organization, usually operating within an extended block of time in the daily schedule, in which learning experiences are focused directly on problems of significance to students" (cited in Anfara 2006, 48). This core curriculum became an example of democracy at its best. The focus of the curriculum was the social concerns of students. The curriculum was planned collaboratively between teachers and students. Through this core curriculum all students experienced a general education relevant to their lives.

The idea of a core curriculum based on social issues that used a problem-based approach to learning began to lose favor after the Russian satellite, Sputnik, was launched in 1957. The result of the Russians beating the Americans into space was a return to strict content disciplines in schools with a focus on science and mathematics.

Present discussions about a core curriculum have nothing in common with the original concept. Today *core curriculum* refers to a collection of subject matter in specific disciplines that all students have to learn. That is far away from the original meaning.

While the concept of the core curriculum was hidden after Sputnik, it was not forgotten. When Donald Eichhorn first engaged in middle level reform in Upper St. Clair, Pennsylvania, not only did he revamp the organization and structure of the junior high school, he also challenged common assumptions about what should be taught and how best to teach it. He believed that the focus on curricular change would ultimately define what middle level education was all about. As Eichhorn stated in 1967, "The middle school concept, founded in the dramatic developments in human growth and development as well as in the society in which youngsters interact, may emerge into a successful organizational pattern, but only if educators develop programs commensurate with the characteristics of the ten to thirteen year old in all respects" (51).

Eichhorn was not alone in his beliefs about curriculum. In 1969 Conrad Toepfer, another early advocate of middle level education, commented, "It is not difficult to find junior high school administrators who conclude that all that needs be done to achieve the unfulfilled objectives of the junior high school is to replace it with a middle school organization, add water, and stir. The only predictable result of such a nostrum would seem to be a continued lack of definitive curricular programs for early adolescents!" (135).

Early philosophical discussions emphasized the need to design programs that focused on personal growth and would help students develop the responsibility and skills to interact with their world (David 1998; Dickinson 1993). These discussions were only moderately successful in impacting the curriculum of the middle school. In most middle schools, the curriculum remains essentially like the high school's. Middle school reform often focuses less on curricular reform than on organizational changes.

Current Discussions

Conversations among scholars on appropriate middle level curriculum models continue. Authors representing NMSA, in its position paper *This We Believe* (2003), wrote, "As commonly conceived, curriculum refers to the content and skills taught. In developmentally responsive middle level schools, however, curriculum embraces every planned aspect of a school's educational program" (19). The middle school curriculum must touch on those issues that concern young adolescents and help them construct meaning about themselves, their world, and their future. To best meet the needs of young adolescents, NMSA advocates a middle school curriculum that is "relevant, challenging, integrative and exploratory, from both the student's as well as the teacher's perspective" (20).

Relevant

"Curriculum is relevant when it allows students to pursue answers to questions they have about themselves, content, and the world" (NMSA 2003, 20). A relevant curriculum responds to the questions and concerns that students have about their lives and their world and offers students the opportunity to make connections to what they are learning. Such a curriculum engages students as they bridge what is happening in school to the outside world.

Challenging

"Challenging curriculum actively engages young adolescents, marshalling their sustained interests and efforts" (NMSA 2003, 21).

A challenging curriculum provides students with the opportunity to explore significant issues in their lives as they attempt to understand themselves and the world around them. Students become actively engaged in the learning process as they address relevant problems. They are empowered to use their knowledge and skills in significant ways and assume control over their own learning.

Absurd

A million miles from nowhere
Sitting alone in my chair
Listening to them whine
A straight line
Is the best way to lose your mind
Doing paper after paper
Where is the laughter
or the learning
It's disturbing
Rote, Rote, Rote
Whipped at our backs
Age old attacks,
It's a fact.
Change to them
is a four letter word
It's so damn absurd.

RICHARD BORDEAUX (1992)

Integrative

"Curriculum is integrative when it helps students make sense of their lives and the world around them and when students learn how to make significant, meaningful decisions about their learning" (NMSA 2003, 22). Curriculum areas need to be related in ways that help students find answers to their questions. In addition, the skills needed to solve problems are incorporated into the learning process. What happens in the classroom is connected to the students' lives and to the world outside school. Effective curriculum design also integrates issues of diversity and democracy; the multiple perspectives of all students are valued, validated, and explored.

Exploratory

"The middle school is the finding place. The entire curriculum at this level should be exploratory, for young adolescents, by nature, are adventuresome, curious explorers" (NMSA 2003, 23). Young adolescents are intensely curious about themselves and the world around them. Their expanding thinking capabilities open their minds to endless possibilities. Middle school should be a time when they can explore these possibilities. A curriculum rich in opportunities can help early adolescents discover things about themselves as they look at ways to make contributions to society. New forms of knowledge and new ways of looking at ideas can become lifetime pursuits. Students who have never had the opportunity to explore photography, quilting, world languages, kayaking, Internet surfing, hiking, astronomy, and a myriad of other areas can do so, broadening their conceptions of themselves and their world.

Basic Approaches to Curriculum Organization

How can a middle school provide a curriculum that is relevant, challenging, integrative, and exploratory? Does a traditional view of the curriculum embrace these qualities? To help us answer those questions as well as the difficult question of what the curriculum should be for middle level students, we will first explore and analyze the ways that curriculum can be organized. There are two basic ways to organize curriculum: a subject-centered, discipline-based approach or curriculum integration.

Subject-Centered, Discipline-Based Approach

Standard Fare—Subject-Oriented Curriculum
Most middle schools organize their curriculum around discrete subjects, and middle school teachers assume roles similar to their high school colleagues. The teachers are specialists in a specific curriculum area, and their responsibility is to teach the students the knowledge and skills that their subject area requires.

Subject-specific middle school teaching is often implemented by forming a team of teachers, each teacher responsible for a specific discipline. Usually the team consists of a math, science, social studies, and language arts teacher. Two-person teams are used in some schools.

One teacher might be responsible for social studies and language arts while the other handles science and mathematics.

In the purest sense of this approach, the teachers, although a team, are concerned about meeting content standards, covering the subject material in their textbooks, and helping students receive acceptable scores on standardized achievement tests. Teachers do not integrate knowledge across subject areas. Each teacher follows some designated curriculum or textbook and chooses those topics that are mandated by the district, appear in the textbook, or are areas of personal interest. The single-discipline approach to the curriculum tends to be textbook driven and teacher led.

Look at the results. Eighth graders arrive at school. In science class, they learn about the structure of the atom. In social studies, they study Brazil and the Amazon Valley. On to language arts, where they analyze plot and character development in the novel *The Westing Game* (Raskin 1978). Mathematics is next. Half of the students go to eighth grade math, where they work on interest rates and percentages. The other half go to algebra to learn how to solve complex equations. Does this approach make sense for young adolescents? Is a curriculum thus designed relevant, challenging, integrative, and exploratory?

If the answer is no (and it is), why do teachers continue to teach that way? Knowing what we know about schools that implemented the core curriculum in the 1940s why would teachers continue with a subject-specific curriculum? Well, most teachers have been trained as subject area specialists. They are confident about their knowledge and their ability to teach what they know best. Teachers feel successful in planning and implementing lessons in their area of expertise.

Planning using the subject approach takes less time than attempting to integrate subject matter with other teachers on the team. Planning time is a precious commodity. Any type of team teaching requires collaboration, which necessitates common planning times.

Increasingly, teachers and administrators argue for a subject approach based on state and local curricular standards and mandates as well as required standardized tests. The argument goes that if we don't teach specific items, students will score low on the achievement tests, which will reflect badly on students, teachers, and administrators. Furthermore, some educators argue that the structure of the high school mandates that single subjects be taught, each focusing on specific content knowledge.

Concerns about high school and college requirements, state and local content standards, and achievement tests also encourage parents to support the subject approach. Parents wonder, "Will my child do well on the SAT or the ACT? Will he or she have the knowledge needed for high school?" Breaking middle school curricular traditions is difficult for parents to understand.

In his groundbreaking book, *A Middle School Curriculum: From Rhetoric to Reality*, James Beane (1993) questioned the traditional ways of thinking about curriculum and challenged the separate subject approach:

> Life and learning consist of a continuous flow of experiences around situations that require problem-solving in both large and small ways. When we encounter life situations or problems we do not ask, "which part is science, which is mathematics, which is history, and so on?" Rather we use whatever information or skills the situation itself calls for and we integrate these in problem-solving. Certainly such information and skills may often be found within subject areas, but in real life the problem itself is at the center and the information and skills are defined around the problem. In other words, the subject approach is alien to life itself. Put simply, it is "bad" learning theory. (45)

When a curriculum is implemented with few links between subject areas, students have difficulty making connections between what they are learning in school and the significant issues that impact their lives. At a time in development when cognitive processes are expanding and the world is filled with endless possibilities, will standards and textbook-driven topics best help young adolescents understand their world and make sense of who they are?

John Dewey described the problems with the traditional curricular delivery system in a speech made almost one hundred years ago:

> It imposes adult standards, subject matter, and methods upon those who are only growing slowly toward maturity. The gap is so great

that the required subject matter [and] the methods of learning and of behaving are foreign to the existing capacity of the young. But the gulf between the mature or adult products and the experiences and abilities of the young is so wide that the very situation forbids much active participation by pupils in the development of what is taught. (cited in Parkey and Hass 2000, 34)

In a world that may appear contradictory and confusing, such a curriculum requires little student input and does not offer the challenging and integrative experiences that best engage them in learning. Textbooks rarely explore concepts or offer connections, often propagate the status quo, and typically present information from a White, male Western European point of view. The relevance that students crave, the challenge that they demand, and the connections that they require are difficult to find in such a curriculum.

We are not saying that the acquisition of content is developmentally inappropriate for middle level students. We are saying that we must look at the content and ask how it contributes to helping students explore the significant issues in their lives. What knowledge is important? What knowledge is valued? Whose knowledge is it? How should we use knowledge? The fragmented, disjointed approach of a subject-centered curriculum makes it difficult to find continuity in learning. What, we ask, is the potential impact of this meaningless content on students choosing to drop out of school? Brown (2006) noted, "It's no surprise to me that a small proportion of students choose to leave high school before graduating. Staying in school through thirteen years requires considerable patience, in part because of the way students are so often 'inactively engaged' cognitively with the material" (779). Although you may use instructional techniques that make your subject enjoyable, you still must ask whether a curriculum thus conceived is the most appropriate.

When we look at the developing social, physical, emotional, and cognitive needs of the young adolescent, we begin to understand that what young adolescents need is a curriculum that engages them intellectually. They need a curriculum that provides opportunities for wide exploration, encourages interactions with the broader social world, helps them see connections between content knowledge and life, teaches them democratic ideals, and provides active hands-on experiences. All this activity must occur within a context of learning the skills needed to function in society, now and in the future. In many ways, the single-subject approach fails to meet the developmental needs of the young adolescent.

Multidisciplinary Approach—Still Subject Specific

Theme teaching has become popular in many middle schools. In a multidisciplinary curriculum, teachers choose themes that can be correlated across two or more subject areas. The teams then determine what it is that each subject and each teacher can contribute to the theme. The simplest form of multidisciplinary planning is called "parallel teaching." In this approach, two or more teachers analyze their curricula for the year to see if there are common topics to cover, and plan to teach these topics simultaneously. For example, when the history teacher covers the Revolutionary War, students read *Johnny Tremain* (Forbes 1944) in language arts class. As students study World War II in history class, they read *The Diary of a Young Girl* (Frank 1967) in language arts. While students explore the geology of Massachusetts in science class, they study the history of the state in social studies. Although teachers are focusing on a similar topic, no overall goals and objectives are common in the two classes.

A more complex form of multidisciplinary teaching involves the entire team in planning. A common theme or topic is chosen after considering state or local content standards, textbooks, or teacher interests. Once a topic is chosen, teachers engage in discussions about what their specific subject area can offer to the study of that topic. They develop overall guiding questions, identify objectives, plan activities, and devise a final assessment project. As you'll notice in Figure 6.1, once a theme is chosen, each teacher develops the activities and skills relevant to the content in their subject area. There is little actual integration of subject areas.

Let's discuss a specific example. A team of teachers has chosen to do a unit on the Olympics. It's an Olympic year, and they think that the students will be excited about the topic. The social studies teacher

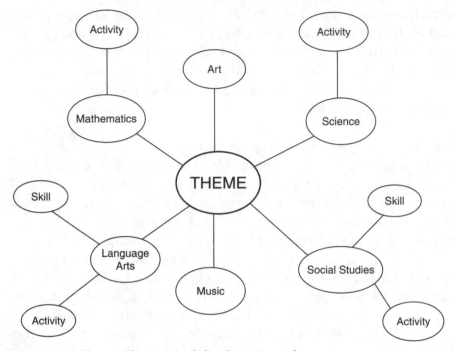

Figure 6–1. *Thematic Planning—Multidisciplinary Approach*

focuses on the history of the Olympic games from ancient Greece through the modern games (after all, ancient Greece is part of the seventh grade curriculum) and discusses how the Olympics have fared during wartimes. Students study world geography. They watch video clips of the parade of nations and investigate why Greece is always first in the parade and why the United States delegation never lowers its flag to the leaders of the host country. Students research countries that have been banned from the Olympics.

The science teacher talks about human anatomy, health and fitness, conditioning, and nutrition. Students analyze video clips of Olympic competitions. They investigate banned drugs and debate the use of drugs to enhance performance and whether rights are being violated with mandatory drug testing (a valid connection to a civics lesson for the social studies teacher). An innovative science teacher might have students research poles used in pole vaults, aluminum versus wooden bats in baseball, why people are running faster now, why changes in tennis rackets have changed the game, the physics of the curve ball, and so on.

In art students construct flags for a parade of nations. In music they learn the national anthems from different countries. In mathematics, they analyze distance, time, rate, height, weight, speed, percentages, runs batted in, earned run averages, and whatever other statistics they can think of. In language arts they read biographies, autobiographies, and novels about former and current Olympians as well as Greek mythology. They reenact the first Olympiad. And of course, the culminating experience is a mini-Olympics in physical education class.

This type of multidisciplinary teaching is common in middle schools. The teachers choose the topics with minimal student input. Despite the connections made between the subject areas, topics remain subject bound. The day is still divided into social studies, mathematics, science, language arts, and reading. Sometimes longer blocks of time are devoted to certain activities, but subject areas remain intact. Teachers choose content that they believe has significance to their students' lives.

There are benefits to a multidisciplinary approach. Such units meet the needs of the young adolescent in a way that discrete subject teaching is unable to do. Students are able to see connections between subject areas. They learn not only content but also how to apply content learned in one area to another.

Affective benefits are just as important. The units can be fun. A sense of team spirit permeates the school day. All the teachers know what's going on in every class. They can talk with the students about their projects for other teachers. Multidisciplinary team teaching assures the students that their teachers are talking to one another.

One drawback of multidisciplinary planning, of course, is limited time for collaborative planning. When teams have little common planning time, the organization and implementation of thematic units are difficult. Activities can become disjointed.

A serious drawback is the tendency to make artificial and contrived connections between subject areas. Sometimes it is difficult to see how a specific subject area fits into a theme. For example, how do you relate mathematics to a study of the rain forest—do you graph all the different kinds of frogs? Thematic units lose their power if there are not clear and meaningful connections made between subject areas and the topics.

Even more problematic is the tendency to focus on teacher-developed, popular, fun themes rather than significant, relevant ones. The unit on the Olympics was fun, but did it provide significant knowledge? Was it, in fact, relevant, challenging, integrative, and exploratory? Was it truly meaningful for young adolescents? Did it help students understand themselves and the world around them? Did it challenge them to explore their world? Was it the best way to spend student time?

Interdisciplinary Approach

In an attempt to better meet the needs of middle level students, some teams choose themes not based on the textbook or teacher interests but on what they think would be meaningful to the students. Since many students have a heightened awareness of their natural surroundings at this time, a team may choose the environment as a theme. Questions to be answered include: What are some of the causes of pollution? What effect does air pollution have on the human body? What can we do to minimize pollution's ill effects? As teacher teams look at the questions, each teacher decides where he or she can best facilitate learning and develops activities accordingly. Although teachers may still ask what their subject area can provide to the study of the theme, more attempts are made to integrate knowledge in meaningful ways. Teaching in this model becomes more interdisciplinary; some of the boundaries between subject areas begin to dissolve. The social studies teacher might talk about the historical implications of scientific research in the rain forest. Together the science and social studies teachers can plan long blocks of time in which students engage in scientific and historical inquiry. On other days, the science and mathematics teachers might have extended blocks of time in which to analyze the data generated by students' questions.

Interdisciplinary differs from multidisciplinary teaching in two significant ways. First, to develop themes, teachers consider what they think the interests of the students are. Second, the boundaries between subjects begin to blur as teachers combine subject areas in order to explore principles.

Nevertheless, themes and activities are still primarily chosen by the teacher. Teachers haven't asked students what is significant in their lives. Although the interdisciplinary model provides more opportunities for middle school students to engage in challenging, meaningful learning, can we in fact go even further and organize the curriculum around the questions and concerns of the young adolescent and not around content standards, textbooks, mandates, or the interests of separate subject teachers? Can we design a curriculum that not only focuses on significant knowledge and teaches the skills to use that knowledge, but also infuses classrooms with the important issues of democracy and diversity? If so, how?

Time for Reflection

In Chapter 1 you were asked what you thought was the most important thing a middle school student could do or learn at school.

- How did you respond then?
- Is your answer the same now?
- What experiences have influenced your response?

What Students Want

Here's what a group of middle school students said when they were asked what was the most important thing to learn in school.

> I think the most important thing to learn is how to live in the real world. . . . We need to learn stuff about life and looking ahead.
>
> EIGHTH GRADER

> I don't think about what job I'm going to get in the future. I think more about what morals I've learned. I think I should first develop a

129

group of morals that I think are right and then I can deal with what job I do later or what I want to learn.

GRACE, SEVENTH GRADER

I don't think that when we grow up anybody will come up on the street and say, "Excuse me, do you know who Constantine was?" We're learning about Constantine and his son and his son's son and his son's cousin. They didn't do anything in history but we learned about it.

JASON, SEVENTH GRADER

The most important thing to learn is to be responsible.

EIGHTH GRADER

A Call for a Democratically Developed Curriculum

We ostensibly live in a democratic society and there are no reasonable grounds that suggest why the democratic way of life should not be extended to early adolescents or into their schools. The democracy I mean, though, is not simply a matter of individuals selecting alternatives from a menu of limited choices nor the pseudo-democratic "engineering of consent" around predetermined possibilities. In short, it is not simply whatever someone wants to do or whatever someone can get them to do. Rather I mean that the curriculum ought to be democratically conceived through collaborative planning with involvement of early adolescents. (James Beane 1993, 19)

The future of a democratic society rests in the ability of each generation to live according to democratic principles and work to propagate and expand those principles for future generations. What are those principles of democracy that we value? In his book *A Reason to Teach: Creating Classrooms of Dignity and Hope*, James Beane (2005) explained,

Democracy is an idea about how people might live together. At the core are two related principles: (1) that people have a fundamental

130

right to human dignity and (2) that people have a responsibility to care about the common good and the dignity and welfare of others. (8–9)

In a democracy, people have a responsibility to themselves and others. That responsibility includes dealing morally and ethically with others, respecting their right to have differing opinions. It means being informed on issues that are relevant to their lives and looking at those issues from many points of view. It means making reasoned decisions on the basis of critical and creative thinking. It means challenging ideas, suspending judgment, and being skeptical. And it means learning to cooperate with others for the common good and thereby assume social responsibility. Developing curriculum using a curriculum integration model is the beginning of creating a classroom environment that is guided by these democratic principles.

Curriculum Integration Model: A Different Way of Thinking About the Curriculum

> A basic principle of a democracy is that those who will be affected by a decision should share in making that decision.
>
> LOUNSBURY AND VARS (2003, 11)

If we are to have a curriculum that makes sense for the young adolescent, it must be one that is infused with democratic principles. That curriculum must respond to young adolescent concerns about the world, to those issues that they feel are important. A curriculum based on the curriculum integration model does just that—focuses on the lives of young adolescents. In such a model, the curriculum is developed collaboratively by teachers and students and arises from the questions and concerns of the students rather than the demands of subject areas or standardized achievement tests. Such a curriculum brings democracy into the classroom.

Teachers who adopt this model don't simply turn to the textbook to determine what content to teach. Instead they ask questions about sources of knowledge and how that knowledge can and should be used within the context of young adolescent lives. Subject area knowledge becomes vital as it helps students answer their questions or solve their problems. The key, however, is that the organizing factor does not focus on the subject areas but rather on student questions and concerns. According to Beane (1997):

> Curriculum integration is a curriculum design that is concerned with enhancing the possibilities for personal and social integration through the organization of curriculum around significant problems and issues, collaboratively identified by educators and young people, without regard for subject-area boundaries. (x–xi)

Young adolescents are intensely curious about their world and their ultimate place in that world. They are developing their own values and learning what it means to have ethical relationships in an often confusing social climate. Given these developmental issues, it makes sense to devise a curriculum that puts them and their concerns at the center.

In *A Middle School Curriculum: From Rhetoric to Reality* (1993), Beane questioned the existing curriculum design of most middle schools. Drawing on the work of the progressive movement in the early part of the twentieth century, he advocated developing a curriculum that has meaning to early adolescents by focusing on their lives to design themes for study. Beane presented eight guidelines for the middle school curriculum:

1. "The middle school curriculum should focus on general education" (17). All students should be exposed to a broad range of educational experiences. Middle school is not the time to sift, sort, and select—to put some students in honors classes while others stay in remedial classes, to expose some to significant issues while providing memory games for other students. A general education focuses on the needs and concerns of all young people in society. We must provide learning opportunities that are accessible to all

students and provide a successful common learning experience for all. We must revive the idea of the core curriculum in its historic sense.

2. "The central purpose of the middle school curriculum should be helping early adolescents explore self and social meanings at this time in their lives" (18). Yes, we have state content standards as well as pressures from parents and society. Those concerns are secondary to meeting the needs of young adolescents. And, as we shall see, designing a curriculum that helps students explore their lives provides access to vast amounts of knowledge and acquisition of skills to adequately process and use that knowledge.

3. "The middle school curriculum should respect the dignity of early adolescents" (18). Young adolescents are not merely hormones with feet, nor are they empty-headed teens with no interests or concerns. Middle school students are dynamic young people who have deep concerns about life and the survival of the world. Their struggles to achieve independence and demonstrate responsibility are genuine. Their faith in their ability to solve problems is immense. The curriculum should be designed to take advantage of these concerns and the energy with which students tackle them. Our faith in students should encourage faith in themselves.

4. "The middle school curriculum should be firmly grounded in democracy" (19). One of the goals of schools is to provide students with opportunities to explore the democratic way of life. Yet the school environment seldom offers the opportunity to practice democracy. More often than not, our schools are run as an autocracy in which one person possesses unlimited power over others. What is learned, how it is taught, and the consequences of behavior are in the hands of that one person.

As Amanda, an eighth grader, put it, "I think students should have more rule over the school. A lot of teachers will say, 'This isn't a democracy' and they're putting us in a

133

dictator's world in this school, and I don't like it at all."
Another eighth grader commented, "In middle school I feel
like a robot. You go where you're assigned to go and do what
you're told."

If we want students to be firmly grounded in the tenets
upon which this country was founded, we must begin in
the classroom, starting with the curriculum. Therefore, the
curriculum must be democratically constructed through
student-teacher collaboration. Control, power, and decision making must be shared. "Bringing democracy to life in
the classroom requires that students have a genuine say in
the curriculum and that their say counts for something"
(Beane 1997, 50).

5. "The middle school curriculum should honor diversity" (19).
In an attempt to honor diversity in the classroom, teachers
often expose students to diverse ways of thinking. After this
exposure, however, students are told to complete the assigned
projects in a timely fashion, following the guidelines and
rubrics prepared by the teacher.

Exposure to diverse ways of thinking isn't enough.
Multiple viewpoints should be at the core of our curriculum, offering students diverse ways of analyzing and
exploring problems and multiple ways of expressing viewpoints. Different ways of approaching knowledge should
not only be valued but also validated. It is through this
validation that students can create personal meaning out
of knowledge.

6. "The middle school curriculum should be of great personal
and social significance" (20). Although fun units can motivate students, teach skills, and expose students to new content, they frequently lack the significance needed for
genuine learning. Fun units are often just that—fun.
Students need to study significant topics and themes that
help them construct meaning from their lives. They should
explore the questions and concerns they have about themselves and the world around them. One eighth grader

mentioned to us, "I think you should be able to pick what you're interested in to study. We don't get choices for most stuff."

7. "The middle school curriculum should be lifelike and lively" (20). Seventh grader Tim said, "Class is so long and boring. Instead of doing fun things, you just read out of a book." Middle school students are and want to be learners. The curriculum should embrace wonder, curiosity, exploration, problem solving, challenges, and action. Lifelike and lively does not mean fun yet insignificant. Young adolescents are ready to use their minds—let's give them the chance to do so.

8. "The middle school curriculum should enhance knowledge and skills for all young people" (21). All students should have access to knowledge and develop the skills to use that knowledge to create a better world. Knowledge is a powerful tool for solving problems and answering questions. Knowledge is most powerful, however, when it is used on a quest for meaning. Skills become the tools to access, process, and use that knowledge.

Curriculum Integration in the Middle School Classroom

A curriculum that embraces a separate-subject approach makes it impossible to achieve Beane's guidelines. Through curriculum integration, however, all students can access knowledge that has meaning and relevance to them. In this approach, students have a true voice in what it is they are going to learn and how they want to learn it. Themes are chosen by teachers and students through a collaborative effort. These themes emerge from students' personal and social concerns. After themes are chosen, teachers do not look at their separate discipline to determine what to study. Instead, students and teachers together determine what activities can be used to explore concepts, solve problems, or answer questions without regard to subject areas. Skills are embedded in the learning process as they become necessary prerequisites for engaging in activities or solving problems. But perhaps most important, as a result of collaboration, students are exposed to the enduring concepts of democracy, including human dignity and cultural diversity (Beane 1993).

While you might agree with the philosophy of curriculum integration, it may be difficult to see how you can implement it in a classroom or team setting. To find themes that revolve around concerns that young adolescents have about themselves and the world around them, teachers must solicit student input. The next step is to identify the skills and develop the activities that will help students explore the issues, answer their questions, and solve their problems.

Beane (1998) described five steps as the most successful way of implementing curriculum integration. These steps may take a number of days to complete. The initial step involves student reflection. Because students are rarely asked to help develop their curriculum, they will be able to do so more easily if they are first given the opportunity to individually reflect and to answer questions about who they are: "I like horses." "I like going to Hawaii." "I am a swimmer, and I like to play baseball." "In my spare time I play street hockey and football."

Students can then be asked to choose the things they like best about themselves and what they would like to change. They can think about what they would like to be like. These ideas can be kept private or shared in small or large groups.

After students have had time to reflect, the second step is to ask students two questions. The first is, "What questions and concerns do you have about yourself?" After individually answering that question, students share their responses in small groups, searching for common questions and combining similar ideas into a group list. Each group presents its list to the class. The key to success is to validate the questions and concerns of all students. Everything gets put on the list during this initial session.

One group of seventh and eighth graders listed the following questions:

- How do you get people to like you?
- How about dating?

- What's wrong with public displays of affection?
- Why do I have to have hair on my legs?
- Why do we have to impress to fit in?
- Why are you judged on appearance (hair, skin color, clothes, jewelry)?
- What will I be when I grow up?
- How do we get money, and how much is enough?
- Why do we alter our looks (hair, plastic surgery, tattoos, piercings)?
- What is your uvula for?
- Why do bones break?
- Why can't you wear hats and coats in schools?
- Why can't you have skateboards in school?
- Why are the lockers so small in the locker room?
- Why do I have to take gym and health?
- Why do you have to take the things you have to take?
- How does high school work—schedules, work, popularity?
- Where will I live?
- Will I be wealthy?
- Will I ever look good?
- Will I ever stop fighting with my sister?
- Will I be successful in life?
- What college will I go to?
- Will I be in peace or in danger?

The second question moves from the personal to a broader category: "What questions and concerns do you have about the world?" Once students have listed, analyzed, and combined the questions they have about themselves, they engage in a similar process with the questions and concerns they have about the world around them—school, family, community, city, nation, world. For example:

- How about the environment—why do we destroy it instead of saving it?
- Why is the world round?
- Why do we slaughter animals for food?

- Will we have World War III?
- Will we ever come in contact with aliens?
- Is cloning a good idea?
- How can scientific progress help the world?
- How do phones and televisions work?
- Why are kids more advanced on the computers than their parents?
- How about prejudice—why do we judge people based on looks or clothes?
- Why are crazy people and murderers that way?
- Why isn't there the perfect crime?
- Why do teachers yell? Why are some people teachers if they don't want to be?
- Will America be the same when I grow up?
- How do diseases start? When will they come out with a cure for AIDS?
- Why do teenagers do drugs?
- Why do adults do drugs in front of teenagers?
- Why are there so many religions and opinions of religions?
- Why do we have gangs?
- Why do we have the death penalty?
- Why do we have war?
- Will the earth die?
- Why does the government cover up things?
- What is the soul? Is there an afterlife?
- Why do sports players make more money than teachers?
- Why is the color of a flame what it is?
- Why do all M&Ms taste the same, and why do some people think they don't?
- How do they get the carbon dioxide in soda?
- How do you read a bar code?

This process takes time. Most students have never been given a chance to talk about those issues that concern them and may begin asking questions we think are superficial: "Why do locker rooms smell?" or "Why are coins round?" In fact, these questions are not

138

superficial at all, but reflect the curiosity that is part of the young adolescent's life. These questions may later lead to a wonderful unit on the mysteries of the world.

As students see that their questions are validated and respected they will begin to list ideas that are of deeper concern to them: "Why do people have to judge you by the way you look rather than by what is inside?" "I'm concerned about the future of cloning, and what it will do to the wonderful diversity that we have today." "Why do we have gangs, and what can we do about all that hatred?" When given a chance to have a voice, young adolescents demonstrate their ability to think deeply about their world.

The third step is for students to analyze both lists to look for connections between their personal and social concerns in order to develop some common themes. Students see that their questions about wearing hats and coats, taking classes they don't want to, teachers yelling, the government hiding things, gangs, crime, and the death penalty might all be related to the theme of power. They might look at their questions about technology, aliens, relationships, what job they'll have, high school, and cloning and come up with a common theme related to the future.

The fourth step is choosing an initial theme. Each group presents the common themes that they developed. These themes are posted and students try to reach a consensus about what they want to study first. Sometimes this process involves identifying what themes were mentioned the most. Other times it might involve looking for correlations between themes and combining them. A decision might be reached by having groups choose their top three and bottom three themes and having students vote. Whatever the strategy, a theme is chosen, and the remaining topics are reserved for later study.

Once a theme has been chosen, the next step is for students to go back to their original lists of questions and identify those that relate to the theme. They generate new questions, concerns, and problems related to the theme. They brainstorm the knowledge and skills needed to understand the theme well. Students suggest activities that will help them explore the concepts. If they choose the topic of the future, the students might have high school students come talk to the class. They might interview computer programmers, learn how to write résumés and fill out applications, or learn how to develop a family budget. Students also identify ways to demonstrate their knowledge.

Teachers' Roles

The teacher facilitates the planning process, helping students explore their concerns and questions. Once a theme is chosen, teachers collaborate with students to develop activities with which to explore the themes. Each teacher on the team analyzes the activities and determines which ones they can best facilitate. Teachers expand and add to student ideas for activities, identify and collect resources, develop lessons related to the activities, create timelines, and integrate the skills students need to answer their questions. Chapter 7 elaborates on the role of the teacher and student in the learning process. Notice in Figure 6.2 that the planning process focuses on the identification of significant concepts needed to explore the theme, rather than identifying how each content area contributes to the theme.

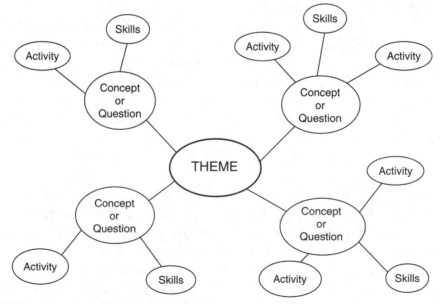

Figure 6–2. *Curriculum Integration Model*

As you can see, developing an integrated curriculum is radically different from developing multidisciplinary units. Curriculum integration begins with and is driven by the questions and concerns generated by students. Activities are chosen because they help students explore the concepts and content needed to answer the questions and concerns. Skills are taught because they are needed in order to solve problems inherent in the theme. Teachers do not adhere to specific subject areas but use subject area knowledge as needed. Content becomes vital and essential as students attempt to explore the significant issues they have raised.

There are compelling reasons for implementing a curriculum integration model at the middle level. It is developmentally responsive; it allows for cognitive challenge, emotional self-exploration, social interaction, and physical movement; and it meets the diverse instructional needs of students and responds to issues of multiple intelligences, ethnic diversity, and students of differing abilities.

The more compelling reasons, however, relate to the focus on genuine problems and concerns of the young adolescent and to issues of democracy in the classroom. A curriculum that focuses on the real concerns of the young adolescent is highly motivating and leads to significant learning. Collaborating with students demonstrates the values and morals inherent in the society in which we live. If we are to teach students the concepts of a democratic citizenship, we must model these concepts in our classrooms. Collaboration between teachers and students gives ownership and power to all involved and respects the knowledge that everyone brings to the learning situation.

Both students and teachers benefit from the curriculum integration model as these comments reveal:

> Having a say is important. It prepares you for later in life when you have to speak out about future issues.
>
> MOLLY, SEVENTH GRADE

> Planning with students is the most challenging and most exciting thing I do.
>
> SIXTH GRADE TEACHER

I would probably quit education if I couldn't do this kind of work.

SEVENTH GRADE TEACHER

There's nothing more important in the world than empowering students. It's exhausting.

SIXTH GRADE TEACHER

I can't imagine doing it any other way.

SEVENTH AND EIGHTH GRADE TEACHER

Ultimately, middle level educators are going to have to ask what curriculum model is appropriate for young adolescents. If we could, in fact, design the perfect middle school, what would the curriculum look like? If curriculum integration is the most effective way to educate the young adolescent, why don't we do it that way? If curriculum integration is such a "perfect" and powerful model, why isn't it more widely used?

Grasping for Air
Four papers
Three worksheets
Too little time
I should have planned ahead
As time passed by
Tick
Tick
Tick
Where are my papers
and my pens
I better begin
Fore the day ends
Too much work
Too little time
Why
isn't quality
more important than quantity?

I know, because it's easier to change lead to gold
than a curriculum that's old.
RICHARD BORDEAUX

The reasons curriculum integration is not more widely used are many and varied. Teacher training, curriculum mandates, pressures from parents, dependence on textbooks, and a society that widely validates the traditional model lead most middle schools to stay with what has always been done.

Teacher attitudes and training are also important variables. Curriculum integration requires a shift in the way that teachers perceive their role in the classroom. The content areas that they have put so much effort into mastering become secondary, and at times insignificant, to their students' search for meaning. Suddenly teachers cannot fall back on what they have been trained to do. Planning is a challenge, as the learning process is dynamic and develops out of daily interaction with students. The uncertainty about what the day will hold can be unsettling when teachers no longer dictate the learning process.

Testing requirements and curriculum mandates are also important variables. Without a doubt, content is important. And without a doubt, curriculum integration provides content and conceptual understanding at a much deeper level than in a traditional curriculum. When a state education department, however, requires the teaching of ancient history in the seventh grade, many social studies teachers feel they will have a difficult time implementing curriculum integration. Teachers who believe in this model must continue to voice concerns about specific curriculum mandates and help other educators, administrators, and legislators explore what curriculum is most appropriate for young adolescents and whether the middle level is the time to engage in content-specific teaching.

Parents create additional pressures. Because most parents grew up learning by means of a traditional curriculum, they feel comfortable with it. They worry about their children's SAT scores, being successful in high school, getting into college, whether their children are learning what they need to learn. Teachers often find themselves having to sell and defend their use of curriculum integration.

Vars (2001) asked, "Can curriculum integration survive in an era of high-stakes testing?" In this era of standards driven curriculum with accountability measured by high-stakes achievement tests, it is becoming more difficult to find schools and teachers who implement curriculum integration. When students and teachers live in fear of high-stakes tests, democracy cannot flourish in classrooms. Despite these concerns, curriculum integration is alive and well, used by progressive educators throughout the country who believe in bringing democracy into the classroom and giving students a voice in their own education. These educators can point to test results proving that their students do as well or better than students educated in conventional class rooms. But they are more likely to point to the other benefits that Vars mentions, "such as love of learning, concern for other people, critical thinking, self-confidence, commitment to democratic group process, and a whole host of other so-called 'intangibles'" (9).

Stuck on a Team

Curriculum integration requires a philosophy of education that puts students, not subject areas, at the center. If a teacher finds himself or herself on a team with others who do not share this philosophy, it will be challenging to implement the curriculum integration model at a team level. What if you believe in the model but are stuck with a mandated curriculum?

Overcoming the obstacles may be difficult, but you can, in fact, do much in your own classroom to propagate the values of democracy and diversity by implementing modified curriculum integration. You can still center your classroom curriculum around students' questions and concerns. You can then connect your subject area teaching to broader understandings relevant to your students' lives.

Have your students identify questions about themselves and the world around them. Help them identify common themes that arise from these questions. Then talk to them about the mandated curriculum and show them the required content standards. If, for example, your seventh graders are required to study ancient civilizations, develop themes related to their questions and concerns, and ask them how they can integrate a study of ancient Egypt into those themes. For example, themes of prejudice or power can govern an investigation into the class structure of ancient Egypt. A technology theme can guide the analysis of pyramid construction and mummification techniques. Disease and medical conditions in Egypt can be explored under the theme of wellness.

As you use curriculum integration, you will find that students learn the content they are supposed to learn, in an environment in which they have ownership of that content. They are, in turn, linking the content to issues that are relevant to their lives. For example, they see that power issues in ancient Egypt are not much different from those encountered in their own lives and world today.

There are other ways to give students voice in the classroom. Students can create the classroom behavioral expectations. They can help design activities or assessments, creating the rubrics by which they will be evaluated. They can evaluate their own work and lead conferences with their parents. You can share unit ideas with them and modify your lessons according to their suggestions for change. Students can help make decisions about how best to meet content standards.

In order to help students perform well on the state tests, teachers in one middle school were told to spend more time on math and reading classes—which, of course, meant less time for social studies and science (Volger 2003). One team of teachers decided to change the way they used the state content standards. These teachers showed the students the standards and had them create units using those standards. Students and teachers worked together to create learning activities and ways of assessment. The project was successful. When achievement tests scores came back, they were higher than in previous years. More important, students were invested in their learning and motivated by the lessons they created. One teacher commented, "Our team's decision to work with students to create an integrated curriculum using state standards was more than just a response to a request. It was a course of action designed to bridge the gap between the need for student-centered curricula and the demands and expectations of a high-stakes testing environment" (10).

The means to give students voice in the classroom are unending. You just have to start doing it. Can you use this model in your own classroom while still being true to curriculum standards? Absolutely. Read the story of one social studies teacher who did just that.

Real Learning in My Classroom? Yes!

By J. SCOTT CLARK (1996)

Teaching: Loftiest of professions or daily drudgery? Tradition of Socrates or foolish frustration? Most of us had hoped that we would teach students who would be thirsting for the gems of knowledge we have to offer them; yet, how often has it felt more like we are casting pearls before swine? In vain we have sought a new teaching method, a new gimmick, a different school, improved technology, a better group of students, the perfect textbook, some way to motivate our pupils into becoming real students, perhaps even scholars. But is our quest all in vain? A recent, ongoing experience has led me to believe that that goal is attainable, right in my own, everyday middle school classroom. My hope is that the following account will provide enough details so that anyone can replicate my success and experience my joy.

In September 1996, I entered my twenty-eighth year as a middle school social studies teacher. I cared deeply about my students and worked well with my interdisciplinary team, but I was prepared for another year of wondering how much my students would really learn, how much they would become engaged in what I had to offer them. I even signed up for one more of those "educational" courses. (You know, the kind where you listen to the drivel from another "expert" professor who you think could never survive an hour with thirty energetic adolescents.)

Little did I realize the "door" she would open for me. Her message was simple and concise: "It's the curriculum, stupid!" She even plastered it across the front of the room with a banner and flaunted it on her baseball cap. She thought the curriculum was the problem? Was she crazy?

Perhaps, but Professor Trudy Knowles introduced me to a small and growing group of reformers led by James Beane who have come to realize that student apathy and uninvolvement cannot be remedied by how we teach, what books we use, or the introduction of new technology in the classroom. No, the solution to our problem lies in the simple but radical notion of curriculum change. They do not simply mean selecting another choice from the menu or even teaching it in conjunction with one's teammates. Instead they suggest that the menu be more relevant to the real world, to the concerns of both adults and adolescents. They suggest that the menu choices be partially determined by student input (What, democracy in the classroom?). They suggest that the classroom experience will be embraced by students when it offers them an opportunity to grapple with the serious, real, and overwhelming issues of our day. Since these issues are not arbitrarily broken down into academic disciplines, neither can educators dissect them into math, social studies, science, and language arts. Teachers must help students to pursue these concerns utilizing all of the disciplines simultaneously. Above all, they must allow their students to seek, inquire, question, probe, and discover what even the teachers may not know. Then and only then will we witness the student involvement and learning of our dreams.

Aha! Pie in the sky, I thought. I would need the cooperation and support of my teaching team, department head, principal, students, and their parents. What materials could I use? How could grades be determined in this process where inquiry would be its own end instead of tests and quizzes? Were my students "good" enough for this? Could I ever implement Beane's ideas in the less-than-ideal conditions in which real teachers labor? My optimism and frustration led me to try.

My "recipe" for success? It is really quite simple. Permission to experiment was readily granted, especially since any success could be shared by supervisors, no new technology was required, and the purchase of a new textbook could be delayed even longer. When I approached my students with the notion that we would, together, actually seek answers to the important issues of their world, enthusiasm was overwhelming. In fact, the decision was made not to stop at answers but to actually attempt to implement solutions. They desperately wanted to make a difference, to improve the world they live in.

What topics would we pursue? Students, individually and privately, listed all of the pressing problems they could think of.

Taking only one "area" at a time, they listed all the problems of world, country, region, school, family, and self. Problems already listed under a previous area were not repeated as they moved down this list of progressively narrower areas. Already they felt that an adult was truly interested in them and their opinions. These private lists were huge, even the lists of students who usually refused to participate in anything I asked them to do. We then consolidated their individual lists into a gigantic whole-class list. We covered one area at a time and filled up all of our blackboard space. At this point, I was little more than a recording secretary who helped students clarify ideas and refine terminology. No attempt was made to edit or criticize ideas. Everyone felt validated when her/his problems were accepted. The students were happy when they found that others shared their concerns and fears, and proud when they pointed out problems that others had not thought of. So far, everyone was a winner.

The next step was critical to our success or failure, to the acceptance of our program by all those "outsiders" like principals and parents. Which one of these problems (well over a hundred in each class group) would they select to study? If their choices proved frivolous, no one would take them seriously. If I exercised control and led them toward the problems I wanted them to study, the students would not take me seriously. Was I in over my head? No! At the end of three days, each class narrowed its list to the seven or eight most serious problems. They did it while I acted only as facilitator. We had to design ways to reach consensus rather than alienating class members. Simple voting that could result in winners and losers was not acceptable.

We began by my reading aloud, slowly and carefully, the entire class list while each student quietly wrote down the problems that were his or her personal top ten to fifteen. I wrote all of these on the board, immediately narrowing our whole-class lists to approximately twenty-five. Students removed problems that seemed less pressing and elevated ones that were more crucial by annotating their personal top ten, marking the three that they considered of paramount importance and crossing out the three that they were most willing to concede. Students suggested such strategies as combining and enlarging to further narrow the lists. After much discussion about the major issues of today (discussions that floored me with their depth, complexity, and passion and for which my presence was totally irrelevant) students reached agreement on their final lists.

What adult leaders would have chosen better? Their class lists were composed of such problems as crime and violence, war, prejudice, disease, rights and freedom, environment, immigration, starvation, employment, poverty and welfare, taxes, drugs, and education. Not a single frivolous problem had even made it to their semifinal lists. Students really are involved with and tuned into their world. All I needed was to have faith in them.

What next? We had to begin our actual inquiry, our problem solving. The only obstacle was that no one had ever entrusted such a task to these eighth graders before. How should they go about it? Here was a job made to order for the teacher in me. After a brief bit of research and some collaboration with my colleagues, I designed a chart that outlined a step-by-step method for solving any problem. It includes:

- careful elaboration of the problem itself
- discovery of the causes
- proposal and analysis of the solutions
- decision as to which solutions to use
- formulation of a plan of action
- implementation of the plan
- a reporting procedure as to what and how it was accomplished.

A simple, hypothetical problem (stolen family car) provided the basis for a practice exercise in using the problem-solving chart. This practice exercise gave both the students and myself a chance to try out our new roles within a classroom. I had to stop thinking of myself as the person with the answers and they had to begin thinking and taking responsibility for their own results. Small cooperative learning groups, often preceded by initial attempts by each individual student, seemed an ideal way to structure the class. It also provided me with more information about how each student performed in a group so that I could form more effective groups for our real projects that would follow.

The choice of our first inquiry topic was determined by the immediate availability of materials. Since prejudice was on each class list and there were ample materials at hand, the selection was easy. My role included material collection and selection, a role I shared more and more with the students as they became accustomed to our new curriculum approach. Textbooks, short stories, newspaper and magazine articles, library materials, computer-generated information, and community resources were all possible materials for students to use as they pursued solutions. I discovered that it was of paramount importance for me to act as a facilitator so that the students could pursue their own inquiries and solutions. I asked only open-ended questions that no one even expected me to answer, for they were coming to realize that only their answers matter.

But what about grades? Oh yes, administrators feel the need for them, parents insist on them, and even students want feedback about how they are doing. This new curriculum holds the promise that all students will do well. We still need, however, to document that progress. Since tests obviously would not do that, I utilized four methods: informal teacher observations; daily journal entries in which students recorded their accomplishments, reflections, and feelings; notebooks that students utilized to record their problem-solving process; and the actual solutions that students devised, contained in written reports documenting what they accomplished (a type of portfolio). This system may not be as mathematically precise as we are used to, but it offers a deeper and more realistic reflection of what a student has really achieved. It even had beneficial side effects. Classes ended on a reflective note as every student spent the last five minutes quietly writing in his or her journal to sum up what had been learned that day. As the time of departure approached, I was surrounded by a sea of hands beckoning me to stamp their daily entries with a "smiley face," my way of acknowledging and thanking them for their participation.

What has all of this accomplished? I am no longer in the memorization business. I am not the game show host who has the answers written out on little cards. I do not have to struggle to motivate bored students. This is real life simply transplanted into a classroom. Real people are seeking real answers to real concerns. As long as it remains their search, the students are the source of their own motivation.

My students are actively engaged in class; they are exploring complex subjects utilizing primary source materials; and they have finally entered into the realms of intellectual problem solving. They feel vibrant and alive because they are not just studying for grades but are actually changing their world. They feel empowered because their opinions and judgments are being actively solicited on a daily basis. They are beginning to understand that problems of this magnitude require cooperation if we are ever going to solve them.

Their journal entries and parents' comments reflect the involvement and interest that has been stimulated. They are preparing themselves for the challenge of the twenty-first century, and I am privileged to witness their progress.

Concluding Reflections

As we look at the realities of young adolescence, we are convinced that curriculum integration most clearly meets the needs of the middle level learner. It directly responds to their concerns about the world as they struggle to find meaning. It addresses cognitive, emotional, social, and physical developmental issues. It responds to issues of ethnic diversity, multiple intelligences, and differing abilities. It focuses on high-level conceptual thinking in addition to the development of necessary skills. And it infuses the classroom with democratic ideals. Who can argue with this?

Chapter 9 introduces several teachers who have implemented curriculum integration in their classrooms and some students who have been fortunate enough to be members of such classes. Their stories demonstrate that the curriculum integration model is practical, possible, and productive. All you have to do is take the first step.

SEVEN

Facilitating Meaningful Learning

___

You are always going to come up with your own way of learning something.

JESS, EIGHTH GRADE

When one approach doesn't work, you don't give up! You've got to go back into that bag and keep pulling out different approaches until the children learn.

MARIA, FIFTH-GRADE TEACHER

School structures, parental expectations, and outmoded testing and accountability procedures keep us from making the kind of changes that cognitive science, literacy research, and our own reflective experience show we need to make.

WILHELM (2006, 19)

Whether you design curriculum and activities collaboratively with students, develop instruction as part of a team, or teach a separate content area, the lessons you plan and the activities you choose determine whether meaningful learning will occur.

In *This We Believe* (2003), the National Middle School Association advocated instruc-

152

tion for middle school students that employs "multiple learning and teaching approaches that respond to their diversity" (7). According to this document,

> Everything we know about the nature of young adolescents and the principles of learning makes it obvious that the most successful learning strategies are ones that involve each student personally. Developmentally responsive instructional practices place students at the center of the learning process. (15)

Instructional practices in middle schools should focus on what we know about the learning needs of young adolescents and their varied cognitive developmental processes, along with what we know about how learning occurs. Although high expectations are set for all students, Jackson and Davis (2000) stated that "uniformly high expectations should not lead to uniformity in instructional practices: teachers need a broad range of approaches to enable students in a heterogeneous classroom to excel" (175). Student success should be a guiding principle for how teachers choose to design instruction.

Time for Reflection
- What is learning?
- How does learning occur?
- How is learning out of school different from learning in school?
- What specific characteristics of young adolescents might affect their ability to learn? How?

How Learning Occurs

Research on cognition and how the young adolescent brain develops impact our understanding about how learning occurs and the teacher's role in the learning process in a middle school classroom (Walsh 2004; Jensen 1998). In addition, understanding how we construct knowledge and the role that socialization plays in that construction helps teachers make better curricular and instructional decisions in the context of young adolescent development.

Brain-Based Learning

Caine and Caine (1994) described some elements of learning that coincide with how the brain operates. Notice the connections between these principles, young adolescent developmental needs, and the curriculum integration model.

1. "Learning Engages the Entire Physiology" (88). Learning is not just a cognitive process. Teachers should consider physical, emotional, and social factors as well. Although relevant for all ages, this principle is particularly significant for young adolescents because of their growth in all areas.
2. "The Search for Meaning Is Innate" (89). All people attempt to make meaning of the circumstances of their lives. Curricular and instructional decisions should establish the necessary conditions for students to create meaning.
3. "The Search for Meaning Occurs Through Patterning" (89). In order to find meaning, students must begin to see the relationship between what they are studying and what is happening in their lives. Finding these relationships requires strategies that engage students in problem solving and critical thinking.
4. "Emotions Are Critical to Patterning" (90). Emotions may have as much (or more) to do with what students learn as their cognitive abilities do, particularly in young adolescents who experience a multitude of emotions each day. Teachers must create emotionally supportive environments in order to ensure that students engage in meaningful learning.
5. "The Brain Processes Parts and Wholes Simultaneously" (91). Bolstered by the books edited by E. D. Hirsch Jr. (1993), *What Your First Grader Needs to Know*, up through *What Your Sixth Grader Needs To Know*, some teachers

believe learning involves mastering isolated skills and memorizing information. Memorizing isolated bits of information disconnected from general principles and broad concepts limits students' cognitive potential and their opportunities for true understanding. Effective teachers help students acquire skills and knowledge within the context of genuine learning situations.

6. "Learning Always Involves Conscious and Unconscious Processes" (92). Teachers must provide time for students to reflect on newfound discoveries in a way that encourages them to accept new theories as they alter previous beliefs. With the emergence of abstract thinking, young adolescents begin to reflect on their own learning.

7. "Learning Is Enhanced by Challenge and Inhibited by Threat" (94). Caine and Caine suggested that teachers create a learning environment for students in which they are in a state of "relaxed alertness" (70). In such a classroom, students are emotionally, cognitively, and socially safe. It is a place where students know they are cared for and valued. In this environment, students are comfortable engaging in challenging learning opportunities.

Constructivism: A Theory About Learning

We constantly construct knowledge and meaning throughout our lives as we are confronted with problems, new ideas, and new knowledge. A toddler learning how to stack blocks, a first grader learning the connection between letters and words, a fourth grader exploring maps, and a seventh grader examining the meaning of prejudice are all constructing knowledge about their world. It is evident from looking at the principles of brain-based learning that in order to construct meaning, students must have opportunities to manipulate ideas and materials. Teachers can't make students construct knowledge— students do this naturally and without external prodding. Teachers can, however, establish an environment that promotes active learning by providing authentic hands-on and minds-on learning experiences

155

within a social context. Michael, a seventh grader, told us, "You've got to learn by doing it. You can't learn about it by taking notes." An eighth grader concurred: "I think kids would learn a lot better if you do something hands-on."

Several significant differences exist between learning in a traditional classroom and learning in a classroom that models the constructivist philosophy. A traditional classroom might be characterized by a focus on discrete, often unrelated skills. Teachers are viewed as dispensers of information and follow fixed curricula, guided by textbooks and curriculum guides. The emphasis in a constructivist classroom is on general principles and concepts. Teachers support learning by providing materials and ideas for students to manipulate and facilitating personal and group reflections as students interact with the material. Teachers carefully introduce and embed needed skills as students engage in the process of exploration. Brooks and Brooks (1993) summarized the principle of constructivism this way: "We look not for what students can repeat, but for what they can generate, demonstrate, and exhibit" (16).

In designing instruction so that students have opportunities to construct their own knowledge, the important consideration is that students are not told what they should find, but are given the opportunity to make sense out of the information themselves. For example, students experiment with pendulums to determine what factors affect their rate of speed. They may analyze lists of words to determine spelling patterns, explore music to develop an understanding of a cultural era, and look for patterns in the survey data they collect. Teachers do not sit on the sidelines as students manipulate and explore ideas and materials. In addition to setting up the conditions for student exploration, they point students in the right direction, providing frequent feedback to ensure accurate understanding.

Constructivist teachers take into account brain-based learning theory as well as what is known about the developing adolescent. When students are provided with opportunities to build their own understandings by interacting with the environment, their knowledge about topics is enhanced in a meaningful way. In addition, providing young adolescents with opportunities to construct their own knowledge enhances their movement from the concrete to formal operational thought processes (Rice and Dolgin 2005).

Helping Students Move Toward Formal Operational Thought

Teaching for understanding provides students with opportunities to touch, see, feel, and hear ideas and principles through hands-on or concrete experiences. Teachers must allow more time for students to experiment with newly taught principles. Constructing new knowledge may mean asking questions of one another and tinkering with new ideas and manipulatives. When teachers do provide direct instruction, they should design lessons that offer more time for students to engage in problem solving, critical thinking, and creative thinking.

Traditional instructional practices often involve asking questions following an assigned reading. Many times only a few students respond, so just how many students are learning? What would happen if teachers let students ask the questions? Although students may not initially have the skills to ask the kinds of questions that reveal the central issues, with teacher guidance they eventually will. Wilhelm (2006) advised, "Students must be the ones asking the majority of the questions and doing the bulk of classroom talk" (10).

Brown (2002a) described how eighth grade teacher Mark Springer develops an atmosphere of student questioning in his integrated curriculum classroom:

> The initial days of the year focus on developing the habits of mind needed to engage in genuine learning. Students must learn to accept responsibility for developing topics that interest them. This personal responsibility for academic growth requires a paradigm shift for many students who have not experienced this kind of responsibility for their learning in previous years. Therefore the teacher coordinators lead activities designed to ask meaningful and insightful questions. (55)

Until students are responsible for asking the questions they have about curriculum, teachers will never really know what students are curious about or what they may misunderstand about the concepts and principles they are learning. Educators may present exciting lessons, but without genuinely knowing what questions students have, they waste instructional time and students' time as well.

One example of academic growth is the new vocabulary students learn in every content area. Teachers introduce a new set of words for a science unit, or the next social studies chapter, or another novel for language arts. A common problem is that students never actually "own" the words once the unit or chapter is completed. They hear them, may memorize a definition, even use the word correctly in a sentence, but they have no long-term memory of the word and are unlikely ever to use it themselves. Beers (2003) described one teacher's realization that she was teaching too many words each week:

> I never really expected that they'd [students] learn them to actually *use* them. It never bothered me that there were so many [words] because I always must have known deep down that they were only learning them for a test. (182)

Teachers must teach fewer new words with each lesson and provide many concrete experiences if they expect students to understand new concepts and principles associated with those new words. They must allow students to use these words in an authentic context.

Encouraging students to explain their thinking and erroneous beliefs about abstract principles also promotes cognitive growth. Asking students to keep journals in which they describe the confusion they experience in understanding new concepts and principles begins the process of deepening their metacognitive awareness—that is, their analysis of their own thinking. Students should also be asked to describe their level of attention to learning and their attitudes toward learning.

Teachers can also encourage cognitive growth by designing time following teacher-directed lessons for students to explain new understanding to one another. This opportunity for collaborative learning may help students clarify confusing principles.

Collaborative Learning

> Only in U. S. classrooms are individuals asked to find every answer,
> solve every problem, complete every task, and pass every test by rely-
> ing solely on their own efforts and abilities.
>
> KLINE (1995, 23)

Brain-based learning, constructivist theory, and the needs of the
young adolescent all point to the positive role that socialization can
play in the learning process. Young adolescents will talk to each other
in the halls, during class, during breaks, at lunch, and on the telephone and computer in the evenings. It should not be difficult then
for teachers to get students talking in the classroom about learning.
A significant step to genuine student learning occurs when teachers
collaborate with students about curricular issues.

In school, students can learn to work collaboratively with others
in developing questions, reaching consensus, solving problems, creating projects, and resolving disagreements. They can learn to become
team players and to understand that there are differences in the way
people think. As Wolfe and Brandt (1998) suggested, "learning is
enhanced when the environment provides [students] with the opportunity to discuss their thinking out loud, to bounce their ideas off of
their peers, and to produce collaborative work" (11).

Never assume that students already know how to work collaboratively. Many students may have had cooperative learning experiences
in elementary school, but often these past experiences resulted in failure and frustration. To ensure success at the middle level, ample time
in the first few weeks of the school year should be devoted to helping
students develop interpersonal strategies needed to progress successfully as a team. Brown (2002a) described how teachers in one curriculum integration classroom encouraged students in their social
development at the beginning of the year:

> During the first few weeks of school, students engage in several
> socialization and trust-building exercises. Cooperative games help
> build a community spirit. Success is defined by everyone's willing-
> ness to cooperate, to communicate clearly, and to be concerned

about and react to the safety needs of others. These activities provide students with the social and emotional tools they need to engage in meaningful learning with one another. (55)

Pairing students together for short periods to work on small projects is one strategy for encouraging students to trust each other and develop productive working relationships. After students have engaged in collaborative activities, teachers should facilitate a discussion on the pitfalls and advantages students experience when working with others. Sharing concerns about the process of teamwork early in the year may help students more successfully navigate future team efforts. Student teams may become the primary learning group in a classroom.

Writing workshop (Davis and Hill 2003; Atwell 2002; Ray 2001) offers the opportunity for students to construct their own knowledge about writing while collaborating with others. Writing workshops feature opportunities for students to choose writing topics, hold student-to-student conferences, take part in peer revision and editing sessions, and have one-to-one conferences with the teacher.

Literature circles are another example of a collaborative activity (Daniels 2002). In a literature circle, four to six students read and discuss books that they choose based on their interests. Literature circles present opportunities for students to process information, create meaning from text, and use critical thinking skills.

Research-team investigations and group oral presentations are other examples of collaborative activities that lead to meaningful learning. Groups of students first analyze primary or other source materials to generate ideas about an event, culture, or historical period. Information is interpreted from diverse and multiple points of view. Students then collaborate on the best way to present their understandings to the rest of the class.

The real value of social learning occurs when students share their questions about issues, offer alternative points of view, devise creative solutions to problems, and provide feedback to each other on the products of their learning. Young adolescents are also more likely to take the risks associated with learning new concepts and principles when they have opportunities to collaborate.

It is not surprising that when structured correctly, collaborative learning provides many benefits. Slavin (1991) described some of the advantages of collaborative learning:

- enhanced achievement
- improved self-esteem
- improved relationships among students of different races, genders, and abilities
- greater acceptance of students with special needs

Collaborative learning is not a cop-out, a way for students to ignore their own academic growth by riding on the coattails of the work completed by more conscientious peers. The intent is for students to grow, which occurs when they have opportunities to speak to one another, share experiences, ideas, and solutions in their daily learning.

The Teacher's Role

To make teaching and learning work . . . teachers must develop an alternative approach to instructional planning beyond "covering the text" or "creating activities that students will like."

TOMLINSON (1999a, 14)

The role of the teacher is to ask questions—constantly! Teachers offer timely intervention when students need help, directing students to resources, suggesting other sources of help in the classroom and out.

MIKE MUIR (CITED IN BRAZEE AND CAPELLUTI 1994, 70)

The teacher is literally a designer who takes bigger ideas and fashions them into learning experiences so young adolescents can learn.

MARY BILODEAU-CALLAN
(QUOTED IN BRAZEE AND CAPELLUTI 1994, 71)

An understanding of the learning process can help teachers make better decisions about what goes on in the classroom. And yet, often, after repeated hours of teacher planning, numerous homework assignments, and all that grading, we dare to ask, "Do you suppose students are really learning?"

Each student encounters new ideas and information and constructs meaning based on his or her own understanding of the world. The teacher is not passive in this endeavor. Teachers play a vital role in helping students acquire essential skills and concepts. Although they may collaborate with students regarding instructional strategies, it is ultimately the teacher who must plan and design the school day.

Effective instructional practice involves more than designing lesson plans to fit the curriculum guides, implementing teaching strategies, and following the steps of the Madeline Hunter (1984) model of instruction in lesson presentation. Teachers who limit themselves to these traditional activities are ignoring the latest research on cognition and discounting the ability of young adolescents to search for their own understanding.

What Does Genuine Learning Look Like?

Teachers often say that students learn best through:

1. experiencing something hands-on
2. collaborating (having conversations) with classmates
3. experimenting with objects and principles
4. taking risks
5. making mistakes and correcting them
6. developing personal theories through experimenting
7. solving problems individually and in groups
8. developing their own questions about content
9. role-playing
10. engaging in case studies (Brown 2003)

All of these processes are components of authentic learning—the kind of learning that is often more likely to occur for students outside school instead of inside. Bringing these activities inside the classroom is how teachers make learning a significant activity.

In talking to students it becomes apparent that they also want something other than traditional forms of direct teacher-controlled lessons. A seventh grader told us:

> Spend more time and try to do creative things, like hands-on. Have kids have their own opinion on something, not just say, "This is the way it is." There are always two ways to learn something. Maybe one way is always easier but you are always going to come up with your own way of learning something so I think they should give kids more of an opinion. They shouldn't just be so out of the book.

Knowles (2006) asked a group of students diagnosed with attention deficit hyperactivity disorder what would help them learn. She summarized their preferences:

> They were the most engaged in lessons that were active, hands-on, and gave them some choices and control over their learning. They talked about making learning relevant, meaningful, and fun. They talked about having direct connections with those things they were learning. They talked about constructing their own understandings about knowledge and about truly understanding something, not just spitting back facts. They talked about what they will truly value and use in their lives. In addition, they saw a great need for flexibility on the part of the teacher. (79)

Teachers who engage in effective instructional practices use everything they know about their content area, learning, young adolescent development, and instruction in order to make the best choices every day. But most important, effective teachers know their students—how they think, their academic backgrounds, previous successes and frustrations as learners, personal interests, and learning profiles.

What Do You Know About Each of Your Students?

Teachers must identify how their students learn, discover their cognitive strengths and weaknesses, and determine how they can help their students grow. In order to know these details, teachers must become expert kid-watchers. Kid-watching begins with an attitude of willingness and a belief that only through knowing students well can we create learning environments for all.

As part of any system for gathering data, teachers should have a three-ring binder or a folder reserved for keeping notes on every student. All pertinent information should be stored in those folders or binders. At the beginning of the year, students can write a letter to the teacher explaining what they know about how they learn. Some teachers ask students to tell them four pieces of information they should know about them as learners and four other details they should know about them as a person. Learning about your students' interests, learning preferences, needs, and personal lives begins in September and continues throughout the school year.

Some teachers carry a clipboard containing notecards or use sticky notes. As they observe or hear something, they note it on the card or sticky note for that student. Some teachers keep notes on address labels that can be peeled and placed in the binder or folder. In addition to keeping notes throughout the day, some teachers reflect on students' behaviors or academic performance for the first few minutes of their prep time or after school, adding notes to the binder. Teachers should discuss students needing assistance at team meetings, gathering information from colleagues about what strategies they use that are effective.

By the end of the first two weeks of school, teachers should have some notes on all students. You may find that you have lots of entries for the students who command your attention, but ask yourself, "Are there students with no entries? Do I have any notes for the quiet student, or the student who completes all the work easily? Are there students who are confusing to me who I should know more about?" These are the students you should begin to focus on. Many experienced teachers will admit to not knowing some students well enough to help them until the last month or two of the school year. We hope this won't happen to you.

Wilhelm (1997) described what he does as a language arts teacher: "I study every student who comes into my classroom. To do less would be to not take each student with the seriousness she or he deserves" (28).

As you become acquainted with your students, you will begin to perceive their learning preferences. You will see how students process information, you will notice the kinds of activities they need in order to be challenged, and wisely, you will assist students in designing learning experiences that capitalize on their strengths and build on their weaknesses. You will take your instructional cues from your students, being sensitive to their needs and challenges.

The observations of student behavior are important, but it is when teachers analyze those notes that they can begin to make decisions about how to help students succeed. Teachers should use the information to individualize instruction, find developmentally appropriate curricula, make appropriate accommodations, or hold conferences with students. The observations should both inform and drive instructional decisions designed to help students reach academic success. Teachers should have frequent conversations with their students to find out what's working and what's not. When teachers know students well, they can help students set daily, weekly, or semester goals for improving their academic progress.

If teachers take the time to help students become reflective, young adolescents will become sensitive to their own learning preferences. Providing examples of different ways to approach a task and opportunities for student choice promotes self-awareness. As students better understand their own learning preferences and differences, they learn to construct knowledge in more meaningful ways. Students are able to identify and engage in projects and activities that promote their way of learning; thus, they become more successful at school.

Establishing Essential Outcomes

Once teachers know their students, they can identify skills and strategies that each one needs to grow. Although students will have considerable input with respect to classroom learning, Voltz (1999) explained that one "important role of the teachers is to conduct knowledge and skill analyses to determine what, if any, important information or aspects of the curriculum have been omitted in student generated topics and activities" (33). The list of desired outcomes does not need to be extensive; however, it should represent a set of cognitive processes that ensure student growth beyond middle school. Students, for example, will develop the ability to:

- communicate their questions and concerns
- hypothesize responses to some of their questions
- develop observation skills and make inferences about these observations
- analyze topics from different points of view
- apply research techniques to gather and analyze primary and secondary sources
- engage in problem-solving strategies using both creative and critical thinking

As you collaborate with students on topics and strategies, an understanding of essential outcomes will help you and your students more effectively structure learning activities.

Facilitators in Action

Teachers take on a variety of roles throughout the school day. The primary role is that of a guide who facilitates the students' search for meaning. "Teacher as facilitator" is perhaps an overused metaphor that some have even interpreted as a way to ignore instructional responsibilities. Being a facilitator, however, requires a great deal of effort, energy, and perseverance. In a curriculum integration classroom, the role is especially challenging. As Nesin and Lounsbury (1999) explained: "[Teachers] have to assist in designing experiments, refining surveys, locating resources, inventing games, resolving conflicts, analyzing data, and delegating responsibility. In addition, they deliver appropriate lectures, organize parts of the unit, monitor student involvement, and assess learning on a daily basis. Teachers also have to create strategies for activities and learning they cannot possibly anticipate" (34).

As a facilitator, some of your primary responsibilities will be to help students develop themes, create the questions they hope to answer as they study the themes, and generate activities through which they can explore their questions. You will then develop a daily plan that will support students as they conduct their inquiry. Your own academic strengths and pedagogical awareness will come into play as you provide historical background or sources of information and embed learning skills and intended outcomes into the study of the topic.

Some teachers use the "KWL" approach in helping students get a handle on their topic. We propose making this a "KWHL" process. Teachers begin by asking students what they already *know* about a topic and then generate ideas about what they *want* to know. As the facilitator, you will assist students in narrowing their ideas into ones that can be reasonably researched. The third step is for students to identify *how* they want to learn the information. Teachers can help them generate ways to locate information from primary and secondary sources. The final step in the KWL process is for students to identify what they have *learned* and to present that information in a meaningful way.

You have several instructional responsibilities during students' search for information. You will teach them the necessary skills to conduct their research. Together with students, you may determine that more background information is needed. You will collaborate on what knowledge is needed and how students can best acquire that knowledge. At times, that may mean direct instruction on a specific topic.

When you collaborate with students on activities, they may suggest a wide variety of ways to approach the acquisition of knowledge. Many students want to do some kind of project to obtain and demonstrate knowledge. As Brodhagen (1998) explained, "Projects . . . provide students opportunities to use multiple resources including technology, popular culture, common 'experts' (people in their personal community who know much about a topic), multicultural resources, and personal experiences" (51).

For example, students might want to interview experts. You could conduct a minilesson on how to generate questions or conduct an interview and then help them set up the interviews. Students might want to conduct a school survey. You will help them develop survey questions and analyze, interpret, and report data.

Two outcomes that you may have identified are improved ability to read and analyze texts and advanced development of writing skills. You might help students choose appropriate novels that address the theme being studied and demonstrate how a literature circle works (Daniels 2002). Students might decide to create a newsletter for the school to present the information they have learned. In order to improve students' writing skills, you might provide skill sessions on such topics as appropriate citations, accurate paraphrasing, use of correct writing conventions, or peer revising skills (Atwell 2002).

This type of instruction requires attention to each student's needs and flexibility in teacher response. It is necessary for teachers to hold frequent conferences with individuals or groups to set goals, establish timelines, and monitor progress toward a final product. Students can focus on their learning during these conferences by responding to teacher questions such as:

- What do you hope to learn as a result of studying this topic?
- What are some ways in which you could demonstrate your learning?
- How does what you know compare with what you would like to know?
- Who would you like to share your new knowledge with once you have researched the topic?
- How would you evaluate your final product?

During conferences, students can explain their work, talk about their explorations, and seek new avenues of research. Your collaboration and conferences with students become paramount in deciding how they will demonstrate their newfound knowledge to others. Students may need extensive instruction, guidance, and feedback as they develop final presentations, pieces of writing, works of art, or scientific demonstrations. Conferences that include parents encourage students to take ownership of their own learning.

As you can see, teachers are highly involved in structuring learning processes. Although you want students to have substantial input, what happens during the school day is ultimately up to you. Your repertoire of strategies must be immense. Brodhagen (1998) discussed some of the instructional strategies that teachers use:

> Cooperative learning groups can be a powerful instructional strategy when used correctly. Direct teaching can be effective when used appropriately. Presenting information through both visual and auditory methods increases retention of material. The use of advanced organizers, anticipatory sets, or scaffolding helps students understand and remember more when ideas or information are connected to prior learning. (50–51)

Nesin and Lounsbury (1999) observed that although many of these strategies can be viewed as traditional and may be used in any classroom, in curriculum integration classrooms "strategies and activities selected result from student-teacher planning rather than teachers' unilateral decisions" (34).

Recognizing Diverse Learners

> A good teacher is one who understands your needs—understands what you need as a student. I'm not saying they have to sit down and write, "Jason needs this, Tom needs this, Anne needs this, Marie needs this." But, they have to be able to know if I don't understand something.
>
> JASON, SIXTH GRADER

It is easy to recognize the physical differences of young adolescents as they enter a classroom; however, perceiving cognitive, social, and emotional differences is challenging, and it is difficult to respond to these differences on a daily basis. It is naïve to think that students in the same grade level are also at the same levels of intellectual processing. Noticing that students look entirely different from one another should signal to you that they are also just as different in what they bring intellectually into the classroom: their background knowledge, previous academic success, levels of basic skills (reading comprehension, mathematical computation), and their attitudes and efforts toward learning.

They differ in the way they process and understand knowledge and in the way they construct meaning from knowledge. Sally, an eighth grade teacher, revealed the diversity she sees in her students: "Each child learns differently. One child might have only a two-minute attention span. Another child might come to school with a host of issues and just be completely exhausted." Students see this diversity also. Jake, a sixth grader, told us, "There is such a wide range of smartness in the school in each class. It's hard because some kids move faster than others, and they [the teachers] have to know the needs of some kids."

Traditional curriculum design and many traditional instructional strategies do not account for the diversity of students' learning needs. The belief that "one size fits all" when it comes to preparing students for life after school results in every student being exposed to the same curricula, reading the same book, receiving the same assignments, acquiring information through the same instructional model, and completing the same tests to demonstrate growth. This philosophy and accompanying instructional practices are accepted by many as the most successful method of educating students. But using the same methods for all students will only ensure that some are not successful. Standardized methods create frustration for many students and their teachers.

Jensen (1998) described one instance of this frustration: "Julie's teacher spends a lot of time reteaching because she doesn't teach in ways that match how Julie's brain learns. This mismatch creates frustration, under performance, and hopelessness" (41). Both the teacher and student are frustrated by the inability to have their needs met—the teacher, who wants to help Julie succeed but is afraid to let go of traditional views of learning, and Julie, who wants to experience academic success.

Differentiated Teaching and Learning

Recognizing diversity in learning means that teachers understand that each student has a unique way of accessing, processing, and applying information. Learning preferences and differences may be based on environmental conditions; on genetic, neurological, or other physical challenges; or on a combination of environmental and physical factors. One student's learning preferences may differ from another's based on broad issues such as developmental level, gender, race, ethnicity, socioeconomic class, or native language. Learning differences may be very specific, such as a preference for learning from parts to whole or vice versa, the need for social interaction versus independent study, the preference for analytical methods of learning, the need to write to enhance learning, or the need to engage in physical movement when learning. Personal interests, learning disabilities, and degrees of background knowledge also impact learning preferences (Tomlinson 1999b).

The causes of individual differences are not as important as the responsibility for teachers to ensure that every student has opportunities to succeed at learning—daily. Teachers' attitudes, philosophies, and ultimately actions in recognizing differences in students determine the degree of success that students will experience. Tomlinson and McTighe (2006) offered the following questions for teachers to respond to as evidence that they intend to help students grow:

> Differentiated or responsive teaching really stems from an affirmative answer to three questions—and dogged determination to live out the answer in our classrooms a little bit better today than we did yesterday.

1. Do we have the will and skill to accept responsibility for the diverse individuals we teach?
   - To develop positive ties with students to encourage their growth?
   - To see their dreams and uncertainties?
   - To study and respond to their cultures?
   - To work with students to build positive learning communities?
2. Do we have a vision of the power of high-quality learning to help young people build lives?
   - To know what really matters in the discipline?
   - To ensure student understanding of what matters most?
   - To discover what's relevant and compelling to individuals?
   - To build student engagement in learning?
3. Are we willing to do the work of building bridges of possibility between what we teach and the diverse learners we teach?
   - To seek out students' strengths and deficiencies?

- To develop flexible scheduling routines?
- To create learning options for varied needs?
- To coach for success?
- To monitor individual growth against goals? (56–57)

Meeting the needs of all learners by differentiating instruction begins with accepting this belief system—one that should influence your practice. Understanding the fact that your students are all cognitively different from one another should encourage you to establish a different set of learning expectations for each student. Accepting this reality will provide you with the opportunity to help every student succeed. Ignoring it will create frustration for you and especially your students.

Students' differing cognitive abilities should determine curricular decisions, instructional strategies, and assessment practices. Educators who seek information about students' abilities and act on them help their students by differentiating their teaching through

- frequent individual and group assessment
- flexible assignments based on students' academic needs and ability levels
- differing curricula chosen to meet the interests and developmental traits of students
- varying sets of expectations for what each student will learn
- flexible time frames for learning
- a variety of grouping arrangements for studying topics (adapted from Tomlinson 1999b, 2)

Differentiated learning involves the use of many varied, intentionally designed instructional experiences to provide multiple ways for students to access, process, and interpret information. In reading assignments, for example, some students may need to be given a list of questions that they stop and think about as they read. Some may need a text in which the important ideas are highlighted. Some may need an abbreviated text or the book on tape. Some may need to be read to or to read it out loud themselves. Varying levels of skill knowledge among students should also induce teachers to develop alternative assessments for students (Tomlinson 2005).

No standardized model for designing learning experiences can meet the needs of all students in every classroom. Understanding, validating, and responding to student learning differences is a professional responsibility of educators. All students have a right to succeed, and teachers must provide the necessary environment for that to happen. Constant traditional whole-class direct instruction makes the creation of such an environment unlikely. When you plan curriculum and instruction collaboratively with students, you are better able to meet their individual needs.

Culturally Responsive Teaching

> I think American society has shortchanged itself and minorities by insisting that immigrants, African Americans, and Native Americans deny their cultures and languages to become "real" Americans.
>
> WEINER (1999, 7)

Immigrants have entered American public schools for centuries. Early perspectives on educating culturally and ethnically diverse students drove educators to use traditional teaching methods in attempts to Americanize students. By using traditional instruction and curricula, educators ignored students' rich cultural and ethnic heritage that they brought from home and also ignored diverse learning profiles that accompanied students' cultural backgrounds. Teachers were well intentioned, yet prevented many students from reaching academic success.

Teaching ethnically diverse students requires specific actions that positively impact student success. Wlodkowski and Ginsberg (1995) explained the need for mandating cultural responsiveness:

> Few of us . . . would care to admit that the way we teach compromises the learning of certain cultural groups. Yet, to avoid or remain insensitive to the cultural issues and influences within our teaching situations under the guise, for example, of maintaining academic standards or treating everyone alike is no longer acceptable. (8)

Culturally responsive pedagogy requires a positive attitude toward change and a commitment to alter instruction and curriculum for the benefit of diverse students. Brown (2002b) noted, "Culturally responsive teaching begins when teachers recognize, demonstrate, and celebrate an equal respect for the backgrounds of all students" (21). Ladson-Billings (1994) further explained, "Culturally responsive teaching is about questioning (and preparing students to question) the structural inequality, the racism, and the injustice that exists in society" (128).

It may be easy, particularly for White teachers, to believe that no injustices exist for our students or to be unaware that much of American teaching reflects traditional cultural norms about how learning occurs. Those beliefs reveal ignorance about the lives of our ethnically and culturally diverse students and their families. Ethnically diverse young adolescents recognize the differences in how they are treated by peers and also by teachers who may ignore how their students' lives are affected by their ethnicity (Brown and Leaman 2006; Sheets 2005). Sheets stated, "Adolescents notice that their groups' accomplishments may be missing or distorted in the school curriculum" (61).

Cultural responsiveness begins by engaging in frequent conversations with students about their families, backgrounds, language, and preferred learning styles. Cultural responsiveness does *not* imply that, "I treat all my students the same—I don't see color." If you believe this, then you may completely ignore your students' differences and the behaviors and learning preferences associated with their ethnic profiles, and you may reduce their chances for academic success.

A primary goal of culturally responsive teaching is to adjust instruction and curriculum so that ethnically diverse students will have equal opportunities for learning (Ruddell 1999). Gay (2000) described many diverse students' needs for more active instructional processes. English language learners have a particular need for direct contact with information through manipulatives and hands-on experiences (Brown 2002c). That means teachers should use more *inductive* teaching rather than *deductive* teaching. Inductive approaches provide students with opportunities to see the whole picture of new principles first. Inductive learning provides students with opportunities to construct their own knowledge by designing and conducting an experiment, handling manipulatives, or being involved in a simulation activity.

Presenting new concepts and principles within a meaningful context that most students have some experience with improves students' chances for comprehending new material. One example of when to provide a meaningful context is when introducing new vocabulary. Teachers who purposely connect those words directly to their students' contextual experiences have a better chance of helping their students genuinely understand new principles.

Gay (2000) contends that African and Hispanic American students need more contextualized learning experiences. Brown (2002c) sees these as opportunities for

- telling stories
- sharing experiences related to new vocabulary and content
- engaging in kinesthetic reenactments of historical events
- designing physical models of new principles
- drawing graphic organizers
- taking field trips associated with key units (adapted from 65)

Contextual instruction requires that teachers know enough about their students' lives to connect content to their personal circumstances.

The cognitive growth and social and emotional needs of young adolescents make collaborative learning an essential aspect of effective cultural and developmental responsiveness. English language learners (ELL) would especially benefit from the opportunities to engage in conversations about content as a way to simultaneously understand new principles and learn English.

An essential component of culturally responsive teaching is educators' ability to respect and respond to their ethnically diverse students' communication styles and native languages. Howard (2001) has discovered that "the achievement of students is increased when teachers modify their instruction to make it more congruent with the cultures and communication styles of culturally diverse students" (183). Several nonstandard forms of English are spoken at some of our students' homes: Hawaiian Creole, Appalachian English, and Black English Vernacular (BEV). Teachers demonstrate their awareness and respect for their students' culture and ethnicity by not correcting them each time they use their language or dialect of origin. Teachers can emphasize the differences between standard English and the discourse students' families speak at home politely and in the context of class discussions, writing assignments, and private conversations. As Brown (2002c) noted in response to some African American students' use of BEV, "To overly correct or dismiss students' use of BEV denigrates young adolescents' ethnic and cultural backgrounds while creating negative feelings between students and teachers" (67).

ELL students need many opportunities for public and private conversations during class time. Teachers must permit them to *code switch* during these conversations, that is, to use both English and their native languages in order to effectively learn English. Frequent conversations with your ELL students will give you an idea of their English skills and the help they need to improve their use of academic English. Garcia (1999) suggested teachers use these instructional strategies in order to improve students' academic success:

- increase wait time following your questions and after their responses to promote elaboration and more processing time
- simplify your language—don't speak louder; rephrase comments or questions instead
- don't force students to speak
- pair ELL students with proficient English speakers
- adapt instructional materials to make them more comprehensible
- support the student's home language and culture (cited in Brown 2002b, 178)

Conversational exchanges among students and between students and teachers during lessons better match the learning profile of ethnically diverse students. Quick responses to questions during recitations and discussions may prevent many ethically diverse students from engaging in learning activities. This type of quick exchange also discourages some students from becoming engaged in learning activities.

Becoming a culturally responsive teacher requires developing and believing in a philosophy of differences among students—differences that must be studied and that teachers must respond to through explicit efforts. Making a difference in our ethnically diverse students' lives depends on our willingness to plan curriculum and instruction collaboratively with students and to make instructional and curricular decisions that take into account all the learners in the classroom.

Living with Content Standards

Many of you will be or are employed in schools that mandate specific skills and topics to be covered in a certain grade—generally known as *content standards*.

Content standards are usually designed by personnel in state departments of education and may often be influenced by college professors, school board members, professional organizations, master teachers, or politically active organizations concerned with a specific agenda (e.g., science curriculum associated with the study of evolution versus other theories). Sometimes these content standards are locally determined, but they are frequently adopted by state education departments and required by every school district in the state. Since the No Child Left Behind (2001) legislation has been passed, many states have aligned their state content standards with the standardized tests required of students.

These realities and concerns may make you reluctant to use a curriculum model and instructional strategies that are developed through substantial student input. Many teachers, however, have discovered that collaborative planning with students has, in fact, raised achievement levels. Alexander, Carr, and McAvoy (1995) described what they discovered when their sixth graders designed their own curriculum and instructional strategies: "In most areas we found that these sixth graders met or exceeded the content coverage of previous classes. Some of what they learned arose from student inquiries and some from teacher givens. The big bonus was all the other learning that took place simultaneously" (56). That other learning included high levels of thinking, cooperative skills, and independence and responsibility for learning. And according to the teachers, "These lessons were not learned at the expense of 'traditional content'" (56).

Other researchers have discovered that students believe they have learned more when they are fully engaged in curriculum integration experiences (Brown and Morgan 2003; Powell and Skoog 1995). Many teachers recognize that thinking processes, interpersonal skills, research abilities, technological skills, and problem solving are the essential outcomes that really matter in the lives of our students (Brown 2006). Helping your students learn to use these strategies in the context of meaningful curriculum is your job as a middle level educator.

We are fully aware of the position in which teachers are sometimes placed when they don't cover the curriculum or complete the textbook; however, time, textbooks, and curriculum guides do not have to be impediments to implementing active learning activities within your own classroom. If you are in a school with departmentalized subject areas, as many of you are or will be, you still have the primary responsibility of meeting students' learning needs within the context of your subject area. Despite the mandates of your subject area, you may continue to engage students in making curricular decisions and encourage them to select among several methods of learning and assessment. After you collaborate with students to develop themes based on their questions and concerns, you can then show them the list of mandated topics and have them work with you on developing ways to integrate those topics into their investigations. A traditional school structure is no excuse for refusing to use best practices based on effective research-based pedagogical principles (Bizar and Daniels 2005; Daniels, Hyde, and Zemelman 2005). Adding content standards to student-designed curriculum can be accomplished without denying students the genuine learning that occurs with curriculum integration (see Chapter 9).

Concluding Reflections

Being a teacher is a complex task. You will not find a recipe that tells you what ingredients to use in order to be successful. You must first remember the young adolescent population with whom you are working. Young adolescents are vibrant and alive, curious and questioning, passionate and intense. If you can capture and use their vibrancy, curiosity, and passion and see learning through their eyes, you have taken the first step toward facilitating meaningful learning. Couple that with your extensive content and pedagogical knowledge as well as the flexibility to use what you know in response to student needs, and you will be able to develop an environment in which students are genuinely encouraged to construct knowledge to make sense of their world.

EIGHT

Assessment That Promotes Active Learning

I went to school where we didn't have grades, and we didn't have tests. We never got a report card. I was much more willing to learn.

DAN, SIXTH GRADER

I'll never forget the expression on the principal's face when I told him that the district's standardized tests could not help me know what the students in my English classes needed to learn.

MARY A. BARR (2000, 20)

Decisions about whether or not students are learning should not take place in the legislature, the governor's office, or the department of education. They should take place in the classroom, because that is where learning occurs.

DOUGLAS CHRISTENSEN CITED IN ROSCHEWSKI, GALLAGHER, AND ISERNHAGEN (2001, 611)

What Is Assessment?

A message posted on the campus where one of us teaches states, "Good luck on exams!" You have undoubtedly heard the same "good luck" from friends and family as you prepared

180

to take tests. We find it humorous that luck would have anything to do with determining what you have learned. How can students spend so much time learning in school only to have the level of their knowledge determined by a test that relies as much on luck as it does on skill or knowledge?

The kind of assessment that takes luck to succeed involves students memorizing facts, then attempting to recall them for the test. Students who experience assessment this way usually have no knowledge of the questions they will be asked to answer until the day they take the test. This reminds us of owl pellets—those small, cylinder-shaped, gray hair balls that owls regurgitate after they eat because they can't digest the hair and bones of field mice. All of us have taken a test in which we regurgitated pellets that represent the information we could not digest! We don't consider that type of assessment an accurate measure of learning. We question the validity of such tests; that is, do these traditional assessment strategies measure what they claim to measure? Do they measure what teachers want students to know?

We need to develop a more genuine view of assessment and increase our understanding of how to help young adolescents become more involved in assessing their own learning. When we think about determining what students know, we may think of words such as *testing, evaluation,* or *grading.* These words do not have the same meaning as *assessment.*

Testing is the traditional term for determining what someone knows. We usually think of teacher-generated tests as multiple-choice, true/false, or essay questions. Testing may come in several other formats, but the questions usually are generated from an outside source rather than from students. Tests may not actually measure what teachers want students to know or be able to do as a result of studying a particular topic.

Evaluation is another word commonly used in place of assessment. Evaluation is a value assigned to student performances and a judgment about the quality of a child's performance or product of learning (Educators in Connecticut's Pomperaug Regional School District 15 1996). Like testing, most evaluation of student learning utilizes external sources instead of being personally generated by students. The typical end products of evaluation are grades.

Grading is another word that is frequently confused with assessment. Grading is an arbitrary label teachers use to place students along a continuum from best to worst or to compare students with one another. Grades in any format, such as A to F, satisfactory, or at grade level, describe student performances over a period of time on a number of tasks. Although grading has a strong tradition, a number of problems exist with this practice. Tombari and Borich (1999) described some of these: "[Grades] assume equal amounts of learning have occurred for individuals who achieve the same grade, fail to acknowledge continuous progress or development in learning, and may mask an individual student's learning strengths and needs" (39). Marzano (2000) noted "Grades are so imprecise that they are almost meaningless. This straightforward but depressing fact is usually painfully obvious when one examines the research and practice regarding grades with a critical eye" (1).

Convincing parents and other educators of the insufficiency inherent in grading is a lifetime battle. A most unfortunate fact is that grades are not motivating for many students and rarely have little to do with learning. If you need any evidence of this, then you should respond to the question Marzano is fond of asking teachers: "How many believe that the grades you received in school were not an accurate representation of your academic achievement?" (9). Every teacher who has attended Marzano's presentations has raised his or her hand to confirm that this accurately describes his or her beliefs about grades; it may reflect your views as well. Marzano added: "A single letter grade or a percentage score is not a good way to report student achievement in any subject area because it simply cannot present the level of detailed feedback necessary for effective learning" (106). The two essential words in this comment are *feedback* and *learning*. When students receive credible feedback about how to improve or where substantial growth has occurred, then the chances for academic growth are greater than when grades are merely used to summarize a teacher's opinion.

Assessment has a more generalized meaning than testing, grading, or evaluation. Assessment is a set of strategies for discovering what students know or can do as a result of engaging in learning experiences. It involves a number of activities designed to determine the level of student learning. Assessment is a comprehensive act that includes consideration of a student's goals for learning, processes of learning, progression toward established goals, and revision of goals when needed. All assessment should have as its primary purpose the improvement of student learning.

Effective assessment begins with discovering what students know when they enter your classroom each fall. Brown (2002b) suggested teachers be aware of the following information about each student:

- attendance records
- comprehensive reading strengths and weaknesses
- writing level and strategies
- study skills
- personal interests not associated with school
- leisure activities
- parents' beliefs about their child's academic progress
- health issues that may affect learning
- personality traits that may affect learning
- English proficiency level
- grade level abilities in major subject areas (adapted from 187–88)

These activities require systematic kid-watching throughout the year (as we described in Chapter 7).

Finding the answers to all this information about students takes time—especially if you are responsible for as many as 100 to 150 students a day. However, without understanding your students' baseline skills and knowledge, you miss the opportunity to determine if genuine growth is occurring each day.

Time for Reflection

- Make a list of the reasons for assessing students.
- Discuss with a classmate or colleague how the reasons you've listed support young adolescents' cognitive growth.
- Describe some of the frustrations you've experienced with traditional assessment techniques.

The Problems with Standardized Tests

Much has changed in the world of assessing students since we wrote the first edition of this book in 2000. The pressure placed on teachers and students by the No Child Left Behind (2001) legislation (NCLB) may have already altered the way you teach students, what you teach students, and how you determine what they know. Despite these pressures, you as a teacher are the only one who can know if your students have gained the necessary skills, strategies, and attitudes they need to successfully complete a year of learning.

Many tests are incapable of assessing students in ways that help teachers improve instruction, but national or state standardized tests may be the *worst* measuring devices for helping teachers and students. We know that each state department of education has mandated specific standardized tests for your students. NCLB legislation mandated that each state department of education choose a way to determine if students have reached certain levels of proficiency. Each state education department was to involve local educators in this process of deciding how each district would assess its students; however, most state personnel chose instead, without any external input, to use traditional standardized tests to determine students' proficiency. Standardized test scores don't necessarily ensure genuine learning of the concepts and principles important to you or your colleagues.

Standardized tests are not generally given as pretest/posttest assessments to determine student gains in knowledge, but instead are administered to students in April or May of each year for a one-time-only view of students' learning of concepts and principles—content that may not even match what you are required to teach. Popham (1999) cited a study in which researchers found that between 50 and 80 percent of the questions found on many national standardized tests did not match the curricula from several textbooks teachers were using. As Popham noted, "The companies that create and sell standardized achievement tests are all owned by large corporations. Like all for-profit businesses, these corporations attempt to produce revenue for their stakeholders" (11). With each state and school district having a different set of learning outcomes for students, it is highly unlikely, if not impossible, for these test corporations to find enough test items that match your district's curricula.

Students should know what content is going to be on a test so that they can prepare for success. Logic tells us, therefore, that all teachers should also know explicitly the items that are to be on a test that has high stakes for students and teachers such as the state tests mandated by NCLB. Yet each year teachers have no idea what the content of the test will be. How can it be considered cheating to prepare students for success? Popham (1999) suggested that educators be provided with an opportunity to "scrutinize the test's items one at a time to see what they are really measuring" (15). Until teachers know what will be tested, many students will suffer the consequences associated with unacceptable scores, and teachers will continue to alter instruction and curricula in ways that discourage meaningful learning.

Proficiency as used by the NCLB authors does not describe genuine student learning. Proficiency may have nothing to do with students learning the critical principles that they need to know. Your students may be proficient in the skills measured by a mandated standardized test yet lack the necessary information and strategies needed to achieve the learning outcomes you have identified for them. "Proficient in what?" is what you should ask following your students' experiences each year with state or national standardized tests.

The difficulty with most of the external examinations required for students throughout America is that these tests in no manner help students learn better or teachers instruct better. Students are given the tests in April or May, and the results are released after students that you taught for the year have completed that grade, meaning you'll never teach them again. Reeves (2004) noted, "By the time the results are published, they are ancient history in the eyes of the student and the teacher" (71).

The results of these state tests are seldom if ever indications of students' academic growth during the year. Teachers for years have proclaimed the folly of taking these tests seriously as a way to determine genuine student learning and growth. Popham (1999) noted, "The better the job that teachers do in teaching important knowledge and skills, the less likely it is that there will be items on a standardized achievement test measuring such knowledge and/or skills" (12).

Teachers are less likely to use creative teaching strategies or spend as much time as is needed to study topics that interest students when they feel pressured and responsible for raising students' scores on external standardized tests. Instead of improving the curriculum and instruction, high-stakes standardized tests tend to narrow the curriculum, increase dropout rates, and decrease graduation rates—especially for ethnically diverse students (Stiggins 2006; Kohn 2000). Stiggins noted that despite legislators' desires to improve student performance by using high-stakes standardized tests, there has been no significant improvement in students' test results since the 1960s. Brown (2002b) added, "Shouldn't standardized tests at least help students and teachers, considering all the money and time spent purchasing, administering, and scoring them" (220)?

The reality is, however, that most teachers believe that they are responsible for helping students learn the content and skills they need to score well on high-stakes tests. Many educators believe that changing instruction to a skill-based, direct-instruction approach will improve students' chances for test success. Adopting this structured teaching approach ignores what is best for young adolescents and may in fact prevent students from learning enough.

Wilhelm (2006) discovered in reporting on an analysis of test score data from the National Assessment of Educational Progress (NAEP) and the Third International Mathematics and Science Study (TIMSS) "that better student test scores are associated with inquiry approaches that emphasize deep understanding" (14). This research runs counter to the belief that structured teaching improves test scores. Instead we find that implementing active instructional processes, student-designed curriculum, and genuine assessment practices assists your students in reaching learning gains on meaningful outcomes.

Other Misuses of Assessment Strategies

Assessment *should not* be about sorting students into categories to determine their opportunities for the future; however, this is how assessment is commonly used. We do not believe that assessment should be used to motivate students. Motivation is an intrinsic thinking process initiated by students rather than an extrinsic one controlled by teachers. When assessment is used to sort, motivate, or determine whether a student will graduate or be promoted, students lose interest in learning opportunities and begin to focus instead on their ability or inability to reach arbitrarily established standards.

Assessment focused on specific standards emphasizes competition instead of creating diverse opportunities for student growth and academic success. Meaningful assessment focuses on learning as a *process* instead of on single performances such as occurs with most standardized tests.

Think about your experiences with multiple-choice tests, essays, projects, or demonstrations. Do these activities contribute to students' overall knowledge or abilities? Do they demonstrate what students genuinely understand? Do assigned grades reflect what students learn or understand? What do students' scores on tests say about their actual learning? How much information do students retain after they complete a test?

As you recall your struggles and successes in mastering content information sufficiently to pass standardized, end-of-unit, and teacher-made tests, you may also remember that memorizing information for the purpose of passing a test led only to a short-term memory of most significant points. The information you memorized may have significance to you, but the way in which you learned it made it seem as if the information was useful only to the extent that knowing it helped you pass the test.

Teachers may design elaborate lessons that are engaging and meaningful, and students may gain much from the learning activities; however, when students are tested by means of a multiple-choice test, the value of the content is often diminished. Traditional assessment instruments, with their emphasis on simple recall, fail to encourage the development of students' abilities in the specific kinds of strategies needed to succeed in life (Schurr 1999).

Assessment FOR Learning

Assessment is not the end product of a unit of study. It should not be focused on the number of facts students have memorized but rather on meaningful learning experiences. Stiggins (2006) described a critical distinction between assessment *of* learning and assessment *for* learning. Assessment *of* learning is the traditional and standardized testing view of assessment that notes how much students have learned as of a particular point in time (the day of the test). Assessment *for* learning, in contrast, is based on the idea and practice of assessing students so that teachers can help each of them grow cognitively (Stiggins).

Schurr (1999) reinforced the importance of learning during assessment activities: "Assessment is about determining what one knows and can do and what one doesn't know and cannot do. Yet, if the true mission of teaching is to help students learn, the measurement must foster growth and development" (17). Assessment is meaningful when it drives instruction and helps students reflect on their own learning.

Another essential component of assessment is feedback, which should occur as soon after a task as possible. Reeves (2004) described effective feedback:

> The best practice in assessment [occurs when] . . . students are required to complete a task and then very soon—within minutes, hours, or days—they receive feedback that is designed to improve their performance. (71)

Genuine feedback should routinely provide students with enough detail and accuracy to ensure that students know what to do to improve their performance. Frequent one-on-one conferences with students to review and discuss their work and written comments that provide analyses of mistakes are examples of productive feedback.

Students need opportunities to hear, see, or reflect on their academic performances and become familiar with the strategies needed to improve their next performance. The emphasis of meaningful assessment is on individual growth—not student-to-student competition. Every student should understand that he or she is responsible for improving *his or her* knowledge, skills, and strategies. There is a better chance of that occurring when students receive appropriate, timely, and frequent feedback (Stiggins 2006).

Assessment is *not* the end product of learning. Assessment becomes meaningful only when curriculum is designed collaboratively and students decide how they will learn information. In this scenario, assessment comprises the meaningful learning activities students engage in throughout their studies. A culminating project or demonstration integrates the essential knowledge and skills that students have obtained.

Connecting Assessment to Curriculum and Instruction

The strategies chosen for determining what students know differ considerably from those of traditional practice when *learning* is the anchor of one's assessment philosophy. Assessment practices must be closely connected to curriculum and instruction. The beliefs that a teacher holds regarding these three components affect the choice of how he or she determines what students know or are able to do as a result of learning. Separate-subject curricular design, teacher-centered instruction, and traditional testing techniques often fail to meet the criterion for connecting curriculum, instruction, and assessment in a meaningful way. When teachers design the curriculum collaboratively with students, students become responsible for helping to design not only how they want to learn information but also how they want to demonstrate their learning. The assessment is in fact part of the instruction and drives the learning experiences.

For instance, students who choose as a small group to study the source of pollution in a local stream are engaged in learning a topic of interest. Students take part in genuine learning as they develop hypotheses, determine how to collect information, analyze samples, and reach conclusions about the stream. Learning occurs through the reflective processes of determining how to design a project that demonstrates their newfound knowledge and in the method they choose to present their findings. Students' assessment decisions provide direction to purposeful learning activities. Student motivation is an end result of the powerful connection of curriculum, instruction, and assessment.

Alternative Assessment

Alternative assessments are strategies for determining what students know or are capable of doing that don't rely on standardized, multiple-choice, short answer, true/false, or essay tests.

Students develop research skills and problem-solving abilities, think creatively, debate, engage in authentic writing experiences and mapping activities, and collaborate successfully among themselves when they have opportunities to personalize curriculum and the ways in which they learn. These are the cognitive activities that students must be engaged in each day for genuine learning to occur. Traditional assessment strategies do not enable students to demonstrate the growth they have acquired as a result of engaging in these meaningful activities.

Meaningful assessment embodies the following characteristics:

- It begins with student goal setting.
- It provides choices for students in demonstrating what they know.
- It allows for flexibility in its design.
- It is developmentally appropriate for each young adolescent.
- It provides opportunities for self-evaluation.
- It encourages development of students' thinking processes.
- It creates authentic connections.
- It permits demonstrations of learning that build on strengths and weaknesses.

Students' Roles in Assessment

Young adolescents are capable of being active participants in both assessment and evaluation and judging their accomplishments. (NMSA 2003, 27)

Differences in the way we act or changes in our lives as adults occur only when we take responsibility for making the changes. When adults decide to search for a new job, stop smoking, lose weight, or get a new haircut, the change occurs when they take direct action, that is, as a result of their own awareness and need for change. Sometimes this change is initiated as a result of a conversation with loved ones or that look in the mirror that surprises us. No matter what event starts the change in motion, these changes occur only when we say they do and as a result of our own motivation to make a change.

Young adolescents are quite similar to adults when it comes to the decisions these students make about their learning and academic growth. Young adolescents can easily blindly follow teachers' leads in completing academic tasks required of them. Of course, many students regularly choose to ignore teachers' requests for completing assignments and acting responsibly about their academic growth. A fascinating and encouraging cognitive growth process among young adolescents, however, is their expanding abilities to determine just how much effort they are expending, how positive or negative their attitudes toward learning are, and just what they are capable of producing cognitively. Put simply, young adolescents are in a perfect position to learn how to be responsible for monitoring their own academic growth with some assistance from their teachers.

One way to help students identify their strengths is to use inventories that assess their learning strengths and preferred ways of learning. Making students aware of their learning preferences is an aspect of handing responsibility for learning to the students themselves. Teachers can demonstrate how they too use their own learning profiles in designing lessons or in their own learning experiences.

Young adolescents must learn to be aware of not only their learning preferences but also their attitude, attention and effort. You should never believe that you, as a teacher, are responsible for students' actions in these three metacognitive areas. You may, however, need to demonstrate explicitly what positive attitudes look like, how students can attend efficiently during lessons, and what maximum effort means in your classroom. Teachers should never assume that all of their students know how to demonstrate appropriate attitudes, give a consistent effort, or monitor their level of attention.

Young adolescents should be involved in goal setting in order to begin taking responsibility for their own learning. These goals should relate to what students expect to learn or be able to do, or behaviors they want to acquire over a period of a week, month, semester, or year. Young adolescents' growing abilities to assess their academic strengths and weaknesses enable them to develop a set of personal learning outcomes.

Student-teacher conferences should be conducted frequently to determine student progress in developing outcomes and to reassess goals if necessary. A copy of these outcomes should be placed in a student's portfolio as a reminder of the direction the student intends to take to reach desired ends. Revisiting and possibly revising these academic goals is imperative to ensuring appropriate academic growth.

When students have helped to develop goals for their learning, they then can use those goals to reflect on themselves as learners. As they share their new understandings about themselves with teachers, parents, or peers, they learn to take increasing responsibility for their learning. Davies (2001) explained the value of students communicating to others about their learning:

> Involving students in communicating their learning signals a shift in roles and responsibilities. Instead of searching for evidence that students have learned, teachers now help students find evidence of their own learning. . . . This shift in roles and responsibilities occurs over time as teachers learn and gain expertise in involving students in their own learning. (49)

A critical aspect of this type of frequent communication between students and teachers and possibly peers is the constant feedback that students receive about their progress toward meeting their personal learning outcomes—feedback that helps them make adjustments and ensures academic growth. One eighth grader in the Soundings curriculum integration experience provided this perspective on his frequent teacher feedback and self-assessment: "The way we were assessed in Soundings gave me constructive advice about how to better my performance in school. I also received feedback from my own reflection on my writing and presentations" (Brown and Morgan 2003, 19).

192

Davies (2001) noted the opportunities for student growth through communication:

> When students communicate with others about their learning, they learn about what they have learned, what they need to learn, and what kind of support may be available to them. Research shows that when students are involved in the assessment process and learn to articulate what they have learned and what they still need to work on, achievement improves. (47)

Students can focus on assessment issues during student-teacher conferences by responding to these questions:

- What do you hope to learn as a result of studying this topic?
- How might you show your understanding of this information?
- How does what you already know compare with what you'd like to know?
- Who would you like to share your new knowledge with once you have researched this topic?
- How would you evaluate your final product with respect to this topic?

Helping students develop a course of study, choose strategies for learning information, and select ways of presenting their learning to classmates, parents, and teachers is a journey that is continually evolving. Teachers help students identify process skills and work habits they need to develop, such as analytical and research skills, time-management strategies, persistence, and collaboration with classmates (Educators in Connecticut's Pomperaug Regional School District 15 1996).

This process involves ongoing teacher guidance and conferencing, student risk taking and experimentation, and careful design and possible redesign of final projects. Learning occurs as much in the unfolding of the process as it does in the completion of the final product or culminating performance.

Stiggins (2004) believes as do we that educators must "stop being so adult centered in our thinking about assessment. We must build classroom environments in which students use assessments to understand what success looks like and how to do better the next time" (25). We can only hand responsibility over to students if we believe that they are capable of communicating about their own learning needs and if we provide them with the strategies and time for reflection on their effort and progress.

Few middle level schools have adopted a student-managed assessment philosophy, in part because of a belief that young adolescents are incapable of independent learning and reflection. We know, however, that their emerging metacognitive abilities permit young adolescents to evaluate their performance on academic tasks. Young adolescents are able to see their mistakes and correct them without intensive teacher direction, think creatively when given opportunities for reflection, use analytical strategies that they had not been capable of prior to this growth period, and develop advanced questioning strategies that provide teachers with insights into their depth of understanding.

Eighth graders in a class that used the curriculum integration model believed that they improved their critical thinking skills more than they would have in a traditional classroom as a result of "thinking about and critiquing what others said or presented; the many circumstances of evaluating each other; their responsibilities for frequent self-evaluation; and their need to review and consider the constructive criticism received" (Brown and Morgan 2003, 23). Stiggins (2006) insisted that students be involved in their assessment so that they develop an understanding of what academic success looks like and have the opportunity and take the responsibility of reaching it. He added that teachers are responsible for helping students believe they are capable learners and that self-assessment leads to this possibility.

Considering the extent of young adolescents' cognitive abilities, we are dismayed with the overuse of traditional standardized assessment instruments such as multiple-choice tests. These instruments can have a negative influence on instructional decision making and often do. They discourage teachers from using alternative instructional strategies that provide students with the time and opportunities to exercise their newfound cognitive abilities (Brown 1990).

Wiggins (1993) noted that in examining the true meaning of the word *assessment*, "It is something we do *with* and *for* the student, not something we do *to* the student" (14). As Marzano (2000) explained, "Wiggins' comments capture the true spirit of effective assessment: teacher and student jointly analyzing the students' strengths and weaknesses relative to specific outcomes" (104).

Accepting Diverse Products

Teachers who use alternative assessments provide options for students in developing individual plans for demonstrating their knowledge. Individualized assessment plans allow students to choose how they will demonstrate their learning so that assessment matches their abilities while strengthening their weaknesses. Teachers who adopt individualized assessment practices accept and account for differences among learners, whether created by culture, gender, developmental stages, or special learning needs.

One expectation of a meaningful assessment environment is that students demonstrate essential thinking processes in a variety of ways. Seasoned teachers understand that students develop competencies at varying levels and times. Saying that you recognize student differences is a beginning, but we have found that few teachers respond to these differences in how they assess students. Failure to adapt curricular and assessment decision making leads to teacher frustration and a likely decline in students' motivation as performance standards are established that some students are incapable of meeting. Establishing realistic individual outcomes results in more meaningful student learning and growth.

Authentic Assessment Leads to Meaningful Learning

Authentic assessment refers to genuine learning activities—opportunities students have to connect curricula to events occurring in their lives and to people with whom they interact. Authentic assessment emotionally engages students, as they use information in real-life contexts that have meaning to them (Schurr 1999). Students engaged in authentic assessment activities often present information that they have learned to selected audiences—from peers to community members.

Examples of authentic assessment include student-generated activities such as developing oral presentations to explain research findings, constructing timelines, creating slide shows, writing song lyrics, creating maps, submitting a short story for publication in a local journal, or devising a research plan. These activities demonstrate how young adolescents are able to use many of their developing cognitive skills such as creative thinking and problem solving, rather than their ability to memorize isolated facts.

Perhaps the greatest advantage of authentic assessment over traditional testing is the chance it provides young adolescents to extend their knowledge through reflection and application of information to real-life contexts. Authentic assessment is a dynamic process that cannot be confined to a forty-two-minute period one day a week.

Schurr (1999) summarized the main components of authentic assessment. It:

- involves an audience or the public
- is not constrained by arbitrary or unrealistic time limits
- requires collaboration with others
- employs higher-level critical and creative thinking
- is complex, open ended, and draws on many capacities
- uses students' own research or background knowledge as a means not an end (3)

Of primary importance in using authentic assessment is that young adolescents need to be challenged in a way that encourages them to find solutions to personally developed questions and hypotheses.

Performance Assessment

Performance assessments provide students with the opportunity to demonstrate what they know or understand through a performance task. We have all participated in performance assessments such as athletic events, musical contests, dance recitals, driving tests, and submission of letters to the editor. Some common classroom performances include writing stories, designing science laboratory experiences, and engaging in debates. Students participating in performance assessments demonstrate deep understanding of a topic by engaging in personally meaningful learning activities.

Students engaged in performance assessments must learn processing strategies and content knowledge simultaneously. In designing a visitors' guide to encourage people to visit a state, for example, students must use many cognitive processes: research skills to locate information, critical thinking abilities in choosing pertinent facts to include, creative thinking in designing the layout of the guide, and metacognitive strategies in designing rubrics to evaluate their final product.

As they develop student assessment practices, teachers should identify the specific process skills they want their students to acquire in order to more effectively connect the processes and the products of assessment. That's the value of performance assessment—it encourages students to engage in specific processing strategies to reach desired results.

Effectively designed performance assessments become the uniting force for content and process. These assessments provide the learner with the opportunities to make connections more meaningfully than he or she would with teacher-designed or externally administered tests. Teachers are responsible for monitoring students' efforts while they develop their end products. Extensive teacher feedback ensures that students are acquiring necessary strategies and accurate beliefs about new principles and concepts.

Rubrics

One effective means of assuring that students' progress meets realistic, quality expectations is the development of rubrics to evaluate performance and products. Rubrics are scoring guidelines that provide a scale and a set of descriptors for varying levels of performance (Lewin and Shoemaker 1998).

Rubrics have become a common avenue for communicating clearly to students what is expected of them to successfully complete academic tasks. Many teachers, school districts, and state departments of education use rubrics to evaluate students' performance and to describe expected student academic behaviors. Many school districts use common rubrics for the evaluation and feedback of students' writing at all grade levels. Computerized rubric scoring mechanisms have become popular in some schools and states as a way of tracking students' academic performances year to year throughout their basic education.

Although there may be numerous advantages to this constant record keeping, we caution the use of a standardized rubric that becomes foreign to students—that is, denies them the opportunities to engage in designing, evaluating, and altering rubrics to fit their learning needs. The more localized assessment processes are, the greater likelihood that the assessment processes will improve learning.

The use of rubrics encourages students to become more reflective about their work. Rubrics can be used as guidelines if students are given access to them *before* they begin their projects. Rubrics are much more descriptive than letter grades or percentage scores because they provide students with the specific feedback needed to improve on past performances and redirect their efforts as they work toward a finished product. Unlike traditional evaluations, these descriptors encourage growth.

Rubrics should not be designed and used as grading mechanisms. The clearly stated expectations for performance that well-designed rubrics provide are meant to show students how they can improve their performance. If you recall that the purpose of assessment is genuine student learning, you will see the advantage of using rubrics to inform and provide specific feedback to students rather than to evaluate them.

The most powerful rubrics are those that are designed with student input. When students are involved in determining what a quality product should look like, they become more aware of what they need to do to reach acceptable performance levels. As students help design rubrics, teachers become aware of the level of knowledge that students bring to the class about specific curricula and can determine how to help students grow in that content area.

Advantages of Using Rubrics as Assessment Tools

Seventh graders using rubrics to conduct a classification task performed better on tests to check for content knowledge than those students who did not use rubrics (Andrade 2000; Goodrich 1996). Andrade stated, "Instructional rubrics provide students with more informative feedback about their strengths and areas in need of improvement than traditional forms of assessment do" (15). It may be no surprise to you that students who actually see the rubrics beforehand and receive an explanation of how they are used are more likely to use the rubrics effectively to improve their performance (Andrade 2000).

Rubrics have been created for the purpose of assessing every strategy and skill that students are expected to know—from critical thinking strategies to the essential basic components of reading. Every content area teacher can design a rubric with student assistance that provides the necessary guidelines for effective academic performance.

Portfolio Assessment

Portfolios are another meaningful assessment tool for young adolescents. Schurr (1999) described portfolios as a "systematic, integrated, and meaningful collection of a student's day-to-day work showing that student's efforts, progress, or achievement in one or more subjects" (4). Students are the primary decision makers regarding which items to include in the portfolio and are also responsible for evaluating its contents (Schurr 1999). Teachers, parents, and peers might also have a voice in deciding what to place in the portfolio. No mandates should govern portfolio creation; however, below are some examples of items that may be included in portfolios:

- student-established goals
- journal entries
- pertinent questions

- written hypotheses
- book reviews
- creative writing and graphic designs
- peer reviews
- videotaped presentations
- parents' comments on work
- teachers' comments
- self-evaluations
- self-designed rubrics
- evidence of collaboration with other students
- computer-generated projects

These are only a few suggestions for what you and your students may choose to place in a portfolio. Certainly the list and variety of items are endless. What is important is that the items represent the essential strategies and knowledge the student uses to explore significant themes.

It is not the collection of student work that makes portfolios an important form of assessment but rather the students' analyses and reflections on their work. Student-developed rubrics or checklists can offer guidelines for how to construct, design, and decide what may go into a portfolio and help students engage in personal reflection of their progress in achieving personal academic goals.

Growth portfolios (Stiggens, cited in Willis 1997) contain items that represent evidence of students' increased proficiency in specific areas of the curriculum. Students have the opportunity to examine their own growth when they are held responsible for collecting and evaluating their schoolwork. Personal attention to their progress can motivate students to improve performance and effort.

Student-Led Conferences

Teachers are encouraged to have middle level students conduct their own conferences with their parents. Student-led conferences put young adolescents in a position of responsibility for their academic growth (Willis 1997). In student-led conferences, students join their parents to discuss their progress throughout an academic term and are responsible for clarifying what was learned and demonstrating knowledge gained. Students have the opportunity to provide insights about their progress toward personally established outcomes. They share with their parents strengths and areas of needed growth as they display samples of their work. These conferences are empowering for students, because the audience for their growth is more personally focused on them than in traditional teacher-led conferences.

Kinney, Monroe, and Sessions (2000) reported that as a result of using student-led conferences, "Students became much more responsible for completing assignments, more articulate in explaining work, and more accurate at analyzing themselves as learners" (5). Ultimately, student-led conferences should lead to greater learning opportunities.

Organizing Student-Led Conferences

Student-led conferences don't reduce teachers' responsibility for being involved with the parents on conference days. Together the teacher and the student develop plans for collecting data to be put in the conference portfolio. This portfolio should include the student's selected goals and evidence that the student has met those goals. Teacher evaluations and peer reviews may also be included. Kinney, et al. (2000) suggested that student academic work prepared for conferences should meet the following criteria:

- show multiple skills and processes
- address state/local curriculum standards
- emphasize process as well as quality of product
- use examples of "real work," not work contrived for show (13)

Students should have an opportunity to practice conducting their conference. Effective review and organization of the portfolio are imperative if it is to be useful for conferences.

Research in middle schools indicates that parents note considerable honesty and candor from their children during student-led conferences (Marzano 2000). Davies (2001) noted:

When students communicate their learning using a variety of work samples, they go beyond what grades, numbers, and scores alone can

201

show, they are able to examine the depth, the detail, and the range of their own learning to figure out their strengths and what they need to work on next. This is all part of learning to self-monitor—an essential skill for self-directed, independent, lifelong learners. (48)

Student-led conferences are a perfect fit for matching the cognitive growth processes of young adolescents with learning opportunities and self-direction that are necessary for genuine cognitive development.

Support for Alternative Assessment

Assessment does not stand apart from curricular and instructional decisions. The integration of these three components must be accomplished if meaningful learning is to be achieved. The adoption and use of alternative assessments can be challenging. We encourage you to choose assessment procedures that maximize student growth and increase student responsibility.

NINE

Real Teachers Using Genuine Curriculum Integration

We have had the honor of working with many middle school teachers whose practice reflects a student-centered philosophy and honors the developmental capabilities of young adolescents while seeking their input. Their teaching is based on their belief, backed by research, that using curriculum integration in a democratic environment is the most powerful way to engage young adolescents. These teachers become facilitators of learning, involve students in decision making, and use student-determined assessment practices that lead to meaningful learning and growth. Here are some of their stories.

Revisiting Scott Clark

In Chapter 6, Scott Clark described how his thinking about learning and his role as a teacher changed as a result of involving students in the planning and implementation of the curriculum in his classroom. In later conversations with Mr. Clark, he mentioned that curriculum integration particularly helped those students who were generally disconnected from their schooling experiences. When he first informed students that he wanted to know the questions they had about themselves and the world, heads popped up off desks, and students became involved in their learning—some for the first time.

After his students had been looking at their first chosen theme of prejudice for a couple weeks, one group of students told Mr. Clark that the problem of prejudice wouldn't be solved unless the elementary students were taught about the problem. They developed a lesson plan, contacted the elementary principals, arranged transportation, and taught their lesson on prejudice to kindergartners and first graders. After that experience, they wrote an article describing their project.

These were students who had not engaged in thoughtful learning until they were given a voice in what they were going to learn and how they would learn it. Mr. Clark demonstrated what can happen when one person on a team decides that he or she wants to change the learning environment in the classroom. He chose to create a democratic classroom by negotiating curriculum with students.

You will meet four other teachers who have embraced the idea of democratic classrooms and curriculum integration. Like Scott Clark, these teachers took many of the same education courses as other teachers. They are ordinary public school teachers, surrounded by more traditional classrooms. What makes them extraordinary is that they believe that students have a right to have a voice in their education, to be at the center of making decisions about what they learn, how they learn, and how they determine that they have learned.

The Alpha Team

The Alpha team at Shelburne Community School, in Shelburne, Vermont, is a multiage student-directed team that has been implementing the best practices in middle level education for over thirty years. Meghan O'Donnell is a National Board–certified teacher who has been a middle level educator for thirteen years and a member of the Alpha team for ten. In her essay she tells about the Alpha program, describing how her team plans curriculum, implements instruction, and involves students in assessing learning. Cynthia Myers has also been with the Alpha team for ten years. She shares her thoughts on why Alpha has been so successful, focusing particularly on the importance of the relationships that can be built when teachers and students work together and honor one another.

Meghan O'Donnell's Story: Honoring Student Voice

I have had the good fortune of being a middle level educator in Vermont for thirteen years. I taught social studies for one year in ninth and tenth grade, and taught two years on a middle level team as a language arts teacher. For the past ten years, I've been a member of the Alpha team, part of a nationally recognized middle level program in Shelburne, Vermont. Alpha has been in existence for over thirty years and has been organized and structured in many different configurations, but it has kept one component at its core regardless of grade groups and size: student voice. Honoring student voice is the heart of the Alpha program. It is at the center of all aspects of our program and is thus the reason for our continued success. This is no small feat in a time when educators are constantly required to conform and restructure their schools and practice based on legislation that emphasizes improved test score results and increased teacher licensing qualifications.

It is in the Alpha setting that I have found the greatest joy in teaching middle level students. To explore ideas and problems collaboratively with students, to see them assume responsibility for their work, for their peers, for their communities large and small, and to witness their ownership of their learning are all testaments for why curriculum integration works and is an essential practice for middle level education. While the idea appears simple, I recognize that providing students with this much responsibility for their learning is not easy. I hope organizing my thoughts around the triangle of curriculum development (curriculum, instruction, and assessment) may help shed some light on why I feel this practice works and is so vital to student success.

Developing Curriculum

First, it is important to understand how we develop curriculum with our students. Our team is made up of three teachers (certified in the four main disciplines combined) who teach approximately sixty-five sixth, seventh, and eighth grade students in multiage groupings for a three-year cycle. In this setting, we intentionally develop curriculum collaboratively with students. At the beginning of each year, we invite our students to create questions about themselves and their world. We model for students what makes a good question so students spend time considering deep, meaningful, questions that are not simply answered with a yes or a no. Developing questions is a homework assignment, in which we hope to encourage some interesting conversations at home with family or on the bus with peers. Each night, students are responsible for developing one set of ten questions: ten about themselves the first night and ten about their world the next night.

Following this nightly homework, students are organized into multiage, mixed-gender groups to share their questions and identify eight to ten common questions. Following the small-group work, the class meets as a team, and each group presents their common questions. Students begin to see threads of commonality between their "self" and "world" questions.

At this point we, as teachers, introduce the broad state content standards that we are expected to address in this year of our three-year cycle. We immediately recognize the students' questions that connect to the standards. If the standards elicit questions that students didn't generate, those are added.

The students sort the questions around big common ideas, and, together, we create our themes for the year. Students work in small groups to create interesting titles and discuss how they would demonstrate their learning for each theme in some kind of culminating event. Working backward, we and the students plan and organize activities, gather resources, fine-tune the questions, and finally, coordinate each theme with the year's calendar, taking into account duration, time of year, and resource availability. This entire process consumes the first three or four weeks of the school year.

By inviting students to think about questions they have about themselves and their world, we create an environment that instantly engages kids. We create a dynamic of collaboration and mutual respect among students and with teachers. The Alpha process eliminates the us/them dichotomy that can easily develop between teachers and students in traditional classrooms. As a result, as teachers, we rarely have to respond to "Why do we have to do this?" This student decision making certainly helps with student participation and classroom management. I'm not saying we have perfect angels in our classrooms; we have our share of behavior and motivation challenges. But they are on a smaller scale and occur less often because of the nature and organization of student decision making on our team.

Fitting Standards into Curriculum
The challenge we have as teachers each year is answering these two questions:

1. How do we reconcile content standards and performance expectations with the students' chosen questions about self and world?
2. How do we do curriculum integration and still hold our students accountable for learning content-specific standards and prepare them for success on standardized tests?

To address the standards, we outline the broad content standards we are accountable for teaching in our three-year cycle. There is a balance in each year of science and social studies standards. Literacy content standards are woven throughout all the student-chosen themes.

Asking students questions about self and world first in our process honors their thoughts, ideas, questions, and concerns and makes the subject matter instantly relevant. By intentionally introducing the standards later in the process, students see that there is an inherent connection between what they *want* to know and what they are *expected* to learn. It is validating for them and for us. Students' questions are fresh and current, inviting new perspectives to standards that reflect current issues, concerns, and events. No two themes in our cycles from year to year have ever been exactly the same.

What I find equally compelling is the universality and depth of student questions. Modeling this process with students from inner-city Philadelphia to rural Vermont shows students' questions mirror large social issues and concerns regardless of background, ethnicity, and socioeconomic status. Students have a lot on their minds: poverty, health care, natural resources, the environment, war/conflict, religions, technology, earth, the universe, economics, life cycles. Clearly, there is rich content here that has meaning for all members of the learning community.

Students are passionate at this age, and they have a lot to think about, a tremendous amount of information coming at them from all directions and sources. They need their learning to have meaning for them. As educators, we feel an obligation and responsibility to teach what the state mandates and standardized tests evaluate. We have been addressing this balance on Alpha for years, and our students achieve well on tests. Our students' results on standardized tests are comparable to or better than their peers from more traditional settings. Most important, our students are well prepared for high school and beyond. They are active thinkers who ask meaningful questions about their learning.

Instruction

Curriculum integration inherently creates a differentiated learning classroom. Inviting students to design and implement curriculum they helped create addresses various student learning styles from the start. We have the flexibility to organize students in many different groupings, and we work to vary these groupings often—another aspect of a differentiated classroom. Our roles as teacher are also varied.

A common misconception often associated with student-centered classrooms is that "teacher-as-facilitator" means we don't ever deliver curriculum. Because we move from theme to theme, our roles as teachers change accordingly. At times we act as facilitator, coach, or manager. But we also act as leaders and can deliver an aspect of curriculum in a more traditional manner when we believe that is needed. This theme variation affects students' roles as well. At times, they are expected to be more independent; at other times, more collaborative with their peers; and often, a participant in the classroom with the teacher.

Our classrooms remain vibrant and engaging. The simple act of inviting student questions fuels pure energy in the classroom and encourages student cooperation that's necessary to make education meaningful and enduring.

Meaningful Assessment

Three times a year, at the end of each trimester, our students put together a portfolio that is organized around Alpha's five vital results:

- communication
- functioning independently
- reasoning and problem solving
- personal development
- civic and social responsibility

For the first trimester, students collect their work from all aspects of their learning (on the team, in Unified Arts, and outside school) and then sort that work as evidence of how they have met these vital results. For example, a piece of writing might be evidence of communication, functioning independently, or personal development. Students decide which category their pieces fit into. They receive guidance from their peers and teachers on how to best categorize their work.

During conferences in November, students present their portfolio to their parents. Students identify areas of success and challenge from the trimester's work, and together with their teacher and their parents set goals for the next trimester based on evident challenges. The process for the March portfolio conference is the same, except that students match their "vital results" with the goals set from the November conference. Students complete a portfolio for the end of the year that goes home with them over the summer.

It would take an entire book to explain the benefits and empowerment that the portfolio process brings to students. Student self-assessment is an invaluable part of our program, in tandem with our curriculum development. The portfolio provides a safe, organized, and manageable vehicle for new sixth graders and advanced eighth graders to speak openly and honestly about their work. Early in the year they see failures or challenges as opportunities for new learning. They see for themselves, with hard evidence from their trimester's work, where they were successful, and can identify what they did specifically to create that success. This self-assessment has far more impact on who they are as learners than a letter grade or a percentage score. Our reporting process includes student and teacher narratives on students' successes and challenges in each vital result area. This, with local and standard assessment results, provides the assessment profile for each student. Alpha students speak differently about how they learn. The differences in their learning from their previous experiences are noticeable, and they are the greatest advocates for themselves and this process because they speak genuinely, articulately, and openly about learning.

Questions and Answers

During the fall of 2005, a small group of Alpha students were invited to make a presentation to a University of Vermont class of preservice teachers. Students explained the curriculum process and their portfolios, and as always, they were far more articulate in their explanation than I would have been. One preservice teacher posed a question in relation to the curriculum development process: "But what if your questions never get answered?" A seventh grader paused, pondered, and very thoughtfully replied, "Well, my questions change all the time." To me this response spoke volumes. It is certainly important for students to *have* answers and equally important for them to *find* answers. Finding answers comes from asking questions and continuing to ask and revise questions to meet the needs of a given task. Students are infinite in their ability to think, wonder, and imagine. Their thoughts and questions are deep, rich, provocative, compelling, and relevant. Though not easy, this process is simple. It keeps my evolution as a teacher always fresh, interesting, and enjoyable.

Cynthia Myers' Story

I transferred onto the Alpha team ten years ago after having taught family/consumer sciences and general science, both in more traditional settings. I am grateful for the chance to become part of this very special program; it has been a peak teaching experience. The Alpha program, supported for over thirty years by the community, parents, master teachers, and administration, fosters best practice for optimum learning for all. The curriculum is student centered, is connected to real-world experiences, is a testing ground for new ideas and technologies, and models and helps students build skills needed for a democratic society while maintaining high academic standards.

Alpha Students' Stories

Our students appreciate the program and frequently write about their experiences in high school and college applications. One former Alpha student wrote in his college application:

> As Robert Fulgham said, "All I Ever Needed to Know I Learned in Kindergarten." But I must have been a late bloomer because everything I know I learned in Alpha. The relationship between teachers and students is unique. The students refer to themselves as family, and there is a strong sense of community. In Alpha, I learned to evaluate my work and myself and then set personal and academic goals. I also learned to lead groups of students big and small. Alpha stressed the importance of community, responsibility, and leadership. The Alpha experience taught me principles I use every day in high school. My abilities to self-assess, lead others, and set priorities, while maintaining balance, have been instrumental to my success.

The teaching of young adolescents brings great joy and rewards. They have taught me to be a leader, a mentor, a friend, and sometimes an expert. I have also learned that each child is fragile and filled with self-doubt and wants to be valued and respected. I have found that when I have a personal relationship with a student, it leads to them wanting to do well and feeling comfortable to take risks. One seventh-grade girl commented,

> I remember in sixth grade how nervous and small I felt. I was placed in your theme group: "Evolution." I also remember how kind and encouraging you were and how great it felt to come into that classroom every day. I have many more memories like this, and in all of them you remained caring and helpful. When I think of school I think of your warm smile and great attitude. You understand that different people work at different paces and incorporate it into the way we learn. You also understand we have lots of stuff going on outside of school and you help us manage our time.

Being part of the Alpha learning experience builds resiliency for teachers and especially for students. Each fall students become designers of their own learning by linking their questions to the Vermont state standards. They help develop activities and assessments that drive our integrated thematic units each year. Designing units this way makes the work vibrant and relevant. The learning is connected, making it easier to master. Students are motivated to learn and make connections between what they learn in school and their everyday lives. Students are not confined to the boundaries of a subject, and their achievement is maximized. Alpha has many community-building events and leadership opportunities built into the curriculum. Many of these occur outside the school day.

An eighth-grade girl who was on an Individualized Educational Plan described her experiences on the team camping trip. "When we got to the campsite, it was like we were a family laughing and working hard to get a job done. We did everything that a family would do. We slept and ate together. It is something I can't fully explain, it's just there in my heart and in my eyes."

Mission X is a program created by eighth graders nine years ago as a way for them to pass on what they found important and meaningful about the Alpha program to the new students on the team. One eighth grade girl described her experience this way:

> I was nervous for Mission X. The previous year in seventh grade it had been such a special night for me. I wanted to make sure that it was special for the new seventh graders this year. Last year I was sad to see my eighth grade friends leave but being in eighth grade has been the best yet. I liked giving seventh graders advice and helping them understand. It was amazing to watch everyone come together for such a serious and solemn ceremony. It made me proud that I had participated in such a meaningful night. As I enter high school, I know Alpha will stay with me and help me along my future journeys.

Parents' Perspectives
Building strong relationships with parents is key to supporting student success. We encourage parent involvement and have designed many

212

vehicles to encourage open communication. This helps foster understanding and build trust. We know that many Alpha parents feel pressure from other parents who wonder how Alpha students are prepared for high school and grading. Parents can be and are some of our strongest advocates. The support carries on with some even after their child leaves the school. They also give us feedback to help us make the program better.

Here are some comments by parents of Alpha students:

> "High school teachers can pick out the Alpha students because they are organized and ask good questions to help with their learning. They approach learning differently."
>
> "My son knows how to look at his work and find both his strengths and areas he needs to improve."
>
> "They don't work for a grade so their learning goes beyond normal expectations."

Holly Pasackow is a parent who has had a child on the Alpha team for the past nine years. She shares her reflections:

> I have had the good fortune to have my third child "graduate" from the eighth grade at Shelburne Community School. Over the past sixteen years my children have been sprinkled throughout the educational system. I have spent a lot of time, energy, joy, and heartbreak in the halls of our schools. Nine of those years have been spent with a child on Alpha. Amazing. Awesome. Incredible.
>
> On Alpha, my family has seen three teachers come and go, one to reassignment to a lower grade, one to retirement, and the third to another district. We have worked with numerous paraprofessionals and student interns, all who have added to the history of Alpha. We have been there with many dedicated families who believed in their children, and in our children, and in Alpha. We have been one of the fortunate families who have been a part of something bigger than middle school and bigger than public school. These incredible teachers, students, and families believe in community, and they have been willing to be the village that collectively raised all the children on Alpha. Imagine taking on the responsibility of raising sixty adolescents, year after year.

The landscape in Alpha has changed, some of it for the better and some—not. Through these changes my family and I have stretched ourselves and dug down deeply to integrate those changes with our family values: what we know; what we believe; and what our hopes are in regard to our children, their needs, their growth and development, as well as their education. Despite the changes and the pressures from all the different factors that make public school education so special, Alpha remains true to form: it really is all about the students—all the kids, not just mine. If the community continues to focus on the kids, the world will be a better place.

Alpha is big, much bigger than just a middle level team at Shelburne Community School. Alpha is bigger than its dedicated professionals and paraprofessionals past and present. Alpha is about the students, their families, and their community, from yesterday, today, and into tomorrow. Alpha is about many, many, many students. I am proud and privileged to have been a part of Alpha over the years and so pleased and relieved to know my fourth child will have the opportunity to be a part of something so big.

The Power of Caring Relationships

Working with ten- to fourteen-year-olds has taught me that small acts of personal interaction are so important. Often I don't even remember saying or doing something that nevertheless made a difference in someone's learning. When I get positive feedback, it makes me want to live up to students' expectations, and I am constantly humbled by their esteem. We who choose to work with middle school students have a chance to make a difference when children are struggling with who they are as a learner and a person trying to build a life without regret. I cherish the special relationship with students. It is teacher/student, yes, but also something very close to friendship. Their trust is inspiring. A former Alpha student writes,

During sixth period, you sat down with me and Morgan to talk about the book we were reading, *Monster*. I know I had work to do, and I'm sure you did too, but you took the time to just talk. We assumed the boy was innocent, and you showed us some parts in the book that made us question that. This is exactly what you gave to me; the ability to question and be bold. I thank you for your never-failing ability to be my friend, not just my teacher.

The profession of teaching is complex and challenging. We have a huge responsibility as the cognitive and emotional link to the hearts and minds of emerging adolescents. Serving children is a productive way to ensure a better society. As middle school educators, we are given a chance to make a difference in the lives of young people. Alpha students make a quilt each year to fund their team-building camping trip; similarly, the teachers help create something lasting, colorful, beautiful, and whole from each different small piece of the Alpha fabric.

Our greatest rewards are intrinsic: watching the spark of light in her eyes when a student discovers the world of ideas and learning. There is great joy that cannot be measured but must be seen or felt. The payoff is that by nourishing young minds and spirits we, as teachers, reap the rewards of doing something that is meaningful and fulfilling. An eighth-grade boy sums up his feelings about Alpha this way:

I have seen myself change physically and emotionally. I can't say I'm much taller, but I definitely got more mature. From sixth grade when I was so short and shy doing my best to try and understand what was going on, to a mature young adult trying to be the best leader I can be. I don't think I would be the same if I hadn't been on Alpha. I came here a young kid, and I am leaving a capable young adult who feels he was offered all the opportunities in the world, because of what Alpha gave to him.

An eighth-grade girl shared these feelings:

Throughout all of the three years I've been on Alpha, I have never wanted to leave. I liked where and who I was. All good things must come to an end. It is time for me to go. I would be holding myself back if I didn't. I need to face new obstacles and people. I will always have a place for Alpha in my heart and it will keep growing. Even though I may not physically be in Alpha, I can carry my leadership, communication, and skills wherever I go.

Nothing is more special than spending three years in a young person's life watching him or her grow from a shy sixth grader into a responsible adolescent ready to take on life's challenges.

Summing Up Alpha

The Alpha team did not begin because a principal, superintendent, or school board demanded that a group of teachers implement this kind of learning with students. It began because a teacher had a vision of how students learn. She believed in the fundamental idea of a democratic classroom, that students learn more and better when invested in their own work, that students have a right to have a voice in their own education. Alpha continues because of the passion of teachers like Meghan and Cynthia.

Carol Smith (2001) taught on the Alpha team for twenty-five years. She has this to say about the program:

> We have touched the lives of more than 1,000 students who are now in high schools, colleges, and out in the world with careers of their own. Some of them are teachers, some of them work in politics and government and health care. Some are artists. Some are craftsmen and -women. Many of them are raising families. Despite their differences and distances now, they come from common roots—a shared educational experience in their middle grade years that honored them as learners and supported their growth as individuals. (37)

Soundings: An Eighth Grade Curriculum Integration Experience

Mark Springer has taught at Radnor Middle School, in Wayne, Pennsylvania, for approximately twenty-five years. In 1986, Mark and his colleague Ed Silcox initiated an interdisciplinary learning experience called Watershed with seventh graders at Radnor. The entire year was based on studying local watersheds, the theme chosen by teachers that drove learning for social studies, science, mathematics, and language arts. Forty seventh graders conducted most of their learning in the outdoors as they studied all components of the watershed, from the history and geography of the area to in-depth water quality investigations. Watershed continues to be a meaningful interdisciplinary experience for seventh graders at Radnor Middle School. Mark describes the Watershed program in a nationally known book, *Watershed: A Successful Voyage into Integrative Learning*, published by the National Middle School Association in 1994.

Mark and Ed continued to coteach the Watershed program themselves for approximately twelve years. Nevertheless, they both wanted to expand the opportunity for curriculum integration, both for students at other grade levels and for more seventh graders, based on other themes reflecting the students' needs and interests. Mark's conversations with progressive educators such as James Beane, Barb Brodhagen, Ed Brazee, and Gert Nesin were an added incentive to leave Watershed in the hands of other educators and develop a student-designed curriculum.

In 1998, Mark implemented a fully student-designed curriculum with eighth graders. He called the new program Soundings. Mark describes the reason for choosing the name:

> The word *soundings* connotes probing and measuring depth, and the Soundings program encourages students to explore the topics they study deeply. The name also refers to the sounds of students who have a voice in their own education and opportunities to share their learning with their community. Finally, just as whales *sound* for fresh air, students and teachers in this program are revitalized and refreshed as they experience the benefits of the program's self-directed, integrated curriculum. (Brown 2002a, 54)

As in the Alpha program in Vermont, in the Soundings program these eighth graders determine the curriculum based on their questions about themselves and the world. We asked Mark to provide his perspective on the program.

Mark Springer's Perspectives

Every middle school teacher should know that there are viable alternatives to the conventional curricular formats used in most schools serving young adolescents. What is more, some of these alternatives can better serve our students because they more closely fulfill characteristics that research has shown improve learning.

For the past twenty years I have been implementing student-centered curriculum integration practices in the Watershed and Soundings programs at Radnor Middle School, in Wayne, Pennsylvania. Curriculum integration (CI) is purposefully designed around the needs of young adolescents, and it uses their questions as the essential organizing principle driving curricular content and pedagogy. As a result, CI empowers students to take charge of their learning, which, in turn, provides students with both the vested interest and a meaningful context for learning. Because they have asked the questions important to them, the students want to discuss possible answers; this enables students to approach required skills and standards as means to that self-determined goal. In addition, this approach establishes and reinforces the validity of the students' questions and concerns, thus giving them confidence in their cognitive abilities and a willingness to push themselves even further.

Having witnessed amazing growth of young adolescents who experienced curriculum integration practices, I believe success stems in part from the atmosphere promoted by CI. By definition, the CI learning community is a truly democratic one and supportive of each individual—a claim most traditional, teacher-directed classrooms cannot make. Students empowered to determine their curriculum start to see themselves in a different light from those in conventional curricula. These young adolescents see themselves in a working partnership with their mentor-teachers and with each other. They are being invited to share in the decision-making process, rather than being told what to do. One student, Mike, put it this way: "Since we determined these guidelines, I feel that this is the most fair and just school environment that I've ever been part of." This climate fosters respect, a shared sense of purpose, and a level of personal security and support that allows young adolescents to move beyond their comfort zones to take the academic risks necessary for deep learning. As another of my Soundings students, Megan, once said, "The program gives us a great responsibility and gives us motivation to do things well." To which Stephanie added: "I can already feel my self-confidence increasing. The deep discussions and issues being brought up in class are so much more advanced and intriguing that I feel I must share my thoughts."

Sentiments such as these, expressed every year by students in Watershed and Soundings, are indicative of a learning environment that promotes exploration, questioning, discussion, and constructive debate. In such a milieu, most students show some accelerated growth in reading and writing skills, as well as information acquisition, because their interest and commitment levels are heightened through the process of curriculum integration. Equally important, however, are the democratic skills and attitudes that the students learn through firsthand experience with curriculum integration.

Schools often talk about democracy, but they tend to be the least democratic institutions in our nation. Every middle school teacher should know that there are ways to put democratic ideals into practice. Curriculum integration is not easy; neither is democracy. The two go hand in hand, however, and I would argue that the future of democracy in America may well be decided in our public schools over the next few decades.

Concluding Remarks About Soundings

Mark Springer is another teacher who has chosen to help young adolescents demonstrate the depth of their cognitive abilities and their curiosity about life through self-directed learning via curriculum integration. Like many other teachers, his experimentation with alternative curricular experiences started early in his career. His development of Soundings is evidence of Mark's continuing professional development and understanding about how teachers can positively affect their students' lives through curriculum integration and democratic classrooms. You can read more about Mark Springer's program in his book *Soundings: A Democratic Student-Centered Education*, published by the National Middle School Association in 2006.

Starting with Our Little Corner

Gert Nesin embraced the curriculum integration model in 1992 while teaching in Maine. Throughout her years as a middle school teacher, she created democratic classrooms that included collaboratively planning curriculum with students. She currently teaches at the University of Maine where she uses that model in creating curriculum with her college students.

Gert Nesin's Journey

When I started practicing integrative curriculum in 1992, I was a teacher at a small, rural, traditional school—Caravel Middle School, in Carmel, Maine. I was teaching math, social studies, computer, and art to students. In those first years, our collaborative planning process revolved around social studies themes I determined, such as Conflict, Balancing Economy, and Environment in Maine. I continued the work at Shapleigh Middle School, in Kittery, Maine.

Since it was my ideal situation—working on a partner team with my sister, Janet Nesin Reynolds, and approximately forty students—we incorporated the curriculum planning process proposed by James Beane (1990). In addition to middle schools, I have also incorporated integrative curriculum at the college level, first teaching at the University of Georgia and, since 2002, at the University of Maine. At the college level, the parameters and processes of curriculum integration are different, but the intention and philosophy—democratic classrooms and collaborative planning of meaningful curriculum, instruction, and assessment—remain constant.

When I started teaching, I made all the decisions about teaching and learning without significant input from students. It was how I was taught through school and college, and I never knew there was or should be any alternative. My students and I were mostly successful because of the caring relationships we developed. I chose to start including students in the process of learning when I took a class, based on John Dewey's *Experience and Education* (1938), that opened my eyes to the idea that students could learn better and more when content started with their experiences, interests, and concerns. I tried it that school year with one group of students, and it really worked! It was reinforced the following summer when I watched James Beane and Barb Brodhagen plan curriculum with students in Maine. At that point, I began to connect with a network of educators who believe in the value and dignity of all students in the learning process and in society. Since then, I have never considered returning to teacher-centered education.

Standards never disappear in my college or middle school classrooms. At the beginning of our time together, I make sure students understand that there is required content, which we spend time looking at and defining. As we plan learning, we carefully include knowledge and process standards on which we will focus. Those standards become the substance that helps them answer their questions rather than an end in themselves.

College students and young adolescents respond similarly to collaboratively achieving common learning goals. At first they are hesitant to believe that they truly do have significant input into the content and direction of their own education. They look for manipulation, unstated expectations, and hoops. When students finally figure out that no hidden agenda exists, they relax and get down to the business and fun of learning together. Some students, usually the individuals who have been successful in more traditional classrooms, hold on to their skepticism further into the school year.

After a year of integrative curriculum, most of my students have changed in significant ways. Probably more important than any other outcome I've observed is that students think they matter, both personally and as part of a learning community. Their ideas, concerns, and talents are valued and they are supported in their challenges. Every student becomes part of the community, with all of his or her abilities and disabilities.

I have also seen many other important changes. The students become expert in how they learn. They become skilled at the process of making decisions that work for individuals while also considering and meeting the needs of diverse group members. They learn content in depth, and they learn how to apply it in important ways. They figure out how they can make a difference in their classrooms, schools, communities, and the world. They become effective researchers—finding, evaluating, understanding, and synthesizing a variety of primary and secondary resources and reaching logical conclusions. They find confidence in who they are and their abilities and contributions. Given significant choice and input, they take responsibility for their learning and behavior. These changes are especially pronounced for students who usually flounder in school, academically and/or behaviorally.

Students overwhelming approve of integrative curriculum. Seventh-grade students in Kittery anonymously responded to the question "What are the benefits of being in this class?" in the following ways:

> "I learned to think about what I am going to do when I get older and choices I have."
> "We learned to be more independent."
> "I've become more responsible, and I've learned how to get involved in activities and stay committed to them."
> "I've gained more knowledge about different topics in my class than I probably would in any other. Our program is more 'advanced' than other classes."
> "I think I do my homework more, and school is more interesting."

As a teacher, I find benefits that improve my teaching and me as a person. Teaching becomes a process of solving problems *with* students rather than dispensing knowledge *to* them. We're all in it together, and I mostly get to enjoy them and their learning rather than finding a way to force them to do what I perceive as best for them. I am absolved of the sole responsibility of being the one who creates interesting and engaging learning activities, since the students share that responsibility. I help students build relationships with one another, me, other adults, and the larger community. I can truly know who they are and what makes a difference to them. For me, I have felt most privileged to watch students who think little of themselves and their abilities realize that they are competent and valuable. Working with students to develop meaningful relationships and learning experiences gives me hope that we can create a better world, starting with our little corner.

Concluding Reflections

The Alpha teams, the students in the Soundings program, Gert Nesin's two-person team—these are different classrooms with different structures, yet the philosophy underlying all of them is the same. They are all based on the belief that the most effective and powerful learning occurs in a democratic classroom in which all involved are given a voice. These classrooms are designed around the philosophy and belief that students have a right to a voice in their learning and that teachers have an obligation to honor that right by listening to what students have to say.

In these classrooms, significant learning is occurring and students are performing well on high-stakes tests. But more importantly, these students are attaining meaningful learning, using thinking processes daily, and living by democratic values that will carry them through life. In interviews, several former Soundings students from three separate years noted that by participating in curriculum integration, they made significant growth in their creative and critical thinking, decision-making, and problem-solving abilities (Brown and Morgan 2003). They also believed that their oral communication skills and ability to work well with others developed better in Soundings than they would have in a traditional classroom.

These former Soundings students mentioned the following as memorable experiences of curriculum integration:

- selecting topics to learn throughout the year
- expressing their beliefs about topics discussed
- working collaboratively in groups
- thinking and learning independently
- becoming more intimate with teachers and students
- exploring topics in greater depth than in traditional classrooms (Brown and Morgan 2003, 17)

With an insight reflective of adult maturity, one student revealed the following about learning via curriculum integration: "Standardized tests are not designed for the kind of thinking we do in Soundings" (28). That testimony alone should be enough encouragement for many more middle level educators to make the transition to curriculum integration teaching and learning.

It seems that many educators, and parents as well, are concerned that if students spend a year or two in a curriculum integration classroom during middle school, they will not be prepared for the traditional curricular experiences and academic expectations of high school. Two Soundings students who were in their junior year of high school when interviewed refuted that unfounded belief with these comments:

> I remember thinking how ridiculous that people would think that Soundings wouldn't prepare you for high school. I think Soundings prepared me better for high school than regular classes would have. I was bored in regular classes in ninth grade—I mean, did someone think the information we're learning this way [teacher directed] was supposed to stick?

> I may have been better prepared because of writing and research skills. Soundings also helped me to be self-motivated—something you need in high school. (Brown and Morgan 2003, 27)

Middle school educators can play a large role in helping students know themselves as learners and as people. Teachers can make all the excuses they can think of for not implementing these kinds of student-directed learning experiences. The truth is, *you* can make your classroom more democratic, and *you* can give students a voice in how the classroom is structured. You just need to use your courage and your willingness to take risks as a professional educator and begin.

TEN

Altering School Structures

In the ideal middle school, we'd have soda and snack machines. You could have your choice of lunches instead of horsemeat. Classes could be twenty-five minutes long. We'd have a free class where you could do whatever you want as long as you get your work done. Classes wouldn't be as boring. We'd have no lectures, and we'd have recess after lunch.

JUSTIN, EIGHTH GRADER

There is now evidence that middle schools demonstrating high levels of implementation of the eight Turning Points recommendations show positive results across the core curriculum. This means understanding the importance of supporting structures such as interdisciplinary teams and taking these very seriously.

TOM ERB (2000, 5)

Responding to the needs of the young adolescent requires that we face the challenging tasks of reevaluating current curriculum models and instructional strategies. We've suggested that the most appropriate middle school curriculum is one that focuses on the questions and concerns that students have about themselves and their world; one in which students collaborate with teachers in

developing themes for study; are the driving force in developing ways to best explore those themes; and make decisions about what and how information should be studied.

Implementing a curriculum design that focuses on student concerns and values student-centered instruction necessitates making changes in the structure and organization of the school day. Early adolescents' needs for movement and socialization, as well as their desires to be known and valued, also have implications for how staff, time, space, and resources are used. A number of structures have been implemented in exemplary middle schools to respond to student needs: teaming, advisory programs, alternative scheduling, exploratory curriculum, and looping.

Teaming—The Heart and Soul of the Middle School Concept

Teaming is often considered the most vital aspect of the middle school structural design and an identifying feature of true middle schools. The need for alternate educational structures was identified more than thirty years ago when William Alexander, a prominent figure in the early middle school movement, called for "a fundamentally different kind of organization utilizing team teaching and some aspects of a nongraded structure to provide a much richer experience for all the children" (Alexander 1998, 26).

The use of teaming has increased dramatically in the past thirty years, most significantly after the publication of the Carnegie Council's original *Turning Points* (1989). From the council's first recommendation—"School should be a place where close, trusting relationships with adults and peers create a climate for personal growth and intellectual development" (37)—came two specific suggestions that advocate the use of teams to transform middle level education.

> First, the enormous middle grade school must be restructured in a more human scale. The student should, upon entering middle grade school, join a small community in which people—students and adults—get to know each other well to create a climate for intellectual development. Students should feel that they are part of a community of shared educational purpose.

226

Second, the discontinuity in expectations and practices among teachers, the lack of integration of subject matter, and the instability of peer groups must be reduced. Every student must be able to rely on a small, caring group of adults who work closely with each other to provide coordinated, meaningful, and challenging educational experiences. In turn, teachers must have the opportunity to get to know every one of their students well enough to understand and teach them as individuals. Every student must have the opportunity to know a variety of peers, some of them well. (37)

The Carnegie Council specifically recommended that middle schools change by "creating smaller learning environments, forming teachers and students into teams and assigning an adult advisor to each student" (37). The authors of *Turning Points 2000* (Jackson and Davis 2000) added, "Large schools should be divided into smaller learning communities, with teams of teachers and students as the underlying organizational structure. Schools should also attend to critical issues affecting team success, such as team size, composition, time for planning, and continuity" (24).

The rationale for the development of teams focused on the problems inherent in the traditional structure of middle level schools—a departmentalized system based on the factory model (see Chapter 4). When students change classes every forty-two minutes for six to eight periods a day and are continually confronted with a new teacher and a new group of students, the close relationships that are so important for the young adolescent are more difficult to develop. The departmentalized, separate-subject model also provides little opportunity for students to make sense out of the curricular material or to integrate knowledge across subject boundaries.

The team solution organizes teachers and students into small groups. The most predominant structure consists of four teachers from the four major content areas (math, science, language arts, and social studies) who have shared responsibility for 100 to 125 students and are empowered to make decisions about what is best for these students. The students move from teacher to teacher with the same group of peers throughout the school day.

In many middle schools, the team teachers serve as subject specialists. Much of their curricular decision making throughout the school year reflects the dictated state or local mandates for their areas of expertise. Often, however, teachers are able to correlate topics so that ideas studied in one subject area complement what goes on in another area. An example of such "parallel" teaching, as described in Chapter 6, is the study of the Revolutionary War in history class correlated with the reading of *Johnny Tremain* (Forbes 1944) in language arts.

Well-functioning teams and teams that have common planning times have the opportunity to move beyond the departmentalized approach and engage in collaborative planning. Teachers may develop multidisciplinary thematic units that involve all teachers on the team. These themes are chosen by teachers, and each teacher determines how his or her subject area can contribute to the study of that topic. The most powerful use of the teaming concept, however, is in the context of curriculum integration (see Chapter 6), when themes are chosen and units developed collaboratively with students. The boundaries between subject areas dissolve, and team teachers ask not how their subject area expertise can contribute to the theme topic but how they can best facilitate student learning.

Some middle schools use teams comprising two teachers and a smaller number of students. The advantage of the smaller teams is fewer students for teachers to get to know. As Nesin and Brazee (2005) explained, "In small teams it becomes easier to know and act on individuals' learning styles, challenges, and strengths" (43). Others add a fifth member to the four-person teams, such as a reading teacher or special-subject instructor (for example, music, art, physical education). In some schools, multigrade teams are developed with seventh and eighth graders on the same team and often in the same classes. Team structures can be as varied as the students they serve. Decisions about teaming should be made after considering space, time, staffing, and student demographic issues.

Less than 10 percent of middle schools in the late 1960s were using a team structure (McEwin 1997). This amount had increased by the late 1980s to about 33 percent and by 1993 more than 59 percent of middle schools were using this approach. Still, despite teaming, "in the majority of all middle level schools, departmentalization continues to dominate—isolating teachers, fragmenting curriculum and letting thousands of young adolescents 'fall through the cracks'" (McEwin 1997, 322).

Benefits of Teaming

Benefits to Students

> The best thing about school is that in some ways I like the teams. I know my teachers and like being with other grades. The teachers get close to you.
>
> MEG, EIGHTH GRADER

In order to be an effective organizational scheme, teaming must produce a learning environment that meets the needs of middle level students. Can teaming, when implemented correctly, support the young adolescent's growth toward independence by providing a means to enhance cognitive growth, nurture emotional growth, enable social growth, and recognize the realities of physical growth?

Curriculum and instruction are most definitely enhanced by the effective use of interdisciplinary teams. We have already discussed how thematic teaching helps students make connections across subject areas, thus avoiding the fragmentation that is often experienced in a departmentalized structure. Learning can be integrated throughout the school day, with each teacher providing specific content and skills to help students explore significant themes. In addition, collaboration with students increases motivation and enthusiasm for learning.

When teams have some control over the class schedule, students have the opportunity to explore ideas for longer periods of time. Flexibility in teaming allows for time to engage in the in-depth research, analysis, and project development that is difficult using a traditional approach.

Teaming helps nurture emotional growth in two ways. First, the team approach helps students cultivate closer relationships with teachers and with one another. Students begin to develop a sense of belonging and community that enhances their own personal identity. Students know that there is always an adult they can turn to for assistance. Second, teachers develop a better understanding of student needs. Teachers are able to discuss individual student concerns at team meetings, analyze problems, and develop solutions to better meet the needs of each child. In departmentalized middle schools, collaborating with colleagues about student needs is difficult because of time restrictions and isolation of both teachers and students.

When students spend the entire day with a single group of peers, they have more of an opportunity to develop close relationships with them. Teachers can involve students in cooperative activities and encourage social interactions. Peer relationships are thereby improved.

Teachers who have control over the scheduling of classes and instructional strategies are better able to respond to the physical needs of young adolescents. When students are in forty-two-minute-long classes, teachers often feel pressured to meet curricular deadlines. They may feel that they don't have time either to allow students the freedom of movement they need or to discuss young adolescent health and personal concerns that are often central to students. Teaming allows more time for varied instructional strategies that focus on active learning, not only enhancing cognitive growth but responding to students' physical needs. Middle level schools with a high commitment to interdisciplinary teaming have significantly stronger academic programs (Epstein and Mac Iver 1990).

Building a team identity is an important aspect of developing a team community. Forte and Schurr (2002) suggested thirty activities that support building a team identity; among them are:

team name/logo/mascot/colors/slogan
team decorations for door, hallways, rooms
team newspaper/newsletter
team rules and codes of conduct
team intramurals
team meals
team T-shirts

team song
talent shows, spirit days, dress-up days
cleanup days, community projects (110)

This is a beginning list that you and other team members can add to based on your interests as well as your students' interests.

Benefits to Teachers

While the benefits of teaming are clear for students in terms of both cognitive growth and school climate, teachers also reap rewards from this structure. For many teachers, teaming improves the work climate and lessens the isolation that often exists in self-contained classrooms. Teaming reduces the fragmentation of learning from one discipline to another and allows teachers to coordinate assignments, testing schedules, classroom expectations, and classroom procedures. Through common planning time and team meetings, teachers can better serve the needs of students and deal proactively with problems (Forte and Schurr 2002).

Research indicates that teachers involved in teaming perceive that they participate more, have more opportunities for decision making, and experience more cooperation than teachers in traditional departmentalized settings (Walsh and Shay 1993). Teachers also believe that they are more supportive of students and more receptive to their needs and ideas. In contrast to teachers in traditional settings, teachers involved in teaming see their students as more motivated and involved.

Certainly teachers in schools that support a team concept experience less isolation than teachers in departmentalized schools. They can collaborate on instructional issues as well as share their concerns about students. As teachers become empowered to make more decisions about what's best for their students, morale is improved and a sense of increased professionalism permeates the school.

Instruction also becomes more effective. Teaming allows for diversity in teaching styles, flexibility in scheduling, and expansion of professional input. Improved relationships with students and parents are also apparent.

Drawbacks to Teaming

I don't have any idea why they have us on teams.

ROB, EIGHTH GRADER

In a perfect world, with a perfect school run by perfect administrators filled with perfect teachers, we would see perfect teams. These teams would be empowered by the administration to make curricular, instructional, and scheduling decisions for their students based on a shared vision of the purpose of education and their role as educators. They would have a common planning time in which decisions could be made and concerns discussed. Teachers would develop their strengths and rely on other teachers to support and nurture them.

But it's not a perfect world. As with any organizational structure, the promise of the team's benefits is at times overshadowed by the reality of its implementation. In the world that we live in, personalities clash, philosophical differences exist, teachers feel threatened, and planning time is limited. Some of the difficulties in teaming are the result of ineffective whole-school policies. Adequate planning time depends on the availability of shared space and time.

More difficult problems arise because of teachers' personalities, insecurities, inflexibilities, and fears. When a teacher becomes certified, that does not automatically ensure that he or she knows how to work with other professionals on a team. The most effective teams have had to work very hard to get where they are. Tuckman (1965) described four levels of team development. A good professional development program in a school can enhance and ensure the success of most teams as they work their way through these stages.

In stage one—*forming*—the team of teachers experiences the excitement of starting out on a venture that they believe will benefit students. The team seeks a purpose and a vision and works to build community.

Relationships are not always easily formed, hence the next step—*storming*. This stage arises as different personalities and differing philosophies about curriculum, instruction, discipline, and student expectations come into play among the members of the team. Poor communication skills may contribute to conflict. Teachers question their values and procedures and must learn how to meld personalities and differences into a system that works.

With good facilitation, during the next stage—*norming*—teachers can develop a clearer vision of the team goals and the role of each member in achieving those goals. Teachers begin to feel confident in their strengths while recognizing the strengths of the other teachers on the team. On the flip side, they become willing to acknowledge their weaknesses and learn how to accept the weakness of other team members. Ideally, they begin to see how their strengths and weaknesses can complement those of the other team members. Roles are defined, and trust between team members is achieved.

The team is then ready to act—this is the *performing* stage. Planning begins and choices are made. Members are committed to the vision of the team. In forming teams, teachers must learn to focus on students. It's a challenge replete with pitfalls. But as Erb (1997) commented, "Teams where teachers engage in dialogue about matters of mutual concern do reflect new levels of teacher interaction leading to the creation of novel solutions to educational problems" (39).

Successful teams are generally made up of a heterogeneous group of students with a strong team identity. In addition, the most successful teams have a balance in terms of teachers' expertise, age, gender, and race (K. Brown 2001). Brown noted that the best chance for successful teaming lies in the leadership of the team, with a formal team leader having specific responsibilities. Effective leadership involves being a liaison between administration and the team, communicating effectively with team members and administration, and keeping team goals in mind by being "task-oriented" (George and Alexander 1993, 293).

Another successful aspect of teaming is common planning time. Researchers found that common planning time was an important element that permitted teachers to focus on curriculum and instructional issues to better meet the needs of students in their classrooms (Flowers, Mertens, and Mulhall 2000). Hart et al. (2002) found that teamed teachers used their common planning time wisely in making decisions that affected students and the entire school.

Although teaming has the potential to enhance socialization, some students feel that it actually impedes their social interactions. Seventh grader Sheila didn't like the team concept at her school. "I don't get to see my friends very often. We're all mixed up on weird teams with eighth graders. Half of my friends are all the way across the school, and we only get to see each other during extra-help period. One of my best friends from last year I never get to see." LeAnne, a seventh grader at a different school, agrees. "I have to stay with the same seventy people all day long. I never get to see the people I got close to last year."

Another potential problem facing the use of teams relates to those students with special needs or diverse learning styles. Not all teachers work equally well with all students. Should we, in fact, be placing students on teams regardless of their specific learning needs or should we be choosing the teachers that will best respond to their needs? One eighth grader with special learning needs commented, "I don't like teaming. I have ADHD. My science teacher is okay, but I don't really get along with the rest of my teachers. I know there are probably other teachers in the school that would understand me better but they won't let me off team."

Incorporating the contribution of teachers of special subjects such as music, art, physical education, computer technology, and foreign languages presents another challenge to teaming. Teams do not usually include teachers of these subjects, because grade level teachers are best able to meet together when all of their students are attending classes with the music, art, or physical education teachers. Not including special-area teachers on the teams once again fragments student learning and may give the message to students that those classes are less important. Administrators must work to ensure that special-area teachers are a vital part of the overall planning process for students.

Frequently teams exist in name only. Although teachers may share students and at times are able to meet to discuss their concerns about them, middle level educators often remain subject bound, engrossed in their own area of expertise without regard to what the rest of the team is doing. If teaming is simply an organizational structure, the full benefits of this construct will not be obtained. If students are still sent through the day as in a factory, traveling from class to class on a rigid forty-two-minute schedule, with no integration throughout the school day, faculty may as well revert to the departmentalized model. Despite those drawbacks "teams provide friendship in a hostile world, a point of reference in the endless cycle of schools. Perhaps this is why inter-disciplinary teaming has become the key to the most effective middle schools" (Golner and Powell 1992, 32).

Advisory Programs

> The quality of the relationship between teachers and students is the single most important aspect of middle level education.
>
> VAN HOOSE (1991, 7)

> In our advisory, the topics we discussed were peer pressure, safety, how to stay away from drugs, and how to bring our careers together.
>
> MICHAEL, EIGHTH GRADER

> Only 39 percent (of middle school parents surveyed) felt that "There is an adult in this school who knows my child well and can offer advice and assistance."
>
> JOHNSTON AND WILLIAMSON
> (1998, 47; CITED IN ANFARA 2001, xvi)

When we look at the multitude of issues facing young adolescents, it is amazing that anyone gets through middle school without incurring some type of permanent emotional disorder. On a daily basis, young adolescents face:

- dealing with physical changes
- making new friends
- being a member of the "right" peer group
- developing independence from parents
- avoiding peer pressure
- going steady with boyfriends/girlfriends then breaking up
- finding a sexual, cultural, or ethnic identity
- being harassed by other students
- handling the pressures of academic demands

These can be and are stressful and anxiety-ridden events for many students. Nesin and Brazee (2005) added another valid reason for providing a supportive culture during the middle school years: "Effective curriculum, instruction, and assessment mean little if the environment in which both educators and young people work does not provide safety, caring, and support" (41).

Some middle schools develop advisory programs to provide the social and emotional support that young adolescents frequently need. The National Middle School Association (NMSA) identified advisor/advisee programs as an essential element of effective middle school design (2003). In addition, as you recall, the original Carnegie Council report focused on the need for teachers to develop close relationships with their students (1989). Specifically, the authors stated, "Every student needs at least one thoughtful adult who has the time and takes the trouble to talk with the student about academic matters, personal problems, and the importance of performing well in middle grade school" (37). This idea was supported in *Turning Points 2000*: "When students make a lasting connection with at least one caring adult, academic and personal outcomes improve" (Jackson and Davis 2000, 143).

Despite these endorsements, few middle schools have adopted advisory programs. Junior high and high schools initiated the homeroom period during the early twentieth century as a way of encouraging positive student-teacher relationships. Anyone who's been in school knows how innocuous and ineffective homeroom periods were in establishing relationships between teachers and students. In many middle schools, advisory programs haven't fared too well in becoming a reality. Several reports during the 1990s revealed that fewer than half of middle schools surveyed had developed advisory programs (Galassi, Gulledge, and Cox 1998a). George and Oldaker (1985), on the other hand, reported that of those schools identified as exemplary, 93 percent used advisory programs.

In an advisory program, an advisor (usually a teacher) meets with a small group of students on a regular basis for the primary purpose of helping students develop trusting relationships with an adult and close social bonds with a small group of classmates. Advisory sessions may be designed for student-to-student and student-to-teacher discussions about personal topics related to young adolescence. These sessions are essentially nonacademic, ungraded, and planned with young adolescents' social and emotional interests and needs in mind.

Advisory sessions can be designed in any number of flexible arrangements to meet the scheduling demands of each school. For instance, some schools have advisory sessions that meet once a week for thirty to forty-five minutes; other schools schedule advisory sessions twice a week; alternately, an advisory session may take place every day for fifteen to thirty minutes. A study by McEwin, Dickinson, and Jenkins (1996) revealed that in schools with advisory programs, most met daily, with the most common length being from sixteen to thirty minutes.

The time at which advisory sessions are offered and the length of the sessions may have an impact on the effectiveness of the programs in meeting students' needs. Sessions scheduled for the end of the school day may be perceived as of low priority; earlier scheduled sessions are more likely to be viewed as a priority by teachers and students. Short durations (less than fifteen minutes) may not provide adequate opportunity for students and teachers to engage in conversations that address students' social and emotional needs.

Students can be grouped with grade-level peers during advisory sessions. Some schools have multiage advisory sessions in which sixth, seventh, and eighth graders are grouped heterogeneously. The developmental differences among young adolescents at each grade level may lead to the belief that separating students by grade level would best meet the needs of the students. Data collected from middle level students in one study, however, indicated that the majority of students surveyed preferred cross-grade advisory groups (Ziegler and Mulhall 1994). An advantage of cross-grade advisory groups is the opportunity for younger students to become acquainted with and receive support and advice from the older students in the building.

In some schools, students remain with the same advisor and advisory group for their entire middle school career, providing increased opportunities for students and advisors to become well acquainted. Gill and Read (1990) reported that fifteen nationally recognized experts in middle level education suggested that students remain with their advisors for all of their middle level years. Students surveyed in one study indicated, however, their preference for changing advisors each year (Sardo-Brown and Shetlar 1994). Not surprisingly, students prefer to choose their own advisor and undoubtedly would like to have the opportunity to switch to a different advisor if they feel the need.

It is primarily teachers who serve as advisors, but to reduce the ratio of advisees to advisors, other professionals in the building, including counselors, administrators, librarians, and district specialists, are often assigned a group of advisees as well. Becoming a proficient advisor requires initial training and regular attention to the specifics of how to organize and deliver an effective program to students. Advisors must be willing to develop a relationship with students different from the one they experience as a regular classroom teacher—one characterized by caring, not authoritarianism (Cole 1992). James (1986) suggested that many students view their "advisor as more of a friend or advocate than a teacher" (53). The primary responsibility of the advisor is to provide a caring and nurturing relationship with students. The advisor must also work with guidance counselors to ensure that students are receiving the services or interventions they may need. The advisor becomes the advocate for the student's academic, personal, and social development (Forte and Schurr 2002).

The expectations for teachers to develop caring and trusting relationships with students and to be willing to discuss personal thoughts and feelings during an advisory session are frequent obstacles to obtaining teacher support for an advisory program (Galassi, Gulledge, and Cox 1998b). Some teachers are not comfortable with or accustomed to becoming socially and emotionally involved with their students. These teachers will struggle as advisors if not properly trained prior to the initiation of an advisory program. Despite some teachers' reluctance to become involved in advisory programs, MacLaury points out to teachers (2002) some advantages of participating in them.

Teacher-advisors often develop closer relations with students, which in turn may increase their motivation to guide and listen to their students. The classroom environment may improve measurably as students also develop closer relationships with others they may not typically socialize with and learn from one another, making the teacher's job easier and ultimately more enjoyable. (249)

Why Young Adolescents Need Advisory Programs

Advisory groups do respond to young adolescent needs for positive social interactions. A seventh grade teacher, Pamela, describes some social issues that create a need for advisory sessions: "I think grades are important to these students, but I think their number-one thing is friends, and that's their biggest fear: not having the right friends, not having certain friends, and being accepted." Advisory sessions provide students with a base, if you will—a place that they can call their home away from home. In a set of interviews from six middle schools, teachers reported that advisory sessions help to create a sense of community in their buildings (Anfara and Brown 2001).

Advisory groups also provide young adolescents with the opportunity to discuss issues and questions about their personal lives—particularly health- and sex-related issues. When asked about her advisory sessions an eighth grade student, Karen, from an urban school district, said, "I'd like to talk about sex education, 'cause most kids when they're at home with their parents don't talk to them about what happens during puberty." We expect middle students' questions about such personal issues to be answered by an adult. If parents aren't comfortable speaking about these sensitive topics to their children or if their children won't allow them to, then teachers must take the responsibility for doing so.

Recent gun violence at middle and high schools is evidence of the great need for emotional support that an advisory group can provide. Cole (1992) suggested, "When a crisis hits a school, such as the death of a student or family member . . . the TA [Teacher Advisory] group may become literally a life saver as all students have an immediate way of talking about the incident in a place where they already belong, with an adult whom they trust" (32). Advisory groups can provide more than a safe haven in a crisis. The presence of an advisory program can, in fact, help stem such violence. We will see violence decrease when all children feel a part of a group and feel valued and wanted.

Choosing an Appropriate Focus

A major objective of many advisory programs is the development of meaningful relationships between students and teachers. Advisory programs, however, may be designed for other reasons. John Galassi, Suzanne Gulledge, and Nancy Cox, in their NMSA publication titled *Advisory: Definitions Descriptions Decisions Directions* (1998b), describe possible emphases for advisory programs:

1. *advocacy emphasis*—focuses on addressing students' individual needs and personal concerns in the development of close relationships between the student and teacher in delivering a developmental guidance program
2. *community focus*—emphasis is on addressing students' social needs; providing a feeling of belonging for students as advisory groups develop a family atmosphere
3. *skills program*—focuses on helping students develop skills in the areas of understanding self and others, problem solving, decision making, academic success, community involvement, and career awareness
4. *invigoration type*—an activity emphasis where students and teachers engage in fun activities to reduce the stress associated with academics with offerings such as intramurals, club activities, or service projects
5. *academic emphasis*—promotes academic growth through activities such as sustained silent reading or the introduction of study skills
6. *administrative emphasis*—much like a homeroom; students are given information or money is collected for lunch or field trips—mainly involves housekeeping tasks

The program developed at each middle school may have one of these foci as its primary objective, or a faculty may decide to combine several of these or other objectives throughout the year. Cole (1992) suggested a daily advisory session with a different focus each day. For example:

Monday—relationship-building activity
Tuesday—intramurals
Wednesday—silent reading
Thursday—relationship-building activity
Friday—tutorial or independent study (10)

Reviews of the literature on advisory programs indicate that "students prefer activities that are fun, less structured, stimulating, relevant to their own lives, and over which they can exercise some degree of choice" regardless of the advisory focus (Galassi, Gulledge, and Cox 1998b, 51). Bushnell and George (1993) discovered that males and females had a different set of criteria for judging the effectiveness of their advisors: females wanted advisors who showed they cared and wanted to talk; males were interested in advisors who showed respect for their opinions and joked around.

Many practical details must be resolved before an advisory program can be implemented. Cole (1992) suggested that the following issues be addressed:

- Who [will] serve as an advisor?
- What training do advisors get?
- When and how often do advisories meet?
- Which students are assigned to which advisors?
- What resources are available for the advisory program? (12–13)

Teachers and administrators should collaborate with students to develop the most effective program for their school. When teachers unilaterally make decisions about how the advisory program is structured, student needs may not be addressed. One sixth grader, Peter, commented, "I think advisory groups are pointless because you don't really do anything. We play silent ball—just throw a ball around and if you drop it you're out. We just play stupid games and do stupid papers. It would be worthwhile if we did something in it but we don't."

Implementation of an advisory program can be quite challenging. Some parents, teachers, administrators, and students may be heavily opposed to adding a nonacademic program to the school's schedule. Teachers may be especially concerned that they are not trained in counseling techniques. In addition, some teachers feel that their job is primarily academic, and they should not be required to help students with challenging emotional issues or other personal concerns. Despite the problems involved in developing an advisory program, such a structure can play a vital role in helping students through the social and emotional challenges they experience during their young adolescent years. Many sensitive issues are on students' minds, and by ignoring these issues, teachers may prevent classrooms from becoming true learning environments.

Anfara and Brown (2001) offered the following suggestions for developing a successful advisory program:

- develop both short- and long-range goals
- be cognizant of students', teachers', and parents' needs
- provide for initial and ongoing staff training and development
- provide an orientation for students, teachers, and parents
- honor small student-teacher ratios
- be structured in the daily schedule of the school
- be very aware of school climate/culture
- involve students, parents, and faculty in the planning phase
- respect teachers and students' rights to privacy. (23)

Initiating an advisory program must be undertaken with much commitment, focus, attention to detail, and patience. Developing a program is a timely process that cannot be delivered in a traditional top-down manner. The philosophy behind the need for a program, the roles and responsibilities of teachers, the appropriate focus of advisory sessions, and the possibilities for a structured curriculum must be discussed in detail among all stakeholders—students, teachers, parents, and administrators—to ensure a successful launch of an advisory program.

Studies that provide direct evidence to support the effectiveness of advisory programs in altering student behavior and improving middle school environments are few; however, those studies that have been conducted report favorable views on the value of advisory programs (Galassi, Gulledge, and Cox 1998b). We believe that a program that can provide student support through this challenging stage of development should be implemented in middle level schools for the sake of young adolescents. Advisory sessions are not wasted time in an academic setting. The resulting relationships that develop between students and teachers can result in greater cognitive growth through whole-child growth. Noddings' (2005) comments about educating the whole child reveal a critical philosophy of effective schools at all levels and one that can be advanced through advisory programs:

> We will not find the solution to problems of violence, alienation, ignorance, and unhappiness in increasing our security apparatus, imposing more tests, punishing schools for their failure to produce 100 percent proficiency, or demanding that teachers be knowledgeable in "the subjects they teach." Instead, we must allow teachers and students to interact as whole persons, and we must develop policies that treat the school as a whole community. (13)

Alternative Scheduling

> Time is the key to working effectively with young adolescents. Schedules can open up and provide that time or constrict and limit it. Days filled with numerous 45-minute periods make it almost impossible to build relationships and learning.
>
> NESIN AND BRAZEE (2005, 43)

A key feature of the transformed middle grade school should be flexibility in the duration of classes. Teacher teams should be able to change class schedules whenever, in their collective professional judgment, the need exists. They should be able to create blocks of time for instruction that best meets the needs and interests of the students, responds to curriculum priorities, and capitalizes on learning opportunities such as current events.

CARNEGIE COUNCIL (1989, 52)

How can the critical middle school feature of relevant curriculum that leads to genuine learning be implemented in schools structured in a traditional forty-five minute, seven-to-eight period day? Perhaps the greatest barrier to any substantial change in middle schools is the common complaint and ever present 800-pound gorilla in the room depicted in the phrase, "we don't have *time* to do that, because our schedule won't permit it." Teachers clearly recognize the types of activities students need to engage in to ensure genuine learning, but they know that a lack of time influenced by traditional school structures will always prevent them from implementing middle level reforms that genuinely affect student learning.

According to the "NMSA Research Summary #2: Flexible Scheduling" (1999), the primary organizational structure for the middle schools is still the factory model, in which students attend seven or eight forty-two-minute classes throughout the day. The bell announces when students move on to the next class, and they must get there in three or four minutes. Teachers provide volumes of factual information through content and little time exists for in-depth study, research, or analysis.

Such an organizational structure results in numerous difficulties. According to Canady and Rettig (1995), one of the greatest problems of a traditional schedule is the effect on a school's climate. Many of the discipline problems that occur in school happen during the time that students are changing classes. With a traditional schedule, you may have one thousand students in the hall at the same time six or seven times a day.

Another difficulty with traditional scheduling is that it does not provide students an opportunity to become deeply involved in their studies or to see connections in their learning. Because the school day is broken up into small segments, students can't do extended research or get involved in major projects. In their look at innovative scheduling, Canady and Rettig (1995) maintained, "Students traveling through a six-, seven-, or eight-period day encounter the same number of pieces of unconnected curriculum each day, with little opportunity for in-depth study" (5). Students require more time to learn—especially young adolescents who are moving from the concrete to the formal operational stage of cognitive development. This time is not available in the traditional schedule. Instead, the traditional factory schedule of most middle level schools continues to provide students with the mile-wide, inch-deep surface knowledge that rarely represents genuine understanding of the concepts and principles critical to understanding the content that is taught.

One solution to the above problems is the development of a flexible schedule—one that optimizes learning experiences for the students. Time then becomes a positive resource rather than a barrier to student learning. Teachers are not bound by the clock and the bell, but are free to make professional decisions regarding the best ways to meet the needs of students. Classes can meet for any number of minutes and on different days of the week. Teachers make decisions as a team about how long their classes will last based on learning needs of both students and teachers.

Many teachers have noted positive results of alternative scheduling formats, especially in improved student behaviors and attitudes (D. Brown 2001a; Hannaford, Fouraker, and Dickerson 2000; Queen 2000; Hottenstein 1998). Other studies noted that teachers implemented more active instructional processes as a result of longer class sessions, such as lessons involving more creative and critical thinking, more time for student reflection, and greater opportunities for student-to-student collaboration (D. Brown 2001b; Reither 1999). Greater time available is the most significant factor in noting the changes in teachers' instructional behaviors.

D. Brown (2001a) interviewed several teachers from two middle schools and received the following comments. Chuck, a seventh grade social studies teacher, saw a positive change in the school climate when his school instituted flexible scheduling. "From a discipline standpoint, block scheduling is definitely affecting kids in a positive way. When teachers spend less time on classroom management, there's more instruction happening."

Dan, an eighth grade social studies teacher, noted that because of increased instructional time, his students' achievement changed. "I teach it better, and the kids understand it better." Jim, who teaches mathematics in seventh grade, agrees. "I think more information is sticking with these students with eighty-minute periods. They have opportunities to think about why they are performing certain functions and operations. I find most of my former students are doing better in eighth grade after they've had the block." Over eight thousand sixth graders who were tested from five middle schools in a North Carolina school district showed considerable gains as a group in their mathematics test scores after the schools switched from a traditional schedule to extended periods or block scheduling (Mattox, Hancock, and Queen 2005).

Ronald Williamson (1998), in his book *Scheduling Middle Level Schools: Tools for Improved Student Achievement*, supports the idea that the traditional six or seven learning periods a day, in addition to inhibiting teachers' creativity, constrains learning and does not respond to the developmental needs of the young adolescent. He says, "Examining and refining the structure of the school day—the use of time—has a profound impact on the school's ability to provide for the learning needs of its students" (8–9).

Teachers who are challenged by the expectations of inclusion may also see an advantage to helping students with special needs if they have longer class sessions. D. Brown (2001a) found that middle school teachers were better able to attend to the individual needs of diverse learners through longer class periods. These teachers also admitted using more partner learning activities to engage diverse learners during block scheduling periods. Teachers who are expected to use differentiated instructional processes also see a benefit to a more flexible schedule. It provides teachers with the time needed to address the varied levels of student abilities through the development and delivery of more appropriate lessons that match students' learning profiles.

The schedule should be a tool controlled by student needs rather than the bell. We need to look at alternative ways to structure learning experiences. Maybe all classes don't need to meet every day. Maybe every subject doesn't need to meet for the same amount of time. Maybe students don't have to have the same number of classes every day.

Types of Alternative Scheduling

Flexible Schedules

Flexible scheduling is just what it says it is—flexible. Successful middle schools create schedules that best meet the needs of their students—accommodating changes as needed. Block scheduling is often not a flexible plan. Flexible schedules are not locked-in eighty- to ninety-minute periods as is common among some middle and high schools. Flexibility in scheduling means that teams of teachers are able to alter the schedule daily to benefit their students. Flexible scheduling implies teacher control of scheduling issues rather than administrator dominance over the schedule.

Block Schedules

Block scheduling offers the advantage of longer time periods for learning. In the block approach, the schedule is designed around blocks of time, usually eighty to ninety minutes. The 4×4 semester block provides students with four core single-subject classes a day, each one meeting for eighty to ninety minutes. Students and teachers in the 4×4 block change classes every semester. In the alternating-day schedule students take eight to ten classes, four or five each on alternating days, for an entire year.

All of these block schedules offer expanded periods of time that provide teachers with the opportunity to engage students in interdisciplinary studies. In addition, students have the time to become involved in in-depth projects and research.

Block scheduling allows and demands that teachers use diverse instructional strategies. Certainly if students are in the same class for extended time, long periods of direct instruction will not work. Chuck, a seventh grade social studies teacher, commented on how block scheduling has changed the way he teaches. "The block scheduling has forced me to be more diverse in my teaching. I tended to be more teacher centered—now, I'm more child centered. . . . I have absolutely changed instruction. I use much more hands-on strategies now,

247

such as Internet activities, projects, research in the library, a lot more in-depth discussion, and a lot more critical thinking."

If teachers do not change instructional patterns, the use of block scheduling could be a disaster. Jesse, an eighth grader, didn't like the use of block scheduling in his school. "I don't like classes that are one and a half hours long. It's kind of stupid to have it that long. They should be like forty-five minutes." Jesse is an adolescent with attention deficit hyperactivity disorder (ADHD). Unless instruction is active and varied, the long block would be very difficult for him.

Block scheduling is not without its difficulties. Schedules must be developed around special classes such as music, art, and other exploratory courses. Teachers must change their teaching patterns, and common planning time for teams becomes an imperative.

Rotating Schedules
A rotating schedule provides flexibility to a block schedule. With a rotating schedule, students meet classes at different times each day. On Monday, students might have one class that meets for the first two periods of the day. On Tuesday, they have an advisory meeting the first period, and the block meets the second and third periods. Blocks in the morning and afternoon might shift. Some students may learn best in the morning, others after lunch. Some teachers do their best teaching in the morning, others after lunch. A rotating schedule gives all teachers and students the opportunity to interact with each other at some time during their optimal learning times.

Dropped Schedules
With dropped schedules, not every class meets each day. This option allows for schools to add advisory periods, exploratory classes, and other special units. In addition, it gives teachers the flexibility of staying with a group for an entire day to complete projects.

No best model for scheduling exists. Each model has its advantages and disadvantages as well as the logistical difficulties inherent in any schedule. How do we schedule lunch, languages, music, art, technology, and other special subjects while still providing a schedule that is responsive to the needs of the young adolescent? Teams of teachers and administrators must work with students to find the model that works best.

NMSA reported in 1999 that only about 20 percent of middle schools implement flexible scheduling of some kind. When looking at exemplary middle schools, however, researchers indicated that approximately 75 percent of those surveyed use some type of flexible scheduling. Bevevino et al. (1999) reported, "Assessment to date has revealed that several areas, including school climate, student learning, and teaching environment, appear to improve with the move to alternative scheduling" (6). Forte and Schurr (2002) warned that "[often] a significant number of faculty members think that the schedule should drive the instructional and assessment process, rather than the other way around. It is imperative that curriculum, instruction, and assessment determine what schedule is most appropriate in any given situation" (148). Middle level educators must begin to focus on maximizing learning opportunities for students. That may mean replacing traditional views of how the school day is structured and making a commitment to designing the school day so that students are engaged in active learning processes.

Exploratory Curriculum

The NMSA (2003) provided the following recommendation:

> The entire curriculum at this level should be exploratory, for young adolescents, by nature, are adventuresome, curious explorers. Exploration, in fact, is the aspect of a successful middle school's curriculum that most directly and fully reflects the nature and needs of young adolescents. Although some experiences or courses may be labeled exploratory, it should not be assumed they are, therefore, non-academic. The reverse is also true; a solid academic, science, for example, when properly taught, clearly is exploratory. Exploration is an attitude and approach, not a classification of content. (23)

Junior highs originally designated courses such as home economics, industrial arts, and foreign languages as exploratory subjects (Waks 2001). Waks noted that a shift exists today in defining exploratories as

"Discovering oneself as a distinct individual" (31). The exploratory emphasis changed during the 1980s and 1990s to unstructured learning opportunities chosen by students and offered generally at the end of the day.

Exploratory experiences in some middle schools during the 1990s and into 2000 were short miniunits lasting approximately six to eight weeks, with titles such as chess club, science exploration, sewing, or some athletic activity. They were offered perhaps once a week for forty-five minutes at the end of the day. These were designed more like interest groups for introductory activities rather than having a specific curricular focus. The intent was to provide young adolescents with opportunities to develop new skills or interests not related to any specific mandated curriculum.

Because of concerns among administrators that exploratory experiences might extract precious moments from the mandated curriculum, middle schools are less likely now to offer exploratories that are unrelated to academic growth (Anfara and Brown 2000). We suspect that some schools may even define standardized test preparation as an example of an exploratory session.

Exploratory experiences should continue to prepare students to enter adult life, but in a way that prepares them to adjust to new learning opportunities as adults, since they are likely to hold several jobs throughout their lives. Waks (2001) suggested using exploratory sessions for introducing problem-solving skills, using resources, and goal setting. Brazee (2000) suggested that exploratory experiences should be offered as complementary to the academic core subjects rather than be unrelated to them.

We believe that young adolescents should explore—in the school setting and in the natural context of learning each day within their classes. This type of exploration requires that teachers listen to young adolescents to discover their interests within the context of integrated curriculum or any traditional curricular delivery system. This emphasis requires that teachers encourage students' questions, seek their interests through lesson planning, alter curricula to match students' questions and concerns, and pursue lessons that improve students' thinking processes as they relate to their futures.

Exploration is a philosophy, an attitude, and an approach with an accompanying way of teaching that emphasizes personal as well as academic discovery.

Looping

Looping is an organizational structure in which teachers move with their students when they pass to the next grade level. In some schools, an entire team of teachers moves with their students from grade to grade. Other schools have multi-aged looping teams. For example, students stay on the Alpha Team for three years. The seventh and eighth graders serve as mentors for the new group of sixth graders who enter each year. Thompson, Gregg, and Caruthers (2005) reported several benefits to looping. Primary is the idea that "since there is no need to start from scratch, learning new names, personalities, and expectations, teachers estimated that a month of learning time was gained at the start of the second year" (140). In addition, because teachers have students for more than one year, stronger relationships are built. Since teachers are already familiar with learning styles, preferences, and interests, time is saved in student assessment and teachers can more readily meet the needs of their students (Thompson, Gregg, and Caruthers 2005). All students can benefit from the predictable learning environment that is transferred from year to year through looping. Multi-age looping teams have as an additional benefit the previous students initiating the incoming class into the structures and routines of the team.

Looping has the possibility of addressing the social, emotional, and cognitive challenges that young adolescents face each year through the middle grades. The opportunity to know students well for two or three years and to be able to immediately assist them each year is an advantage that educators should provide to middle school students.

Concluding Reflections

Making a difference in the lives of young adolescents requires that we reform and transform middle level education. In addition to curriculum, instruction, and assessment that validate students' questions and concerns, changes in the school structure can help create more powerful learning environments. Meeting the needs of middle level learners is a challenging and exciting task. We have the opportunity, through listening to students, to make school a place that makes sense to young adolescents and helps them find meaning in their lives.

ELEVEN

Being an Advocate for Young Adolescents

Adolescence is one of the most fascinating and complex
transitions in the life span: a time of accelerated growth and
change second only to infancy; a time of expanding horizons,
self-discovery, and emerging independence; a time of
metamorphosis from childhood to adulthood. Its beginning is
associated with profound biological, physical, behavioral,
and social transformations that roughly correspond with the
move to middle school or junior high school. The events of
this crucially formative phase can shape an individual's entire
life course and thus the future of our society.

THE CARNEGIE COUNCIL (1996, 7)

One of the most powerful lessons of the past decade is how
important it is to implement multiple elements of middle

grades reform and maintain those elements over time in order to see positive
outcomes for students. Which of the
systems of the human body could you
eliminate that would not be debilitating
if not fatal? Amputations and organ
removals may leave a body living, but
they leave a body with a diminished
capacity. So it is with middle grades
reform. Flexible structures and a shared
vision are important, but without a

253

challenging curriculum, varied learning approaches, and
programs for health and wellness, the middle grades school
will function with diminished capacity.

ERB (2005A, 3)

By now you are convinced that young adolescents need a distinctive learning environment to serve their particular needs, that they deserve an exciting, meaningful learning experience, and that being a middle school teacher is the right job for you—or not.

In the first chapter of this book we asked you to list the characteristics you felt a middle school teacher needed to have. Have your ideas changed? We heard what middle level students told us about the kind of teachers they want. "They should be nice." "They should make learning fun and interesting." "They should care about us." Listen to middle level students. Listen intently to what they have to say to you. Sit at the lunch table with them. Chat with them in detention and as they wait outside the principal's office. Listen to them as they roam through the halls or respond to other teachers. Volunteer to chaperone a middle school dance. Observe band and choral rehearsals. Attend track and soccer practices. Eavesdrop on the conversations that occur during physical education classes or in the bus lines after school each day. Seek their opinions about curriculum, instruction, and assessment, and then listen to their responses.

Young adolescents are vibrant, alive, curious, energetic, and exciting to be around. They need a school environment that responds to these qualities. Too often their schools are dull, detached, sometimes even cruel places. These students are captives of a system that suppresses their natural needs, capacities, and desires. What do young adolescents need?

- curriculum that is relevant, meaningful, and student designed
- instruction that is challenging and active
- varied assessments designed to promote growth rather than simply measure it
- kind, caring teachers who listen to students

254

- adults who constantly strive to know them well and whom they can trust
- opportunities to socialize with peers
- a healthy and physically and psychologically safe school environment
- opportunities to question and explore their social, emotional, cognitive, and identity developmental processes

Young adolescents are changing dramatically, and those changes should translate into the creation of a suitable learning environment. As young adolescents make that often frightening move from the dependence of childhood to the independence of adulthood, teachers need to support them, to enjoy them, and to provide guidance as they search to make meaning from the many changes occurring in their lives.

Misunderstanding the Middle School Concept

The middle school concept is not always supported by those outside education or those associated with education through political appointments. Despite years of research supporting the components of true middle schools, often the public hears a negative report that is unsubstantiated by research. A *Time* magazine reporter, for instance, recently claimed: "A series of studies depict U. S. middle schools as the 'Bermuda Triangle of education'" (Wallis 2005, 50–51). Those who make unsupported claims that misguide the public about the value of middle schools usually lack any knowledge of the developmental traits of young adolescents. School districts that drop their middle school arrangements may attempt to justify their change based on these erroneous claims, thereby creating schools that ignore the needs of young adolescents.

Some urban school districts from 2001 to 2004, for instance, changed the structure of their middle schools to K–8 buildings, but did so primarily in an attempt to improve high-stakes test scores rather than to provide young adolescents with the schools they need. These highly publicized changes often lead to misinformation about the value of a true middle school. George (2005) noted that in these urban environments, abandoning the middle school model is not likely to provide young adolescents with the schools they deserve. He commented:

> "Troubled" middle schools are likely to result from troubled lives—millions of students and families afflicted by the harsh impact of poverty, violence, divorce, homelessness, forced mobility, alcohol and drug abuse, lack of adequate health care, and the studied contempt of policymakers, bureaucrats, politicians, and corporate CEOs who lack the will or the interest to provide the leadership and the resources required for permanent and pervasive improvement in our schools.

Unfortunately, the public doesn't generally access professional educational journals and encounters only the erroneous (and unsupported) perspectives that are often publicized. Fortunately, professional educators, you among them, have many opportunities to promote the middle school concept based on reading valid research and other accurate accounts of effective middle level practices. Erb (2005b), in a *Middle School Journal* editorial, called the attacks on middle schools "The Making of a New Urban Myth"; he cited numerous studies in support of schools that implement a true middle school concept. Recognizing the research of Brown, Roney, and Anfara (2003), he stated, "The evidential base supports the middle school concept as a means to improve student behavior and achievement when it is implemented in healthy schools" (3).

The middle school concept is not an educational "fad" that is doomed for a short shelf life. The middle school concept developed during the 1960s and has been supported by continued research, and more middle schools are being opened each year (Lounsbury and Vars 2005). As you have read, young adolescents have unique developmental characteristics that warrant a learning environment that differs considerably from the high school and the elementary school. The middle school concept exists primarily because of these specific student needs.

Lounsbury and Brazee (2004), in an attempt to dispel misunderstandings associated with the design of the middle school concept, noted the following typical myths about the purposes of middle schools:

- The middle level school is a "feel good" school.
- The middle level school exists to prepare students for high school.
- The middle level school is "fun time."
- Middle level schools have "failed." (38)

None of these statements has any credibility—they are completely false. Some of your colleagues may espouse these erroneous ideas as you begin or continue your teaching career.

Having read this book, you understand how effective middle schools, through their specific design and implementation, respond to the needs of young adolescents to ensure their success during these critical years of their growth. We sincerely hope that you are able to connect young adolescents' traits with the need for student-directed curriculum, instruction, and assessment that leads to meaningful learning. We hope that it is also clear that when students actively participate in their learning, the result far outweighs the learning that occurs in traditional classrooms.

Support for the Middle School Concept

A comprehensive look at research on middle level reform (Lipsitz, Jackson, and Austin 1997) includes the report "The Impact of School Reform for the Middle Years" (Felner et al. 1997). The authors presented results from a longitudinal study that analyzed the degree to which each of the Carnegie Council recommendations in *Turning Points* (1989) had been implemented in specific schools and the resultant impact on student achievement and behavior. The researchers divided the schools into those with the highest levels of implementation of the Carnegie recommendations (including common planning time for teachers, a small number of students per team, the presence of advisory programs, changes in the teaching-learning process, and curriculum reform), those at medium levels of implementation, and those with no implementation. A diverse mix of schools was represented at each level. In the seven years in which data were collected, ninety-seven schools were studied.

The results of the analysis indicated significant academic gains and personal growth when the Carnegie Council recommendations were implemented. Students from those schools reflecting high implementation scored consistently higher than state norms in mathematics, language, and reading assessments. Students' scores from schools with the lowest levels of implementation tended to be at or below state averages.

Similar patterns were found in student behaviors. Teachers from the more fully implemented schools reported far lower levels of student behavioral problems, including aggression, learning difficulties, and emotional distress. On self-reports, students from the more implemented schools showed less fear, depression, and anxiety and had higher levels of self-esteem. As the authors indicated, "Clearly, across quite different types of sources of data (e.g., achievement tests, teachers' reports, student self-reports), there are distinct differences between schools that have attained different levels of implementation of the *Turning Points* recommendations" (Felner et al. 1997, 545).

Partially Implementing the Middle School Concept

Middle school faculty who implement only portions of the Carnegie recommendations are not realizing the full impact that total implementation can have on middle level students. Too often faculty and administrators change the school structure without changing instructional and curricular practices. Many middle level faculty place students on teams; however, the teachers are given little if any common planning time and limited decision-making authority over the schedule or the curriculum. With no opportunities to collaborate on curriculum, no control over instructional issues, and little opportunity to discuss individual learning needs, young adolescents are denied optimal growth opportunities. Felner et al. (1997) found the following problems associated with inadequate implementation of the *Turning Points* recommendations:

- Teams fail to engage in critical teaming activities that focus on curriculum integration, coordination, and collaboration around student needs/assignments.
- Students report a more negative school climate.
- Students and teachers report increased psychological and behavioral problems.
- Student achievement lags. (548)

The authors concluded, "It appears that when schools attempt to implement these practices but do them poorly (e.g., one or two common planning times per week, interdisciplinary instruction without common planning time, large teams), there may be no effect or even negative effects, especially on teacher attitudes and student performance" (548). Since the Felner et al. study in 1997, Erb (2005) has reported that many other studies have been conducted that indicate that "implementing more elements [of middle level reforms] for longer periods of time does, with certainty, lead to improved student outcomes in all three major goal areas—academic, behavioral, and attitudinal" (8). Schools are more likely to meet the academic needs of their students when they simultaneously aspire to address the behavioral and attitudinal areas of development.

Teachers and administrators must pay more than lip service to the implementation of recommendations for middle level reform. Lipsitz, Jackson, and Austin (1997) reported that "reforms implemented independently of one another are likely to produce little or no significant rise in student achievement, especially for disadvantaged youth. Not until a critical mass of reforms is in place and operating together in an integrated manner do significant positive changes in student outcomes occur" (519). Mizell (2005) added, "School systems that embraced the 6–8 middle school configurations also put too much emphasis on changing the organization of the grades and too little emphasis on the new knowledge, skills, and behaviors teachers and principals would have to develop to make middle schools successful" (15).

Middle level faculty that change school structure but ignore altering curriculum or instruction may be seeing positive changes in school climate, but they will not experience the maximum benefits of students' academic growth. Until the integration of curriculum, instruction, and assessment becomes the focus of change and young adolescents' voices are included in these decisions, the development of a true middle school will remain elusive.

Supporting Young Adolescents

What do these research findings mean for you? You must speak out. Do not be content with being a teacher in a middle school in name only. As middle level educators, we have a responsibility to be advocates for those programs that improve the quality of education for young adolescents. The data clearly demonstrate that gains in achievement as well as improved student behavior and emotional adjustment are the result of implementation of recommendations for middle level reform. These gains are representative for all, including at-risk students. If we implement reforms that group students to ensure success, provide a common core of knowledge for all, expand opportunities for learning, maximize the use of time and space, and involve students in decision making with respect to their learning, many of the needs of the young adolescent will be addressed.

Not only must we develop a community of learning in middle level schools, we must also garner parental support and community resources. We have discussed at length the pressures that exist against many middle level reform policies, including societal expectations, legislative dictates, parental fears, mandated tests, and concerns about being able to succeed in high school or college. Joining professional organizations, attending conferences, and reading professional journals are all ways for you to expand your knowledge and keep current on middle level reform. You must share this knowledge with administrators, parents, and other adults so that we can continue to help young adolescents grow.

The *True* Middle School

A primary objective in writing this book was to describe the characteristics and conditions needed to create a true middle school. Some of you will say that creating such a school is not possible or practical. We know it is possible, because year after year more teachers and administrators are establishing a vision, developing a plan, and implementing the components that we have described in this book. They establish teams, collaborate with students on curriculum and instruction, institute flexible schedules, develop advisory sessions, and, in effect, create successful middle schools. Chapter 9, with its stories of teachers who embraced curriculum integration, alternative assessment, democratic classrooms, and dynamic learning experiences, should encourage you also to take the risks associated with developing the true middle school concept.

The critical components needed to establish effective middle schools don't spring from politicians' mandates, administrators' policies, school board members' proposals, or parents' complaints. They develop when teachers speak clearly, loudly, and knowingly about what is best for young adolescents and then act on those pronouncements.

A true middle school reflects much more than program or structural reforms, however. It is more than just a place of learning. It is a place where students experience the support of caring adults who provide liberal amounts of prodding, encouragement, understanding, and celebration to the experiences that young adolescents encounter. A true middle school is a place where students are genuinely valued—not merely in words but in the very way that they are treated. We've asked many middle school students what advice they would give to someone who wants to be a middle level teacher. Their suggestions are straightforward and from the heart.

> "My advice to people wanting to be middle school teachers is
> to be strong. The students are going to give you a hard time.
> You need a lot of patience and you have to make it fun.
> Being in middle school is really hard."

"My advice to teachers is to listen to the kids' half of the story, get to know the kids, get to be their friends and not just a teacher—but don't be too much of a friend."

"Be nice."

"My advice to teachers is that when you're telling someone what to do, don't yell. Be more open minded. Don't think, 'My way or no way.'"

"Teachers need to be more understanding or they won't last."

"Be humorous. Do not be mean to the kids. Don't be strict or very demanding."

"I think anyone who wants to be a teacher better check to make sure they have a sense of humor. It is important to be funny sometimes when dealing with kids."

Interviews by Doda and Knowles (2007) with young adolescents have yielded the following advice for teachers from an eighth grader:

I can imagine that teaching eighth graders must be pretty tough. Half of us don't even know who we are, so how could teachers understand us? It's hard, but I can think of some ways. First of all, it must be understood that we are all trying to fit in. Eighth grade is a hard year and everyone has insecurities. I'm not saying to walk on eggshells around us, but be aware that our emotions can change like the wind. Be firm but understanding and strict but gentle. Also, we need to get breaks from class work and homework. We have a life outside of school. Parts of us wish we were older, but other parts wish we were still in kindergarten, playing in the sandbox. If it's nice weather, don't give a lot of homework. We need time to breathe and enjoy life while we're still kids.

Sharing these students' comments is in keeping with a critical component of effective middle school teachers—listening to your students. Beyond that essential component of teacher effectiveness are the thoughts of Jeffrey Wilhelm (2006) on professional responsibilities. Wilhelm provided the following questions to consider when you enter the classroom each day:

- What kind of teacher do I want to be? Which beliefs about students and theories of learning will help me best become that teacher?
- What quality of experience do I want my students to have in my classroom today?
- How will that experience motivate my students for further learning? How do I want their experience to affect their attitudes toward my subject, learning, school, and their futures?
- How will what I do today help my students internalize concepts and tools for immediate use *today* as well as for future learning?
- What will my students say about today's class to their friends at lunch, and to their parents at dinner? Will their words and feelings match my purposes? Will the quality of my teaching and way of interacting with the ideas and issues of the world stay with my students?
- How will today's learning change my students' ways of thinking, acting, and being? (40)

We ask that you consider these questions each day before you teach, particularly during the planning process when you're thinking of how you will engage students in learning. These are not idle questions in which the responses are purely "academic." The way you respond to these questions determines first whether or not you genuinely care about students and second whether any meaningful learning will occur in your class. Your responses to these questions and the appropriate actions that follow define the term *teacher accountability* better than any test score ever will.

You either already are or want to be a middle school teacher. You want to make a difference in the lives of young adolescents. Right now you are on top of the mountain. If you believe that you have what it takes to work with young adolescents, to validate them and encourage them and help them learn, push your poles into the ground and go. It will be an exhilarating ride. You will surely fall. But you will also fly.

References

Alexander, W. M. 1998a. "The Junior High School: A Changing View." In *Moving Forward from the Past: Early Writings and Current Reflections of Middle School Founders*, edited by R. David. Columbus, OH and Pittsburgh, PA: National Middle School Association and Pennsylvania Middle School Association, 3–13.

———. 1998b. "Program and Organization of a Five Through Eight Middle School." In *Moving Forward from the Past: Early Writings and Current Reflections of Middle School Founders*, edited by R. David. Columbus, OH and Pittsburgh, PA: National Middle School Association and Pennsylvania Middle School Association, 14–26.

Alexander, W., D. Carr, and K. McAvoy. 1995. *Student-Oriented Curriculum: Asking the Right Questions*. Columbus, OH: National Middle School Association.

Andrade, H. G. 2000. "Using Rubrics to Promote Thinking and Learning." *Educational Leadership* 57, no. 5: 13–18.

Anfara, V. A. Jr. 2001. "Introduction: Setting the Stage: An Introduction to Middle Level Education." In *The Handbook of Research in Middle Level Education*, edited by V. A. Anfara, Jr. Greenwich, CT: Information Age Publishing, vii–xx.

———. 2006. "The Evidence for the Core Curriculum—Past and Present." *Middle School Journal* 37, no. 3: 48–54.

Anfara, V. A. Jr., and K. M. Brown. 2000. "Exploratory Programs in the Middle Schools." *NASSP Bulletin* 84, no. 9: 58–67.

———. 2001. "Advisor-Advisee Programs: Community Building in a State of Affective Disorder?" In *The Handbook of Research in Middle Level Education*, edited by V. A. Anfara, Jr. Greenwich, CT: Information Age Publishing, 3–34.

ANFARA, V. A. JR. and L. J. WAKS. 2002. "Developmental Appropriateness Versus Academic Rigor: An Untenable Dualism in Middle Level Education." In *Middle School Curriculum, Instruction, and Assessment: A Volume in the Handbook of Research in Middle Level Education*, edited by V. A. Anfara, Jr., and S. L. Stacki. Greenwich, CT: Information Age Publishing, 41–55.

Anorexia Nervosa and Related Eating Disorders (ANRED). 2006. "Statistics: How Many People Have Eating Disorders?" *Anorexia Nervosa and Related Eating Disorders, Inc.* Available from www.anred.com/stats.html.

ATWELL, N. 2002. *Lessons That Change Writers*. Portsmouth, NH: Heinemann.

AZMITIA, M. 2002. "Self, Self-Esteem, Conflicts, and Best Friendships in Early Adolescence." In *Understanding Early Adolescent Self and Identity: Applications and Interventions*, edited by T. M. Brinthaupt and R. P. Lipka. Albany, NY: State University of New York Press, 167–92.

BANKS, R. 2000. "Bullying in School." *ERIC Review* 7, no.1: 12–14. Champaign, IL: ERIC Clearinghouse on Elementary and Early Childhood Education.

BARR, M. A. 2000. "Looking at the Learning Record." *Educational Leadership* 57, no. 5: 20–24.

BARTH, R. S. 1991. *Improving Schools from Within*. San Francisco: Jossey-Bass.

BEANE, J. A. 1990. *A Middle School Curriculum: From Rhetoric to Reality*. Columbus, OH: National Middle School Association.

———. 1993. *A Middle School Curriculum: From Rhetoric to Reality*. 2nd ed. Columbus, OH: National Middle School Association.

———. 1997. *Curriculum Integration: Designing the Core of Democratic Education*. New York: Teachers College Press.

———. 1998. "A Process for Collaborative Teacher-Student Planning." *The Core Teacher* 48, no. 3: 3–4.

References

————. 2005. *A Reason to Teach: Creating Classrooms of Dignity and Hope.* Portsmouth, NH: Heinemann.

BEERS, K. 2003. *When Kids Can't Read: What Teachers Can Do.* Portsmouth, NH: Heinemann.

BEVEVINO, M. M., D. M. SNODGRASS, K. M. ADAMS, and J. A. DENGEL. 1999. *An Educator's Guide to Block Scheduling: Decision Making, Curriculum Design, and Lesson Planning Strategies.* Boston: Allyn and Bacon.

BIZAR, M., and H. DANIELS. 2005. *Teaching the Best Practice Way: Methods That Matter, K–12.* Portland, ME: Stenhouse.

BLACKBURN, J. 1999. Conversation with the authors, West Chester, PA, 12 March.

BORDEAUX, R. 1992–1994. Unpublished poetry for class project. Sinte Gleska University, Mission, SD.

————. 1993–1994. Unpublished poetry for class project. Sinte Gleska University, Mission, SD.

BOSWORTH, K. 1995. "Caring for Others and Being Cared For: Students Talk About Caring in School." *Phi Delta Kappan* 76, no. 9: 686–93.

BOWER, A., and J. CAPLAN. 2005. "Being 13." *Time,* 8 August, 40–63.

BRAZEE, E. 1995. "An Integrated Curriculum Supports Young Adolescent Development." In *Beyond Separate Subjects: Integrative Learning at the Middle Level,* edited by Y. Siu-Runyan and C. V. Faircloth. Norwood, MA: Christopher-Gordon, 16–28.

————. 2000. *Exploratory Curriculum in the Middle School.* ERIC Document Reproduction Service No. ED447970.

BRAZEE, E., and J. CAPELLUTI. 1994. *Second Generation Curriculum: What and How We Teach at the Middle Level.* Topsfield, MA: New England League of Middle Schools.

BRENDTRO, L. M., M. BROKENLEG, and S. VAN BOCKERN. 1990. *Reclaiming Youth at Risk: Our Hope for the Future.* Bloomington, IN: National Education Service.

BRINTHAUPT, T. M., and R. P. LIPKA. 2002. "Understanding Early Adolescent Self and Identity: An Introduction." *Understanding Early*

Adolescent Self and Identity: Applications and Interventions, edited by T. M. Brinthaupt and R. P. Lipka. Albany, NY: State University of New York Press, 1–21.

BRODERICK, P. C., and P. BLEWITT. 2003. *The Life Span: Human Development for Helping Professionals*. Upper Saddle River, NJ: Merrill Prentice Hall.

BRODHAGEN, B. 1998. "Varied Teaching and Learning Approaches." *Middle School Journal* 29, no. 3: 49–52.

BROOKS, J. G., and M. G. BROOKS. 1993. *In Search of Understanding: The Case for Constructivist Classrooms*. Alexandria, VA: Association for Supervision and Curriculum Development.

BROOKS-GUNN, J., A. C. PETERSON, and D. EICHORN. 1985. "The Study of Maturational Timing Effects in Adolescence." *Journal of Youth and Adolescence* 14: 149–61.

BROUGH, J. A. 1994. "Donald H. Eichhorn: Pioneer in Inventing Schools for Transescents." *Middle School Journal* 25, no. 4: 19–22.

BROWN, D. F. 1990. "The Effects of State Mandated Testing on Elementary Classroom Instruction." Ed.D. diss., University of Tennessee.

———. 2001a. "Middle Level Teachers' Perceptions of the Impact of Block Scheduling on Instruction and Learning." *Research in Middle Level Education Annual* 24: 121–41.

———. 2001b. "Flexible Scheduling and Young Adolescent Development: A Perfect Match." In *The Handbook of Research in Middle Level Education*, edited by V. A. Anfara, Jr. Greenwich, CT: Information Age Publishing, 125–39.

———. 2002a. "Self-Directed Learning in an 8th Grade Classroom." *Educational Leadership* 60, no. 1: 54–58.

———. 2002b. *Becoming a Successful Urban Teacher*. Portsmouth, NH and Westerville, OH: Heinemann and National Middle School Association.

———. 2002c. "Culturally Responsive Instructional Processes." In *Middle School Curriculum, Instruction, and Assessment*, edited by V. A. Anfara, Jr. and S. L. Stacki. Greenwich, CT, and Westerville, OH: Information Age Publishing and National Middle School Association, 57–73.

————. 2003. Informal Assessment of Middle Level Teachers' Perceptions of How Learning Occurs. Unpublished Raw Data, West Chester University, Pennsylvania. 25–30 June.

————. 2005. "The Significance of Congruent Communication in Effective Classroom Management." *The Clearing House: A Journal of Educational Strategies, Issues, and Ideas* 79, no. 1: 12–15.

————. 2006. "It's the Curriculum, Stupid: There's Something Wrong With It." *Phi Delta Kappan* 87, no. 10: 777–83.

BROWN, D. F., and H. L. LEAMAN. 2006. "I'm White: They're Not: Helping Ethnically Diverse Students Develop Healthy Identities." Presentation at the Pennsylvania Middle School Association annual conference. 20 March in State College, Pennsylvania.

BROWN, D. F., and J. L. MORGAN 2003. "Students' Perceptions of a Curriculum Integration Experience on Their Learning." Paper presented at the American Educational Research Association annual conference. 23 April, in Chicago, Illinois.

BROWN, D. F., and T. D. ROSE. 1995. "Self-Reported Classroom Impact of Teachers' Theories About Learning and Obstacles to Implementation." *Action in Teacher Education* 27, no. 1: 20–29.

BROWN, K. M. 2001. "Get the Big Picture of Teaming: Eliminate Isolation and Competition Through Focus, Leadership, and Professional Development." In *The Handbook of Research in Middle Level Education,* edited by V. A. Anfara, Jr. Greenwich, CT: Information Age Publishing, 35–72.

BROWN, K. M., K. RONEY, and V. A. ANFARA, JR. 2003. "Organizational Health Directly Influences Student Performance at the Middle Level." *Middle School Journal* 34, no. 5: 5–15.

BROWN, L., and C. GILLIGAN. 1992. *Meeting at the Crossroads: Women's Psychology and Girls' Development.* Cambridge, MA: Harvard University Press.

BROWNLEE, S. 2005. "Inside the Teen Brain." *Mysteries of the Teen Years: An Essential Guide for Parents. U. S. News and World Report,* 10 May.

BUIS, J. M., and D. N. THOMPSON. 1989. "Imaginary Audience and Personal Fable: A Brief Review." *Adolescence* 24: 773–81.

BUSHNELL, D., and P. S. GEORGE. 1993. "Five Crucial Characteristics: Middle School Teachers as Effective Advisors." *Schools in the Middle: Theory into Practice* 3, no. 1: 10–16.

CAINE, R. N., and G. CAINE. 1994. *Making Connections: Teaching and the Human Brain*. Menlo Park, CA: Addison Wesley.

CANADY, R. L., and M. D. RETTIG. 1995. "The Power of Innovation Scheduling." *Educational Leadership* 53, no. 3: 4–10.

CARNEGIE COUNCIL FOR ADOLESCENT DEVELOPMENT. 1989. *Turning Points: Preparing American Youth for the 21st Century*. New York: Carnegie Corporation.

———. 1996. *Great Transitions: Preparing Adolescents for a New Century*. Abridged Version. New York: Carnegie Corporation of New York.

CARSKADON, M. 1999. "When Worlds Collide: Adolescent Need for Sleep Versus Social Demands." In *Adolescent Sleep Needs and School Starting Times*, edited by K. Walstrom. Bloomington, IN: Phi Delta Kappa Educational Foundation, 11–27.

CHARLES, C. M. 2000. *The Synergetic Classroom: Joyful Teaching and Gentle Discipline*. Reading, MA: Addison, Wesley, and Longman.

CHARNEY, R. S. 1991. *Teaching Children to Care*. Pittsfield, MA: Northeast Foundation for Children.

CHASKIN, R. J., and D. MENDLEY RAUNER. 1995. "Youth and Caring." *Phi Delta Kappan* 76, no. 9: 667–74.

CHU, J. 2005. "You Wanna Take This Online?" *Time Special Report on Being 13*: 52–55. 8 August.

CLARK, S. 1996. "Real Learning in My Classroom? Yes!" Unpublished Manuscript. Westfield State College, Westfield, MA.

———. 1997. Unpublished Presentation Materials. Westfield State College, Westfield, MA.

COLE, C. 1992. *Nurturing a Teacher Advisory Program*. Columbus, OH: National Middle School Association.

COMER, J. P. 2005. "Child and Adolescent Development: The Missing Focus in School Reform." *Phi Delta Kappan* 86, no. 10: 757–63.

CROSS, W. E., JR. 1991. *Shades of Black: Diversity in African American Identity.* Philadelphia, PA: Temple University Press.

DANIELS, H. 2002. *Literature Circles: Voice and Choice in Book Clubs and Reading Groups.* York, ME: Stenhouse Publishers.

DANIELS, H., A. HYDE, and S. ZEMELMAN. 2005. *Best Practice: Today's Standards for Teaching and Learning in America's Schools.* 3rd ed. Portsmouth, NH: Heinemann.

DANIELS, S. R., R. P. MCMAHON, E. OBARZANEK, M. A. WACLAWIW, S. L. SIMILO, F. M. BIRO, G. B. SCHREIBER, S. Y. S. KIMM, J. A. MORRISON, and B. A. BARTON. 1998. "Longitudinal Correlates of Change of Blood Pressure in Adolescent Girls." *Hypertension* 31: 97–103.

DAVID, R. ed. 1998. *Moving Forward from the Past: Early Writings and Current Reflections of Middle School Founders.* Columbus, OH and Pittsburgh, PA: National Middle School Association and Pennsylvania Middle School Association.

DAVIES, A. 2001. "Involving Students in Communicating About Their Learning." *National Association of Secondary School Principals Bulletin* 85, no. 621: 47–52.

DAVIS, J., and S. HILL. 2003. *The No-Nonsense Guide to Teaching Writing: Strategies, Structures, Solutions.* Portsmouth, NH: Heinemann.

DEVRIES, A. L. C., P. T. COHEN-KETTENIS, H. D. DELEMARRE-VANDER WAAL. 2006. "Caring for Transgender Adolescents in BC: Suggested Guidelines." (cited 27 March 2007). Available from www.vch.ca/transhealth/resources/library/tcpdocs/guidelines-adolescent.pdf.

DEWEY, J. 1938. *Experience and Education.* New York: Macmillan Publishing.

DICKINSON, T., ed. 1993. *Readings in Middle School Curriculum: A Continuing Conversation.* Columbus, OH: National Middle School Association.

DODA, N. M., and T. KNOWLES. 2007. "Listening to the Voices of Young Adolescents." *Middle School Journal,* in press.

DUBAS, J. S., J. A. GARBER, and A. C. PEDERSEN. 1991. "A Longitudinal Investigation of Adolescents' Changing Perceptions of Pubertal Timing." *Developmental Psychology* 27: 580–86.

References

EDER, D. 2002. "Segregating the Popular from the Unpopular." In *Readings on Adolescence and Emerging Adulthood*, edited by J. J. Arnett. Upper Saddle River, NJ: Prentice Hall, 151–60.

EDUCATORS IN CONNECTICUT'S POMPERAUG REGIONAL SCHOOL DISTRICT 15. 1996. *A Teacher's Guide to Performance-Based Learning and Assessment.* Alexandria, VA: Association for Supervision and Curriculum Development.

EICHHORN, D. H. 1998. "New Knowledge of 10- Through 13-Year Olds." In *Moving Forward from the Past: Early Writings and Current Reflections of Middle School Founders*, edited by R. David. Columbus OH: National Middle School Association, 43–53.

Eight Year Study. 1942. *Adventure in American Education*, vol. I. Retrieved from www.8yearstudy.org.

ELIAS, M. J., J. E. ZINS, R. P. WEISSBERG, K. S. FREY, M. T. GREENBERG, N. M. HAYNES, R. KESSLER, M. E. SCHWAB-STONE, and T. P. SHRIVER. 1997. *Promoting Social and Emotional Learning: Guidelines for Educators.* Alexandria, VA: Association for Supervision and Curriculum Development.

ELKIND, D. 1967. "Egocentrism in Adolescence." *Child Development* 38: 1025–34.

———. 1970. *Children and Adolescents: Interpretive Essays on Jean Piaget.* New York: Oxford University Press.

ELLIS, N. B. 1991. "An Extension of the Steinberg Accelerating Hypothesis." *Journal of Early Adolescence* 2: 221–35.

ENGLANDER, M. E. 1986. *Strategies for Classroom Discipline.* New York: Praeger.

EPSTEIN, J., and D. MAC IVER 1990. *Education in the Middle Grades: Overview of National Practices and Trends.* Columbus, OH: National Middle School Association.

ERB, T. 1997. "Thirty Years of Attempting to Fathom Teaming: Battling Potholes and Hairpin Curves Along the Way." In *We Gain More Than We Give: Teaming in Middle Schools*, edited by T. S. Dickinson and T. O. Erb. Columbus, OH: National Middle School Association, 19–59.

———. 2000. "Do Middle Level Reforms Really Make a Difference." *The Clearing House* 73, no. 4: 194–200.

272

————. 2005a. *This We Believe in Action*. Westerville, OH: National Middle School Association.

————. 2005b. "The Making of a New Urban Myth." *Middle School Journal* 37, No. 1: 2–3.

ERIKSON, E. H. 1950. *Childhood and Society*. New York: W. W. Norton.

————. 1968. *Identity: Youth and Crisis*. New York: W. W. Norton.

FELNER, R. D., A. W. JACKSON, D. KASAK, P. MULHALL, S. BRAND, and N. FLOWERS. 1997. "The Impact of School Reform for the Middle Years: Longitudinal Study of a Network Engaged in *Turning Points*–Based Comprehensive School Transformation." *Phi Delta Kappan* 78, no. 7: 528–32, 541–50.

FINN, P. J. 1999. *Literacy with an Attitude*. Albany, NY: State University of New York Press.

FLANNERY, D. J., D. C. ROWE, and B. L. GULLEY. 1993. "Impact of Pubertal Status, Timing, and Age on Adolescent Sexual Experience and Delinquency." *Journal of Adolescent Research* 8: 21–40.

FLOWERS, N., S. MERTENS, and P. MULHALL. 2000. "What Makes Interdisciplinary Teams Effective?" *Middle School Journal* 31, no. 4: 53–56.

FORBES, E. 1944. *Johnny Tremain*. Boston: Houghton Mifflin.

FORTE, I., and S. SCHURR. 1993. *The Definitive Middle School Guide*. Nashville, TN: Incentive Publications.

————. 2002. *The Definitive Middle School Guide*. Rev ed. Nashville, TN: Incentive Publications.

FRANK, A. 1967. *The Diary of a Young Girl*. New York: Doubleday.

GALASSI, J. P., S. A. GULLEDGE, and N. D. COX. 1998a. "Middle School Advisories: Retrospect and Prospect." *Review of Educational Research* 67, no. 3: 301–38.

————. 1998b. *Advisory: Definitions Descriptions Decisions Directions*. Columbus, OH: National Middle School Association.

GARCIA, E. 1999. *Student Cultural Diversity: Understanding and Meeting the Challenge*. 2nd ed. Boston: Houghton Mifflin.

GAY, G. 1994. "Coming of Age Ethnically: Teaching Young Adolescents of Color." *Theory Into Practice* 33, no. 3: 149–55.

———. 2000. *Culturally Responsive Teaching: Theory, Research, and Practice.* New York: Teachers College Press.

GE, X., R. D. CONGER, and G. H. ELDER, JR. 2001. "The Relation Between Puberty and Psychological Distress in Adolescent Boys." *Journal of Research on Adolescence* 11: 49–70.

GEORGE, P. 2005. "K–8 or Not? Reconfiguring the Middle Grades." *Middle School Journal* 37, no. 1: 6–13.

GEORGE, P., and W. ALEXANDER. 1993. *The Exemplary Middle School.* 2d ed. New York: Holt, Reinhart, and Winston.

GEORGE, P. S., and L. L. OLDAKER. 1985. *Evidence for the Middle School.* Columbus, OH: National Middle School Association.

GEORGE, P. S., C. STEVENSON, J. THOMASON, and J. BEANE. 1992. *The Middle School—and Beyond.* Alexandria, VA: Association for Supervision and Curriculum Development.

GIANNETTI, C., and M. SAGARESE. 2001. *Cliques: 8 Steps to Help Your Child Survive the Jungle.* New York: Broadway Books.

GILL, J., and J. E. READ. 1990. "The 'Experts' Comment on Adviser Advisee Programs." *Middle School Journal* 21, no. 5: 31–33.

GLATTHORN, A. A., and J. BARON. 1991. "The Good Thinker." In *Developing Minds: A Resource Book for Teaching Thinking,* edited by A. L. Costa. Rev. ed. Alexandria, VA: Association for Supervision and Curriculum Development, 63–67.

GOLEMAN, D. 1995. *Emotional Intelligence.* New York: Bantam Books.

GOLNER, S. J., and J. H. POWELL. 1992. "Ready for Teaming? Ten Questions to Ask Before You Jump In." *Middle School Journal* 24, no. 1: 28–32.

GOODMAN, J. F., V. SUTTON, and I. HARKEVY. 1995. "The Effectiveness of Family Workshops in a Middle School Setting: Respect and Caring Make a Difference." *Phi Delta Kappan* 76, no. 9: 694–700.

GOODRICH, H. 1996. *Student Self-Assessment: At the Intersection of Metacogition and Authentic Assessment.* Unpublished Doctoral Diss. Harvard University, Cambridge, MA.

References

GRABER, J. A., P. M. LEWINSOHN, J. R. SEELEY, and J. BROOKS-GUNN. 2002. "Effects of the Timing of Puberty." In *Readings on Adolescence and Emerging Adulthood*, edited by J. J. Arnett. Upper Saddle River, NJ: Prentice Hall, 40–49.

GRANTES, J., C. NOYCE, F. PATTERSON, and J. ROBERTSON. 1961. *The Junior High We Need*. Washington, DC: Association for Supervision and Curriculum Development.

GRUHN, W., and H. DOUGLASS. 1971. *The Modern Junior High School*. 3d ed. New York: Ronald Press.

HANNAFORD, B., M. FOURAKER, and V. DICKERSON. 2000. "One School Tackles the Change to Block Scheduling." *Phi Delta Kappan* 82, no. 2: 212–13.

HART, L. E., S. S. McCOTTER, K. D. MUTH, and J. H. LIM. 2002. "Interdisciplinary Teams at the Middle Level: Results of a National Survey." Paper presented at the American Educational Research Association annual meeting. 3 April in New Orleans, Louisiana.

HAYWARD, C., J. D. KILLEN, D. M. WILSON, and L. D. HAMMER. 1997. "Psychiatric Risk Associated With Early Puberty in Adolescent Girls." *Journal of the American Academy of Child and Adolescent Psychiatry* 36, 255–62.

HIRSCH, E. D., JR., ed. 1993a. *What Your First Grader Needs to Know*. New York: Delta.

———. 1993b. *What Your Sixth Grader Needs to Know*. New York: Delta.

HOFFMAN, K. R. 2003. "Messaging Mania." *TIME for Kids*, 2 May.

HOTTENSTEIN, D. S. 1998. *Intensive Scheduling: Restructuring America's Secondary Schools Through Time Management*. Thousand Oaks, CA: Corwin Press.

HOWARD, G. R. 1999. *We Can't Teach What We Don't Know: White Teachers, Multiracial Schools*. New York: Teachers College Press.

HOWARD, T. C. 2001. "Powerful Pedagogy for African American Students: A Case Study of Four Teachers." *Urban Education* 36, no. 2: 179–200.

HUNTER, M. 1984. "Knowing, Teaching, and Supervising." In *Using What We Know About Teaching*, edited by P. Horsford. Alexandria, VA: Association for Supervision and Curriculum Development, 52–65.

JACKSON, A. W., and G. A. DAVIS. 2000. *Turning Points 2000: Educating Adolescents in the 21st Century.* New York and Westerville, OH: Teachers College Press and National Middle School Association.

JAMES, M. 1986. *Adviser-Advisee Programs: Why, What and How.* Columbus, OH: National Middle School Association.

JENSEN, E. 1998. "How Julie's Brain Learns." *Educational Leadership* 56, no. 3: 41–45.

JOHNSTON, J., and R. WILLIAMSON. 1998. "Listening to Four Communities: Parent and Public Concerns About Middle Level Schools." *NASSP Bulletin* 82, no. 597: 44–52.

KAIL, R. 1997. "The Neural Noise Hypothesis: Evidence From Processing Speed in Adults with Multiple Sclerosis." *Aging, Neuropsychology, and Cognition* 4: 157–63.

KERR, M. M. 2006. "Bullying: What the Research Tells Us." Presentation at the Pennsylvania Middle School Association Conference. 19 March in State College, PA.

KIM, K., and P. K. SMITH. 1998. "Retrospective Survey of Parental Marital Relations and Child Reproductive Development." *International Journal of Behavioral Development* 22: 729–51.

KINNEY, P., M. B. MONROE, and P. SESSIONS. 2000. *A Student-Wide Approach to Student-Led Conferences.* Westerville, OH: National Middle School Association.

KLIEBARD, H. M. 1986. *The Struggle for the American Curriculum: 1893–1958.* Boston: Routledge and Kegan Paul.

KLINE, L. W. 1995. "A Baker's Dozen: Effective Instructional Strategies." In *Educating Everybody's Children: Diverse Teaching Strategies for Diverse Learners,* edited by R. W. Cole. Alexandria, VA: Association for Supervision and Curriculum Development, 21–45.

KNOWLES, T. 2006. *The Kids Behind the Label: An Inside Look at ADHD for Classroom Teachers.* Portsmouth, NH: Heinemann.

KOFF, E., and K. RIERDAN. 1995. "Preparing Girls for Menstruation: Recommendations from Adolescent Girls." *Adolescence* 30: 795–811.

KOHLBERG, L., and C. GILLIGAN. Fall 1971. "The Adolescent as a Philosopher: The Discovery of the Self in a Postconventional World." *Daedalus* 1051–86.

KOHN, A. 1986. *No Contest: The Case Against Competition, Why We Lose in Our Race to Win*. Boston: Houghton Mifflin.

———. 2000. *The Case Against Standardized Testing: Raising the Scores, Ruining the Schools*. Portsmouth, NH: Heinemann.

KROGER, J. 2003. "Identity Development During Adolescence." In *Blackwell Handbook of Adolescence*, edited by G. R. Adams and M. D. Berzonsky. Oxford, England: Blackwell Publishing, 205–266.

LADSON-BILLINGS, G. 1994. *The Dreamkeepers: Successful Teachers of African American Children*. San Francisco: Jossey-Bass.

LANE, B. 2005. "Dealing with Rumors, Secrets, and Lies: Tools of Aggression for Middle School Girls." *Middle School Journal* 36, no. 3: 41–47.

LEWIN, L., and B. J. SHOEMAKER. 1998. *Great Performances: Creating Classroom-Based Assessment Tasks*. Alexandria, VA: Association for Supervision and Curriculum Development.

LIPSITZ, J. 1995. "Prologue: Why We Should Care About Caring." *Phi Delta Kappan* 76, no. 9: 665–66.

LIPSITZ, J., A. W. JACKSON, and L. M. AUSTIN. 1997. "What Works in Middle-Grades School Reform." *Phi Delta Kappan* 78, no. 7: 517–19.

LONG, C. 2006, May. "Girl Bullies: Sugar and Spice?" *NEA Today* 24, no. 8: 30–33.

LOUNSBURY, J. H., and E. N. BRAZEE. 2004. *Understanding and Implementing This We Believe—First Steps*. Westerville, OH: National Middle School Association.

LOUNSBURY, J. H., and D. CLARK. 1990. *Inside Grade Eight: From Apathy to Excitement*. Reston, VA: National Association of Secondary School Principals.

LOUNSBURY, J. H. and G. F. VARS. 1978. *A Curriculum for the Middle School Years*. New York: Harper & Row.

———. 2003. "The Future of Middle Level Education: Optimistic and Pessimistic Views." *Middle School Journal* 35, no. 2: 6–14.

———. 2005. "Middle Level Education: A Personal History." In *The Encyclopedia of Middle Grades Education*, edited by V. A. Anfara, Jr., G. Andrews, and S. B. Mertens. Greenwich, CT: Information Age Publishing, 1–14.

MacLaury, S. 2002. *Student Advisories in Grades 5–12: A Facilitator's Guide*. Norwood, MA: Christopher-Gordon.

Manning, M. 1993. *Developmentally Appropriate Middle Level Schools*. Wheaton, MD: Association for Childhood Education International.

Marcia, J. 1980. "Ego Identity Development." In *The Handbook of Adolescent Psychology*, edited by J. Adelson. New York: Wiley, 159–87.

———. 1991. "Identity and Self Development." In *Encyclopedia of Adolescence, Vol. 1*, edited by R. M. Lerner, A. D. Petersen, and J. Brooks-Gunn. New York: Garland, 529–533.

Marzano, R. J. 2000. *Transforming Classroom Grading*. Alexandria, VA: Association for Supervision and Curriculum Development.

Mattox, K., D. R. Hancock, and J. A. Queen. 2005. "Block Scheduling Effects on Middle School Students' Mathematics Achievement." Paper presented at the American Educational Research Association annual meeting. 12 April in Montreal, Canada.

May, F. B. 1998. *Reading as Communication: To Help Children Write and Read*. 5th ed. Upper Saddle River, NJ: Merrill Prentice Hall.

McCarthy, A. R. 1999. *Healthy Teens: Facing the Challenge of Young Lives*. 3rd ed. Birmingham, MI: Bridge Communications, Inc.

McEwin, C. K. 1997. "Trends in Establishing Interdisciplinary Team Organization in Middle Schools." In *We Gain More Than We Give: Teaming in Middle Schools*, edited by T. S. Dickinson and T. O. Erb. Columbus, OH: National Middle School Association, 313–24.

McEwin, C. K., and T. S. Dickinson. 2001. "Educators Committed to Young Adolescents." In *This We Believe . . . And Now We Must Act*, edited by T. O. Erb. Westerville, OH: National Middle School Association, 11–19.

McEwin, C. K., T. S. Dickinson, and M. G. Jacobson. 2005. "How Effective Are K–8 Schools for Young Adolescents?" *Middle School Journal* 37, no. 1: 24–28.

McEwin, C. K., T. S. Dickinson, and D. M. Jenkins. 1996. *America's Middle Schools: Practice and Progress—A 25-Year Perspective*. Columbus, OH: National Middle School Association.

Meeus, W., J. Ledema, M. Helsen, and W. Volleburgh. 1999. "Patterns of Adolescent Identity Development: Review of Literature and Longitudinal Analysis." *Developmental Review* 19: 419–61.

Milgram, J. 1992. "A Portrait of Diversity: The Middle Level Student." In *Transforming Middle Level Education: Perspectives and Possibilities*, edited by J. L. Irvin. Needham Heights, MA: Allyn and Bacon, 16–27.

Mills, R. C., R. G. Dunham, and G. P. Alpert. 1988. "Working with High Risk Young in Prevention and Early Intervention Programs: Toward a Comprehensive Wellness Model." *Adolescence* 23: 643–60.

Mizell, H. 2005. "Grade Configurations for Educating Young Adolescents Are Still Crazy After All These Years." *Middle School Journal* 37, no. 1: 14–23.

Muuss, R. E. 1988. *Theories of Adolescence*. 5th ed. New York: McGraw Hill.

National Middle School Association. 1982. *This We Believe: A Position Paper of the National Middle School Association*. Columbus, OH: National Middle School Association.

———. 1995. *This We Believe: Developmentally Responsive Middle Level Schools*. Columbus, OH: National Middle School Association.

———. 1999. "NMSA Research Summary #2: Flexible Scheduling." National Middle School Association. www.nmsa.org.

———. 2003. *This We Believe: Successful Schools for Young Adolescents*. Westerville, OH: National Middle School Association.

Nechochea, J., L. P. Stowell, J. E. McDaniel, M. Lorimer, and C. Kritzer. 2001. "Rethinking Middle Level Teacher Education for the 21st Century: A Systems Approach." In *The Handbook of Research in Middle Level Education*, edited by V. A. Anfara, Jr. Greenwich, CT: Information Age Publishing, 161–81.

Nesin, G., and E. N. Brazee. 2005. "Creating Developmentally Responsive Middle Schools." In *The Encyclopedia of Middle Grades Education*, edited by V. A. Anfara, Jr., G. Andrews, and S. B. Mertens. Greenwich, CT: Information Age Publishing, 3–44.

NESIN, G. and J. LOUNSBURY. 1999. *Curriculum Integration: Twenty Questions— With Answers*. Atlanta, GA: Georgia Middle School Association.

NEWMAN, D. L., D. T. SPALDING, and L. YEZZI. 2000. "Cognitive and Social Emotional Growth of Early Adolescents: A Longitudinal Study of Middle School." Paper presented at the American Educational Research Association Annual Conference. 5 April in New Orleans.

No Child Left Behind Act. 2001. Retrieved from www.ed.gov/policy/elsec/eg/esea02/index.html. Public Law No. 107–110.

NODDINGS, N. 2005. "What Does It Mean to Educate the Whole Child?" *Educational Leadership* 63, no. 1: 8–13.

NORTH CENTRAL ASSOCIATION. 1919. Bulletin. North Central Association of Colleges and Secondary Schools.

NOTTELMANN, E. D., E. J. SUSMAN, J. H. BLUE, G. INOFF-GERMAIN, L. D. DORN, D. L. LORIAUX, G. B. CUTLER, and G. P. CHROUSOS. 1987. "Gonadal and Adrenal Hormone Correlates of Adjustment in Early Adolescence." In *Biological-Psychological Interactions in Early Adolescence*, edited by R. M. Lerner and T. T. Foch. Hillsdale, NJ: Erlbaum, 303–323.

OGBU, J. U. 1991. "Cultural Diversity and School Experience." In *Literacy as Praxis: Culture, Language, and Pedagogy*, ed. C. E. Walsh. Norwood, NJ: Ablex Publishing, 25–50.

ORNSTEIN, P. 1994. *School Girls: Young Women, Self-Esteem, and The Confidence Gap*. New York: Anchor Books, Doubleday.

OZER, E. M., M. J. PARK, T. PAUL, C. D. BRINDIS, and C. E. IRWIN, JR. 2003. *America's Adolescents: Are They Healthy?* San Francisco: University of California, San Francisco, National Adolescent Health Information Center.

PADDACK, C. 1987. "Preparing a Boy for Nocturnal Emissions." *Medical Aspects of Human Sexuality* 21: 15–16.

PARDINI, P. 1999. "Battling Bullies: Teasing and Taunting Can Threaten School Safety." *Middle Ground* 3, no. 7: 25–29.

PARHAM, T. A. 1989. "Cycles of Psychological Nigresence." *The Counseling Psychologist* 17: 187–226.

References

PARK, A. 2004. "What Makes Teens Tick?" *Time*, 10 May, 58–65.

PARKEY, F. W., and G. HASS. 2000. *Curriculum Planning: A Contemporary Approach.* 2nd ed. Needham Heights, MA: Allyn and Bacon.

PERRY, B. D. 1996. *Maltreated Children: Experience, Brain Development, and the Next Generation.* New York: Norton.

PETERSEN, A. C. 1987. "Those Gangly Years." *Psychology Today* September: 28–34.

PIAGET, J. 1977a. *The Development of Thought: Elaboration of Cognitive Structures.* New York: Viking.

———. 1977b. *The Essential Piaget.* New York: Basic Books.

POLLOCK, S. L. 2006. "Counselor Roles in Dealing With Bullies and Their LGBT Victims." *Middle School Journal* 38, no. 2: 29–36.

POPHAM, W. J. 1999. "Why Standardized Tests Don't Measure Educational Quality." *Educational Leadership* 56, no. 6: 8–15.

POWELL, R., and G. SKOOG. 1995. "Students' Perspectives on Integrated Curricula: The Case of Brown Barge Middle School." *Research in Middle Level Education Quarterly* 18: 85–114.

QUEEN, J. A. 2000. "Block Scheduling Revisited." *Phi Delta Kappan* 82, no. 2: 214–22.

RASKIN, E. 1978. *The Westing Game.* New York: Puffin Books.

RAY, K. W. 2001. *The Writing Workshop: Working Through The Hard Parts (And They're All Hard Parts).* Urbana, IL: National Council of Teachers of English.

REEVES, D. B. 2004. *Accountability for Learning: How Teachers and School Leaders Can Take Charge.* Alexandria, VA: Association for Supervision and Curriculum Development.

REITHER, G. 1999. "When There Aren't Enough Hours in the Day. . . ." *Momentum* 30, no. 2: 63–67.

RICE, R. P., and K. G. DOLGIN. 2005. *The Adolescent: Development, Relationships, and Culture.* 11th ed. Boston, MA: Pearson.

RIGBY, K. 2001. *STOP the Bullying: A Handbook for Teachers.* Markham, Ontario, Canada: Pembroke Publishers Limited.

RIMM, S. 2005. *Growing Up Too Fast: The Rimm Report on the Secret World of America's Middle Schoolers*. New York: Rodale.

ROSCHEWSKI, P., C. GALLAGHER, and J. ISERNHAGEN. 2001. "Nebraskans Reach for the STARS." *Phi Delta Kappan* 82, no. 8: 611–15.

RUDDELL, R. B. 1999. *Teaching Children to Read and Write: Becoming an Influential Teacher*. 2nd ed. Needham Heights, MA: Allyn and Bacon.

SADKER, D. 1999. "Gender Equity: Still Knocking at the Classroom Door." *Educational Leadership* 56, no. 7: 22–26.

SARDO-BROWN, D., and J. SHETLAR. 1994. "Listening to Students and Teachers to Revise a Rural Advisory Program." *Middle School Journal* 26, no. 1: 23–25.

SCHURR, S. 1999. *Authentic Assessment: Using Product, Performance, and Portfolio Measures from A to Z*. Columbus, OH: National Middle School Association.

SHEETS, R. H. 2005. *Diversity Pedagogy: Examining the Role of Culture in the Teaching-Learning Process*. Needham Heights, MA: Pearson, Allyn, and Bacon.

SIMMONS, R. 2002. *Odd Girl Out: The Hidden Culture of Aggression in Girls*. New York: Harcourt.

SLAVIN, R. E. 1991. "Synthesis of Research on Cooperative Learning." *Educational Leadership* 48, no. 5: 71–77, 79–82.

SMITH, C. 2001. "Becoming Worthy: A Journey of Teaching and Learning." In *Living and Learning in the Middle Grades: The Dance Continues*, edited by K. Bergstrom, P. Bishop and J. Carr. Westerville, OH: National Middle School Association, 26–38.

SPRENGER, M. 2005. "Inside Amy's Brain." *Educational Leadership* 62, no. 7: 28–32.

SPRINGER, M. 1994. *Watershed: A Successful Voyage into Integrative Learning*. Columbus, OH: National Middle School Association.

———. 2006. *Soundings: A Democratic Student-Centered Education*. Westerville, OH: National Middle School Association.

STEPHEN, J., E. FRASER, and J. E. MARCIA. 1992. "Moratorium-Achievement (MAMA) Cycles in Lifespan Identity Development: Value Orientations and Reasoning System." *Journal of Adolescence* 15: 283–300.

STIGGINS, R. 2004. "New Assessment Beliefs for a New School Mission." *Phi Delta Kappan* 86, no. 1: 22–27.

———. 2006. "Assessment for Learning: Creating a Culture of Confidence." Presentation at the National Middle School Association Annual Conference. 3 November in Philadelphia, PA.

SWAIM, S. 1993. "Curriculum Change—The Time Is Now." In *Readings in Middle School Curriculum: A Continuing Conversation*, edited by T. Dickinson. Columbus, OH: National Middle School Association, xi–xiii.

SWANSON, H. L., and G. HILL. 1993. "Metacognitive Aspects of Moral Reasoning and Behavior." *Adolescence* 28: 711–35.

TANNER, J. M. 1972. "Sequence, Tempo, and Individual Variation in Growth and Development of Boys and Girls Aged Twelve to Sixteen." In *Twelve to Sixteen*, edited by J. Kagan and R. Coles. New York: W. W. Norton, 1–23.

THOMPSON, S. C., L. GREGG, and L. CARUTHERS. 2005. "Using Action Research for Aspiring Middle Level Administrators: Going Beyond the Traditional Practicum Experience." In *Making a Difference: Action Research in Middle Level Education*, edited by M. Caski. Greenwich, CT: Information Age Publishing, 125–45.

TICE, D. M., J. BUDER, and R. F. BAUMEISTER. 1985. "Development of Self Consciousness: At What Age Does Audience Pressure Disrupt Performance?" *Adolescence* 20: 301–305.

TOEPFER, C. 1969. "Curricular Imperatives for the Middle School." In *Moving Forward from the Past: Early Writings and Current Reflections of Middle School Founders*, edited by R. David. 1998. Columbus OH: National Middle School Association, 134–39.

TOEPFER, C., JR. 1992. "Middle Level School Curriculum: Defining the Elusive." In *Transforming Middle Level Education: Perspectives and Possibilities*, edited by J. L. Irvin. Needham Heights, MA: Allyn and Bacon, 205–43.

TOMBARI, M., and G. BORICH. 1999. *Authentic Assessment in the Classroom: Applications and Practice*. Upper Saddle River, NJ: Merrill.

TOMLINSON, C. A. 1999a. "Mapping a Route Toward Differentiated Instruction." *Educational Leadership* 57, no. 1: 12–16.

————. 1999b. *The Differentiated Classroom: Responding to the Needs of All Learners*. Alexandria, VA: Association for Supervision and Curriculum Development.

————. 2005. "Differentiating Instruction: Why Bother?" *Middle Ground* 9, no. 1: 12–15.

Tomlinson, C. A., and J. McTighe. 2006. *Integrating Differentiated Instruction + Understanding by Design: Connecting Content and Kids*. Alexandria, VA: Association for Supervision and Curriculum Development.

Tuckman, B. W. 1965. "Developmental Sequences in Small Groups." *Psychological Bulletin* 63: 384–99.

Tye, K. 1985. *The Junior High: School in Search of a Mission*. New York: University Press of America.

Umana-Taylor, A., and M. A. Fine. 2001. "Methodological Implications of Grouping Latino Adolescents into One Collective Ethnic Group." *Hispanic Journal of Behavioral Sciences* 23: 347–62.

Van Hoose, J. 1991. "The Ultimate Goal: AA Across the Day." *Midpoints* 2, no. 1: 1–7.

Van Hoose, J., and D. Strahan. 1988. *Young Adolescent Development and School Practices: Promoting Harmony*. Columbus, OH: National Middle School Association.

Vars, G. F. 2001. "Can Curriculum Integration Survive in an Era of High-Stakes Testing?" *Middle School Journal* 33, no. 2: 7–17.

Vogler, K. E. 2003. "An Integrated Curriculum Using State Standards in a High-Stakes Testing Environment." *Middle School Journal* 34, no. 4: 5–10.

Voltz, D. L. 1999. "Empowering Diverse Learners at the Middle Level." *Middle School Journal* 30, no. 4: 29–36.

Waks, L. I. 2001. "Exploratory Education in a Society of Knowledge and Risk." In *The Handbook of Research in Middle Level Education*, edited by V. A. Anfara, Jr. Greenwich, CT: Information Age Publishing, 23–40.

Wallis, C. 2005. "Is Middle School Bad For Kids?" *Time Magazine Special Report: Being 13*, 8 August.

WALSH, D. 2004. *Why Do They Act That Way? A Survival Guide to the Adolescent Brain for You and Your Teen*. New York: Free Press.

WALSH, K. J., and M. J. SHAY. 1993. "In Support of Interdisciplinary Teaming: The Climate Factor." *Middle School Journal* 24, no. 4: 56–60.

WATERMAN, A. S. 1993. "Developmental Perspectives on Identity Formation." In *Ego Identity: A Handbook for Psychosocial Research*, edited by J. E. Marcia, A. S. Waterman, D. R. Matteson, S. L. Archer, and J. L. Orlofsky. New York: Springer-Verlag, 42–68.

WEINER, L. 1999. *Urban Teaching: The Essentials*. New York: Teachers College Press.

WHITE, G. P., P. G. ANDREWS., V. A. ANFARA, JR., D. HOUGH, S. B. MERTENS, and N. B. MIZELLE. 2003. *Research and Resources in Support of This We Believe*. Westerville, OH: National Middle School Association.

WIERSON, M., P. J. LONG, and R. L. FOREHAND. 1993. "Toward a New Understanding of Early Menarche: The Role of Environmental Stress and Pubertal Timing." *Adolescence* 28: 913–24.

WIGGINS, G. 1993. "Assessment Authenticity, Context and Validity." *Phi Delta Kappan* 78, no. 3: 200–14.

WILHELM, J. D. 1997. *"You Gotta BE the Book": Teaching Engaged and Reflective Reading with Adolescents*. New York: Teachers College Press.

———. 2006. *Engaging Readers and Writers with Inquiry*. New York: Scholastic.

WILLIAMSON, R. D. 1998. *Scheduling Middle Level Schools: Tools for Improved Student Achievement*. Reston, VA: National Association of Secondary School Principals.

WILLIS, S., ed. 1997. "Student-Involved Conferences." *Education Update* 39, no. 8: 1, 6. Alexandria, VA: Association for Supervision and Curriculum Development.

WLODKOWSKI, R. J., and M. B. GINSBERG. 1995. *Diversity and Motivation: Culturally Responsive Teaching*. San Francisco: Jossey-Bass.

WOLFE, P. 2005. "Advice for the Sleep-Deprived." *Educational Leadership* 62, no. 7: 39–40.

WOLFE, P., and R. BRANDT. 1998. "What Do We Know from Brain Research?" *Education Leadership* 56, no. 3: 8–13.

WOLFSON, A. R., and M. A. CARSKADON. 1998. "Sleep Schedules and Daytime Functioning in Adolescents." *Child Development* 69: 875–87.

WRIGHT, M. R. 1989. "Body Image Satisfaction in Adolescent Girls and Boys." *Journal of Youth and Adolescence* 18: 71–84.

ZIEGLER, S., and L. MULHALL. 1994. "Establishing and Evaluating a Successful Advisory Program in a Middle School." *Middle School Journal* 25, no. 4: 42–46.

Index

A

Advisory programs: appropriate focus, 240; rationale, 235–239; schedule, 241; student need, 239; successful programs, 242; *See also* Flexible Scheduling; *See also* National Middle School Association

Alexander, W., 76, 77, 86, 177, 226

Alpha Team, 205–214; *See also* Curriculum Integration

Alternative Scheduling: improving learning, 245; teachers' perspectives, 245–246; value, 243–247; improving teaching, 246; Types of, 247–249;

Anfara, V. A., Jr., 75, 118, 235, 239, 242, 250, 256

anorexia nervosa, 23

appetite, 21–23

Assessment: Alternative, 190; Authentic, 195–196; Connecting to curriculum and instruction, 189; defined, 180–183; FOR learning, 187–188, 188; Meaningful, 190; Misuse of, 186–187; Performance, 196–197; Portfolio, 199; Students' Roles, 190–195; *See also* Rubrics

B

baseline data, 183

Beane, J., 123, 130, 132–136, 220; *See also* Curriculum Integration

Black English Vernacular (BEV), 176

Block Scheduling, 247–248; *See also* Flexible Scheduling; *See also* Alternative Scheduling

Bordeaux, R., 34, 38–39, 52, 142,

Brain-Based Learning, 154–155

Brazee, E. N., 113, 205, 236, 243, 257

Brodhagen, B., 167, 169

Brown, D. F., 58, 98, 124, 157, 159, 162, 174–176, 178, 183, 186, 192, 195, 217, 223–224, 245–246

Bullying: Dangers of, 102–103; defined, 103; Teachers' Responsibilities, 104–105

C

Caine, R. N. and Caine, G., 31, 70, 154–155

caring: characteristics of caring teachers, 95; Establishing a Caring Environment, 94–96; impact of care on student learning, 95; Power of Caring, 214–216

Carnegie Council on Adolescent Development: advocating for young adolescents, 81, 253; recommendations for advisory sessions, 236; recommendations for scheduling, 244; recommendations for teaming, 227; implementing *Turning Points*, 257–259; *Turning Points* executive summary, 82–84; *See also Turning Points 2000*

certification, 5

Clark, J. S., 146–151, 203–204

Cognitive development: blossoming, 27; Developmental stages, 29–33: moving between stages, 32–33; myelination, 27; prefrontal cortex (PFC), 27–28; pruning, 27; *See also* Concrete Operational Thought; *See also* Formal Operational Thought *See also* Piaget

Collaborative Learning: Environments, 110–111; value to learning, 159–161

Communicating with Students: empathetic listening, 100; Roadblocks to Communication, 99; strategies for effective, 97–101

Concrete Operational Thought, 29, 32
Conferencing: between students and teacher, 168, 192
Constructivism, 155–157
Content Standards: influence on the middle school, 84–86; Living with, 177–178
Culturally Responsive Teaching, 173–177
Curriculum: Current Discussions of, 119–120, defined, 115; democratically developed, 130–131; historical discussions, 116–119; democratic classrooms, 220; Interdisciplinary Approach, 128–129; Multidisciplinary Approach, 125–127; Subject centered, 121–122; *See also* democratic classrooms; *See also* Exploratory Curriculum
Curriculum Integration: description of, 131–140; developing student themes, 139–140; students' perspectives, 194, 211, 213, 214–215, 219; students' questions for, 136–138; teacher's experience with, 204–211, 216–219, 220–223; teachers' roles, 140–142; teaming issues, 144–145; *See also* Alpha Team; *See also* Beane, J.; *See also* Clark, J. S.; *See also* National Middle School Association; *See also* Nesin, G.; *See also* Springer, M.; *See also* Soundings

D
Daniels, H., 168, 178
Decision Making: sharing with students, 108–109; on curricular issues, 109–110.
Developmental Variations: defined, 14; Gender Distinctions, 14; *See also* Physical Development
diet, 21–23; *See also* appetite
differentiated teaching and learning, 170–173; *See also* Tomlinson, C.
Diverse Learners: Recognizing and Responding to, 107–108; 169–170
Doda, N. M., 39, 72, 262
Dropped Schedules, 248; *See also* Alternative Scheduling

E
early adolescence, 3–4
early physical development: females, 18–19; males, 20–21
Egocentrism, 51–52

Eichhorn, D., 77–78, 118
Emotional Development: 37, 50, Mood Swings, 50–51; developing independence, 45; effects of hormones, 20, 28, 50
English language learners (ELL), 174–176
Erb, T., 89, 225, 233, 253–254, 256, 259
Erikson, E., 53–54; *See also* Identity
Ethnic Identity, 56; Cross's stages, 57; *See also* Oppositional Identity
Evaluation, 181; *See also* Assessment
Exploratory Curriculum, 121, 249–250

F
Facilitators, 166
factory model of schooling, 70; Influence on Teaching Beliefs, 71–72; Influence on Teaching Behaviors, 72–73; *See also* Caine and Caine
Female physical changes, 14–17
Flexible Scheduling: Block Schedules, 247–248; Rotating Schedules, 248; Dropped Schedules, 248; *See also* Alternative Scheduling
Formal Operational Thought, 30–33; emergent, 32; Helping Students Move Toward, 157–158
friendships, 40–41

G
Gender identity, 60–62; *See also* Identity; *See also* Sexual and Gender Identity
George, P. S., 78, 88, 233, 236, 241, 256
grading, 182; *See also* Assessment
Growth spurt, 14

H
high stakes testing, 144
Hormones: testosterone, 16; estrogen, 16; pituitary gland, 14; progesterone, 16; sweat glands, 17; *See also* Emotional Development; *See also* Physical Development

I
Identity: development of, 37; search for, 52–65; Erikson's theories, 53–54; Ethnic, 56–58; Marcia's theory, 54–56; Oppositional, 58–60; Sexual and Gender, 60; *See also* Erikson; *See also* Ethnic Identity; *See also* Marcia, J., *See also* Sexual and Gender identity

imaginary audience, 50–51
independence, 44–45, 49
Intellectual Development, *See* Cognitive
    Development
Interdisciplinary Curriculum Models, *See*
    Curriculum

J
Jackson, A. W., and Davis, G. A., 86, 153, 227,
    236; *See also Turning Points 2000*
Junior High Schools, 74–76

K
knowing students, 163–165
Knowles, T., 39, 72, 163, 262

L
learning: how it occurs, 153–155; teachers'
    roles in encouraging, 161–163; *See also*
    Brain-Based Learning
literature circles, 160
Looping, 251
Lounsbury, J., 32, 89, 131, 166, 169, 256, 257

M
Male physical changes, 19
Marcia, J.: theories on identity development,
    54–56; *See also* Identity
McEwin, C. K., 7, 88, 228, 229
Menstruation (menarche), 17–19; earlier
    occurrence, 18; differences among
    ethnicities, 18
Metacognition: characteristics of, 31; defined,
    31
Meyers, C., 210–211; *See also* Alpha Team
Middle level certification, 4
middle level teachers: characteristics of
    effective, 7–8
Middle school: Appropriate Design, 76, 79–84;
    Concept, misunderstanding of, 255; con-
    figurations, 74–76, 78; history of, 76–78;
    support for, 79, 261
Mood Swings, 50–51
Moral Development, 48–50
multidisciplinary curriculum models, *See*
    Curriculum

N
National Middle School Association:
    Developmentally responsive middle level

schools, 79–80; founded, 79; publications,
    79; advisory programs, 236; assessment,
    190; curriculum, 119–121; exploratory
    curriculum, 249; instructional behaviors,
    153; scheduling, 244; *see also This We
    Believe: Successful Schools for Young
    Adolescents*
Nesin, G., 166, 169, 220–223, 228, 236, 243
No Child Left Behind federal legislation:
    Adequate Yearly Progress (AYP), 84–85;
    certification issues, 5; influence on content
    standards, 84–85; 177; proficiency,
    184–185

O
obesity, 22
O'Donnell, M. , 205–210; *See also* Alpha Team
Oppositional Identity, 58–60; *See also* Identity
outcomes: establishment of, 165–166

P
peers: Roles of, 42
peer group: approval, 43; pressure, 43–44
personal fable, 50–51
Physical development, 12: Appetite, 14; early
    and late maturation, 18-19; Growth
    Spurt, 14; height gain, 14-15; impact on
    self-esteem, 15–16; Individual
    Differences, 14, 24–25; Muscular
    Changes, 15; Skeletal Changes, 15;
    Weight gains, 14
Piaget, J., 29–30
portfolio: Assessment, 199; *See also* Assessment
popularity, 42
Prefrontal cortex (PFC), 27–28; impact of
    lack of development, 35; effects on
    socialization, 41; *See also* Cognitive
    Development
puberty, 13

R
Rice, R. P., and Dolgin, K. G., 14, 18, 19, 29,
    42, 49, 63, 157
Rimm, S., 18, 46, 48
Risk Taking, 35; Encouraging, 105;
Rubrics, 197–199

S
Scheduling, *See* Alternative scheduling
Self-esteem, 63–65; among females, 18–19;

sexual development: 13–14; *See also* Physical Development; *See also* Hormones
Sexual and Gender Identity, 60–62; *See also* Identity
sexual harassment, 60–61
skeletal and muscular development, 15
sleep needs, 23–24
Social Development: 37, 38; opposite-sex relationships, 40; rejection of parental authority, 45; Role of the Community; 46; Role of the Family, 44–45; Role of the Media, 46; Role of peers, 42, 44; same-sex friendships, 40, 43
Soundings, 192, 194; description of program, 216–219; *See also* Springer, M.
spermarche, 20; *See also* wet dreams
Springer, M., 157, 216–219; *See also* Soundings
Sputnik, 86
standards: responding to them, 87–89,
standardized tests: negative effects of, 184;
Stiggins, R., 186, 188, 194, 200
Student-Led Conferences: defined, 200–201; Organizing, 201–202
student psychological safety, 107
student stress: effects on learning, 93–94; fears caused by teachers, 92–93

T
Teaming: activities, 230; Benefits to Teachers, 231, 233; defined, 226; drawbacks, 232; effects on students, 227, 229–230; purposes, 229; stages of, 232–233
technology: affects on, 47–48
testing, 181; *See also* Assessment

This We Believe: Successful Schools for Young Adolescents: advisory, 236; challenging, integrative, and exploratory curriculum, 119–121; developmentally responsive middle schools, 79–80; first edition, 79; instructional strategies, 153; second edition, 1995; student decision making, 110; third edition, 2003; *See also* National Middle School Association
Tomlinson, C., 171–173; *See also* differentiated teaching and learning
Turning Points 2000: Educating Adolescents in the 21st Century, 86; recommendations, 87, 236, 227; *See also* Jackson, A. W., and Davis, G. A.
transescence, 3
transgender issues, 62
Turning Points: Preparing Youth for the 21st Century: first suggestions, 81; executive summary, 82–84; teaming, 226; *See also* Carnegie Council on Adolescent Development

V
Vars, G. F., 89, 131, 144, 256
vocabulary instruction, 158

W
Walsh, D., 16, 24, 26, 28, 35, 37, 153
wet dreams, 20
writing workshop, 160

Y
young adolescence, defined, 3

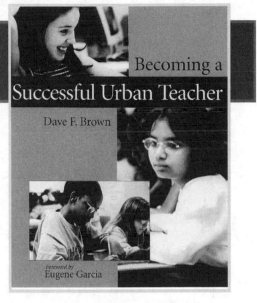